The Great Adventure Films

The Great

BOOKS BY TONY THOMAS

The Films of Errol Flynn
(WITH RUDY BEHLMER AND CLIFFORD MCCARTY)
Ustinov in Focus
The Films of Kirk Douglas
Music for the Movies
The Films of Marlon Brando
The Busby Berkeley Book
Cads and Cavaliers
Song and Dance Man: The Films of Gene Kelly
Burt Lancaster
The Films of the Forties
Harry Warren and the Hollywood Musical
Hollywood's Hollywood (WITH RUDY BEHLMER)

Adventure Films

By
TONY THOMAS

CITADEL PRESS, SECAUCUS, NEW JERSEY

For my children—
Richard, David and Andrea—
in the hope this will help them understand
their Walter Mitty-type father
a little better

ACKNOWLEDGMENTS

The acknowledgments for this book are substantially the same as those in my previous books about the film world, which means I have been fortunate in receiving even more help from the same good people. My Research was done mostly at the Library of the Academy of Motion Picture Arts and Sciences in Los Angeles, for which I am again indebted to Mildred Simpson and her staff, and at the Ontario Film Institute in Toronto, for which I give my thanks to Gerald Pratley and Clive Denton. In solving the considerable problems of finding good photographic illustrations, ever the basic concern in books of this kind, I am grateful to Eddie Brandt, Bob Colman, John Lebold, Gunnard Nelson, Paula Klaw (*Movie Star News,* New York), Warner Bros., Inc. and Walt Disney Productions. And I am most particularly grateful to Rudy Behlmer, who shares my interest in many of these films and who made his own research on them available to me.

TONY THOMAS.

First paperbound printing, 1980
ISBN 0-8065-0747-0

Copyright © 1976 by Tony Thomas
All rights reserved
Published by Citadel Press
A division of Lyle Stuart, Inc.
120 Enterprise Ave., Secaucus, N.J. 07094
In Canada: George J. McLeod Limited
73 Bathurst St., Toronto, Ont.
Manufactured in the United States of America by
Halliday Lithograph Corp., West Hanover, Mass.
Designed by A. Christopher Simon

LIBRARY OF CONGRESS CATALOGING IN PUBLICATION DATA
Thomas, Tony, 1927-
    The great adventure films.

    Includes index.
    1. Adventure films—History and criticism. I. Title.
PN1995.9.A3T5   791.43'0909'1   76-26142

Contents

Introduction

I once asked John Ford why he had specialized in westerns and he replied in his characteristically terse manner, "I like the cowboys. I like the stunt men. I like these people. They're gentlemanly, charitable and easy to work with. It gives me a chance to get out of Southern California and go to Arizona, where I can breathe fresh air. It gives you a different view on life. I can relax." I next asked if he thought the western was particularly good cinema and he snapped back, "The western is the *real* picture. It's full of action and character. You see the outdoors—nature, horses, rivers, valleys. The people *move*. The western is truly a moving picture."

It seems to me that what Ford said about westerns fully applies to the whole genre of adventure films, which of course includes westerns. The intellectual view of such movies is that they are vicarious pleasures for frustrated romantics, would-be heroes, armchair travelers, the dreamers and the discontents. In short, just about all of us. Nobody realized this more than James Thurber, whose Walter Mitty is the alter ego of every man who spent hundreds of hours of his boyhood in the darkness and the escape of the movie theatres, watching the antics of Fairbanks (père et fils), Errol Flynn, Gary Cooper, John Wayne, *et al*. Mitty's imagination was so fervent it allowed him to slip into fantasies as an RAF fighter ace, a western gunslinger, a sailing ship captain, a riverboat gambler and a celebrated brain surgeon. The rest of us had to settle for those flickering images on the screens, sitting there for a couple of hours with reality in abeyance.

The term "adventure film" has a slightly subordinate ring to it, as if it were something less than the dramas and the movies which tackle weighty issues. Perhaps the problem lies in definition. To me Olivier's *Henry V* is an adventure film, as is Lean's *Lawrence of Arabia* and Huston's *The Treasure of the Sierra Madre*—three examples of filmmaking at its highest level. But since adventure films deal in the main with make-believe, with soldiers-of-fortune, explorers, pirates, avengers, rescuers and trouble-shooters, it becomes necessary to defend such pictures with the phrase "good of its kind." If that is the case, then I cannot think of a better scripted, directed, acted, scored, mounted and costumed film "of its kind" than Curtiz' *The Adventures of Robin Hood*. If anything, the making of top-flight adventure films requires even greater effort and even finer craftsmanship than other kinds of movies.

Choosing fifty prime items from any genre of film history is difficult and bound to provoke discussion. I arrived at my choice by setting up certain lines of demarcation for myself. Since the book will likely find most of its customers in the United States and the countries of the British Commonwealth, I decided to list only American and British productions. There is no denying that good adventure films have been made elsewhere but they are not readily available to most of us. I was tempted to deal only

with sound pictures but on reflection it seemed to give a false balance. The style of movie heroics in the sound era took its cue from the best examples done in the silent years, going as far back as Fairbanks' *The Mark of Zorro.* However, I limited myself to four silent pictures, those which I thought had the most influence on the genre as it developed. I took a stand against science fiction adventures and those dealing with fantasy. This is partly a matter of taste— I prefer my adventures to be grounded in basic reality—but also because such films spill over into a genre of their own. I view the disaster films in somewhat the same light. They most certainly are a form of adventure, dealing as they do with the horrors of enraged nature, crashing airliners, capsized ships, burning buildings, and earthquakes, but this is rapidly becoming a separate category and I shall not be surprised at the appearance of a book titled *The Great Disaster Films.* Whoever the author turns out to be, I wish him strength.

I imposed a few other restrictions upon myself. I thought it best to severely ration myself in the choice of war films and westerns, since both kinds

almost always involve adventure. This was not too difficult because with war films and westerns the frameworks tend to be similar in each case, and it was a matter of choosing those I thought most representative. And there was one other limit to which I decided to adhere—Errol Flynn pictures. I settled on *The Adventures of Robin Hood* and *The Sea Hawk* and crossed off such fine adventure specimens as *The Charge of the Light Brigade, The Dawn Patrol, They Died With Their Boots On* and *Objective Burma* simply because it would have made the book Flynn-heavy. Besides, my propensity for this actor's work is documented in *The Films of Errol Flynn,* which Rudy Behlmer, Clifford McCarty and I wrote for Citadel in 1969.

On the subject of Flynn, I feel he most personifies the adventurer, perhaps because that is precisely what he was himself. An adventurer—a man who likes to roam and explore, to live by the skin of his teeth, to take risks, to gamble with his luck and tackle the unknown. If Flynn was good as a pirate captain, a rebel leader and a knight in shining armor it was probably because he really belonged in a previous age. He often said how much he disliked

of sadness in looking through these pages. It is not only a case of a replacement for Errol Flynn but where are the contemporary likes of Ronald Colman, Leslie Howard, Clark Gable, Spencer Tracy, Tyrone Power, Humphrey Bogart, Gary Cooper, Robert Taylor and Robert Donat? Who replaces John Wayne, Burt Lancaster, David Niven, Gregory Peck and Robert Mitchum when they follow Cary Grant into retirement? What has happened to the art of being a *gentleman?* Has Byronic romanticism gone forever? If the answer is "yes," I prefer not to hear it.

To those who feel the lack of adventure films is due to a scarcity of written material, a scanning of these pages should prove otherwise. More than half of these fifty films are based on classic literature, all of it still available. This was something that did not occur to me until after I had made my selection —just how much we owe to the great authors as the whole basis for making adventure pictures. The four masters of historical fiction are all present and accounted for—Sir Walter Scott, Robert Louis Stevenson, Alexandre Dumas and Rafael Sabatini. So too are Jack London, Baroness Orczy, James Fenimore Cooper, Anthony Hope, Mark Twain, A. E. W. Mason, P. C. Wren, Kenneth Roberts, Rudyard Kipling, H. Rider Haggard, Johann Wyss, Samuel Shellabarger, C. S. Forester, Daniel Defoe, Jules Verne, Leo Tolstoy and even William Shakespeare. Only a handful of these fifty films use original screenplays, which tends to suggest that great adventure films need great source material.

Great adventure films also need the services of the very best talents in the film industry. This kind of picture, like opera, must be well done in order to be even tolerable. Look over the listing of these fifty films and note that most of them employ the master cinematographers—men like Freddie Young, James Wong Howe, Robert Surtees, Robert Krasker, Sol Polito, Lucian Ballard, Charles Rosher, Conrad Hall and Lee Garmes. In that other mighty contribution to cinema magic—music—consider how many of these films are scored by Erich Korngold, Miklos Rozsa, William Walton, Alfred Newman, Max Steiner, Ralph Vaughan Williams, Victor Young and Elmer Bernstein. The best adventure films offer marvelous scope for photography and music, and anyone who looks upon this as a sub-genre can hardly claim to be a complete and loving film buff. The only limits of the adventure film are the limits to the talents involved in making them. Few kinds of films offer as much opportunity to the imaginative.

the twentieth century, and toward the end of his rather short life he grew nostalgic for his early days as a drifter in the South Seas. By the time he died in 1959 it had become increasingly difficult for young men to do what he had done only a generation before. How does a man in this day and age reconcile his love of freedom and adventure with socialism, trade unionism, computers and red tape? If he is extremely lucky, and if he lives in a time when there is a market for romanticism, he becomes a movie star. It was Flynn's great good fortune that he had that outlet. On the other hand, an actor needs an adventurous background to be really convincing as a swashbuckling hero, and modern life, with all its restrictions, curtails the young man who would storm his way around the world. It has produced anti-establishmentism, drop-outism and bitter rejection of old social values, all of which is negative—and all of which is apparent on the screen today. What we now lack are young actors who actually *want* to play Robin Hood and Captain Blood.

I have enjoyed writing this book because I love the movies with which it deals, but there is a twinge

Tastes change, with film producers as much as with the public, and the ever-increasing costs of production make the likelihood of costume epics slimmer all the time. Such films do not seem to have a ready acceptance on today's youth-oriented market, as *Cromwell* and *Waterloo* have proved, and in order to impress that market directors apparently need a satirical approach, of which Richard Lester's *The Three Musketeers* is a case in point. I considered this film as the final item in this book but decided it was too flippant. I also considered *The Dove* because it was a story of a young man sailing a small boat around the world, but it lacked the excitement of a really great adventure film. I found it a problem to find suitable subjects after the mid-Sixties. The Thirties and the Forties were rich and the Fifties were fairly well stocked but after dealing with *The Professionals* in 1956 I found myself hard put to make suitable choices. I considered cutting the book off at that point but the thought of doing so bothered me. It would have been a forced surrender. My publisher felt the same way, so we let the project sit for a while. Then, late in 1975, came *The Man Who Would Be King*. For the purposes of this book it was a picture that arrived like the U.S. Cavalry in the last reel of an old-fashioned western.

Having to look so hard for worthy films after 1966 bothers me not so much for my own sake but for my children, who are denied the range of pictures I enjoyed as a child. In fact, just letting them go to the movies at all has become a major consideration, now that producers seem concerned with revealing to us how evil, rotten and shabby we humans are. If this book moves any producer to making a spirited, zesty, uplifting adventure picture I shall be very pleased.

The Mark of Zorro

1920

A United Artists Picture. Produced by Douglas Fairbanks. Directed by Fred Niblo. Screenplay by Elton Thomas (Fairbanks), based on the story *The Curse of Capistrano* by Johnston McCulley. Photographed by William C. McGann and Harry Thorpe.

CAST

Don Diego Vega, Douglas Fairbanks; *Lolita,* Marguerite de la Motte; *Sergeant Pedro Garcia,* Noah Beery; *Don Carlos Pulido,* Charles Hill Mailes; *Dona Catalina,* Claire McDowell; *Captain Juan Ramón,* Robert McKim; *Governor Alvarado,* George Periolat.

It really all began with Douglas Fairbanks, and particularly with *The Mark of Zorro*. There had been some costumed adventure films prior to 1920 but they lacked the style and the spark that Fairbanks brought with him when he turned from being a buoyant comedian and became a movie swashbuckler. Portraying the adventurous hero with conviction has always required more talent that most viewers realize. It obviously demands a splendid physical presence in order to be able to run and jump, fight and fence, ride and rout. And it has to be done with panache, personality and plausibility. That kind of actor has always been in short supply and the prototype was Fairbanks.

He began his Hollywood career in 1914 after a few years on the New York stage and quickly became popular because of his gymnastic verve and his cheerful manner. Fairbanks was an extraordinary man. He fairly glowed with confidence and vigor, and bolstered his screen image by writing a series of books with titles like *Laugh and Live, Initiative and Self-Reliance,* and *Making Life Worthwhile.* There was nothing phony about his advice. This breezy philosophy was fully realized, and by 1919 Fairbanks was a millionaire and monarch of all he surveyed. That was when he married Mary Pickford, with the two of them becoming the King and Queen of Hollywood, living in their own Buckingham Palace of Beverly Hills—Pickfair.

1919 was also the year Fairbanks founded United Artists, with his wife, Charlie Chaplin and D. W. Griffith as partners. In addition to his other attributes Fairbanks was an astute businessman. He had been getting half a million dollars per film, but when he saw his pictures earning huge profits he realized he could do better. United Artists, the first film company formed by actors, thereafter produced and distributed all the Fairbanks and

The villain on the left is Noah Beery.

before the Mexicans cut themselves loose from Spanish control. The story was written by Johnston McCulley (1883–1958), now remembered only as the man who invented Zorro (the Spanish word for fox) but who also wrote dozens of popular adventure novels. Fairbanks was intrigued but cautious and a little unsure about a full plunge into costumed adventure. He decided to gamble but immediately afterwards made a knockabout comedy called *The Nut* just in case his Zorro failed to please. He had no cause to worry. *The Mark of Zorro* captured a large and enthusiastic audience and within a few weeks Fairbanks took it as his cue to immerse himself entirely in the business of producing elaborate action spectacles.

The plot of *Zorro* has become familiar to latter-day audiences through the 1940 remake, which is essentially the same, and through many television treatments. Fairbanks wrote his own scenario, calling himself Elton Thomas, and hired Fred Niblo to direct. Niblo was fairly new to directing, having made only four films prior to this, but he clearly understood what Fairbanks wanted, which was swift pacing and a sense of fun. Fairbanks was a pleasingly egocentric man and he designed the picture as a showcase for his acrobatic ability. Had he been merely an acrobat the results would have palled, but Fairbanks had flair. He was graceful and imaginative, and as entertaining as he was agile. No one has since quite matched this aspect of the Fairbanks films.

This version of *Zorro* has more humor than the versions that followed—Fairbanks had been a light comedian too long to change *that* much. Here he is the aristocratic Don Diego Vega, who returns from his education in Madrid to his home in what now seems like the Los Angeles of prehistoric times. He finds that his father has been deposed as governor and that an avaricious tyrant has taken his place, with a military advisor, Captain Juan, Ramón (Robert McKim), who manages the campaign of suppression and crippling taxation. To rectify the situation Diego allows himself to be known as a pacifist and a fop, this being a cover for his activities as Zorro, the black-costumed avenger who terrorizes, confuses, and retrieves taxation money from the governor's soldiers. In doing this he wins both the love and the disdain of the governor's daughter (Marguerite de la Motte)—she loves the hero and hates the fop, until she discovers they are one and the same. Diego also confuses the buffoonish sergeant of the governor's guards, Garcia (Noah Beery), who finally admits, after several trouncings,

Pickford films, and brought them vast wealth. The idea of making *The Mark of Zorro* grew from Fairbanks' assessment of the changes in public taste following the First World War. He sensed the need of a new image, something more substantial than his former comedic boyishness, and it seemed to him there might be a market for romantic, fanciful escapism.

Pickford and Fairbanks played safe with their first two United Artists productions. She did *Pollyanna* and he did *His Majesty the American,* a Ruritanian adventure in which he actually spoofed the genre in which he was soon to excel. He followed it with *When the Clouds Roll By,* which contained quite a few action sequences, and *The Mollycoddle,* which ranged from motor racing in Monte Carlo to skirmishes with Indians in Arizona. Having broadened his style he now looked around for something even more expansive. Someone brought to his attention a story that had been running as a serial in the pulp magazine, *All-Story.* It was called "The Curse of Capistrano" and it was about a Robin Hood type in the California of 1820, when it was still a colony of Spain, a few years

Douglas Fairbanks, Sr.

Fairbanks with Marguerite de la Motte. The fop does not impress the lady.

But Zorro does!

that Zorro is the better man, and joins him. The heroine is bothered by the lecherous Captain Ramón but this problem is eventually solved when the captain comes face to face with Zorro, and Ramón discovers that he is not the finest swordsman in Olde California.

The Mark of Zorro set high standards for movie adventurers to follow, and the only man to surpass its athletic verve was Fairbanks himself. It altered his career completely. He thereafter specialized in costume epics, following it with *The Three Musketeers,* with himself as D'Artagnan, a role that was really his alter ego. Then came *Robin Hood, The Thief of Bagdad, Don Q, Son of Zorro, The Black Pirate, The Gaucho,* and *The Iron Mask,* again as D'Artagnan. These eight films are the textbooks of film swashbucklers.

The 1940 version of *The Mark of Zorro* is a film in a somewhat different league. It is short on action because Tyrone Power was not an athletic actor but it has a great deal of stylishness and atmosphere due to the taste of its director, Rouben Mamoulian. But the real value of this version lies in the performance of Basil Rathbone, as the military advisor to a cowardly governor. The role was considerably enlarged from the Fairbanks version in order to

6

accommodate Rathbone and the fact that he was one of the very few actors who had mastered stage fencing. The duel in this *Zorro* is among the half-dozen best ever staged for the screen, with Power being doubled in everything but the close-ups by Albert Cavens. Rathbone never won a swordfight in his pictures, but anyone with knowledge of fencing could spot that none of the so-called heroes would have stood a chance against him if they had not had the script on their side.

Basil Rathbone and Tyrone Power in the 1940 version.

Captain Juan Ramon (Robert McKim) doesn't stand a chance, either with Zorro or the girl.

7

Don Juan

1926

A Warner Bros. Picture. Directed by Alan Crosland. Screenplay by Bess Meredyth. Photographed by Byron Haskin. Music by William Axt and David Mendoza. Running time: 125 minutes.

CAST

Don Juan/Don José, John Barrymore; *Adriana Della Varnese,* Mary Astor; *Pedrillo,* Willard Louis; *Lucretia Borgia,* Estelle Taylor; *Rena,* Helene Costello; *Maia,* Myrna Loy; *Cesare Borgia,* Warner Oland; *Count Donati,* Montagu Love; *Beatrice,* Jane Winton; *Leandro,* John Roche; *Trusia,* June Marlowe; *Don Juan, age five,* Yvonne Day; *Don Juan, age ten,* Philippe De Lacey; *Hunchback,* John George; *Nehri,* Gustav von Seyffertitz; *Duke Della Varnese,* Josef Swickard; *Duke Margoni,* Lionel Braham; *Imperia,* Phyllis Haver; *Marquis Rinaldo,* Nigel de Brulier; *Marquise Rinaldo,* Hedda Hopper.

John Barrymore was an ideal actor to play Don Juan. He was romantic in both the Byronic and the amorous sense and he had about him the air of a man who belonged in a fantasy world rather than in real life. His handsome face and his once graceful figure, plus his elegance as an actor and his well-documented interest in women, combined to make him what Byron might well have had in mind when he wrote his epic poem. The poem was the inspiration for this picture but scenarist Bess Meredyth concocted her own concept of the Don and his possible adventures with the infamous Borgias of fifteenth-century Italy. Seen today in its original two-hour form, *Don Juan* cries out for editing, its action sequences being separated by long stretches of tedious plot devices. But in any version

it is Barrymore's stylishness and his image of romantic heroism that gives the film its distinctiveness.

Don Juan is an important item in cinema history because it was the first film to have a fully synchronized musical score, in addition to sound effects, and Warners gave it a gala presentation in New York on the evening of August 6, 1926, complete with a selection of short films displaying operatic, concert and entertainment celebrities. This was a full year before Warners broke the movie sound barrier with *The Jazz Singer.* The Vitaphone sound-on-disc system was the pride of the burgeoning brothers Warner and enabled them to move from minor to major in the picture business. The score and the sound effects were recorded on 33⅓ RPM platters, one for each reel of film (*Don Juan* ran to ten). To add to the prestige value of their picture Warners commissioned a symphonic score from William Axt and David Mendoza, who had already distinguished themselves scoring *The Big Parade* and *Ben-Hur,* and hired the New York Philharmonic Orchestra under Henry Hadley to record it at the Manhattan Opera House. The venture

8

Barrymore, Astor and Montagu Love.

was a success on all counts and helped establish Barrymore as a popular movie star, something he had not been to this point.

Don Juan begins with the Don as a boy, being warned by his father Don José (also played by Barrymore) of the infidelity of women. The elder Don discovers his wife's affair with a lover, then drives the wife from his castle and seals up the lover in a hiding place. His advice to his son is hypocritical to say the least; he is in fact a lusty old man who dies after being stabbed by one of his many mistresses. Years later Don Juan is invited to the castle of the powerful Borgias, where the sensuous, amoral Lucretia (Estelle Taylor) invites him to be her lover. He declines and in so doing incites her vengeance, particularly when he falls in love with the gentle Adriana (Mary Astor), whom the Borgias want to marry off to Count Donati (Montagu Love) in order to strengthen yet another of their political tentacles. It is also their plan to poison Adriana's father, the Duke Della Varnese (Josef Swickard) and appropriate his lands after the proposed marriage. Don Juan is informed he must

marry Lucretia but he claims he would prefer death. He is imprisoned but escapes, swims the turbulent Tiber river and bursts in on the Borgias as they prepare to marry Adriana to Donati. Juan engages Donati in a furious fight with swords and daggers and kills him. He and Adriana are then locked in the dungeon but again he escapes. Later he returns to the prison as Adriana is being tortured and, disguised as a monk, he comforts her and tells her of his scheme of rescue. The scheme involves much chasing and battling but Juan vanquishes the villains and wins his lovely Adriana.

Don Juan met with mixed reactions from the critics, many of whom rightly pointed out that it was too long and too melodramatic. Its importance in a listing of great adventure films is the influence it had on the genre. Barrymore set a high standard

Juan as a boy (Philippe de Lacey) being keenly watched over by his misogynist father (Barrymore).

Mary Astor, apparently overcome by the advances of Juan.

Lucretia Borgia (Estelle Taylor) making a play for Juan, who, among other things, loves tall drinks.

Montagu meets his match.

for future romantic swashbucklers and Alan Crosland's direction of the action sequences was an advance in the right direction. This applies particularly to the famous duel between Don Juan and Donati, which was better staged and photographed than anything done before 1926, even in the Fairbanks pictures. The music scoring helped, and Crosland moved his cameras fluidly in following the duel, even allowing for direct lunges into the lens. This sequence is the only thing the Barrymore film has in common with the Errol Flynn version made in 1949, which copies the duel and has Juan fling aside his rapier and leap, dagger in hand, at the villain down a long flight of stairs.

Barrymore was forty-four at the time of making *Don Juan* and it is somewhat amazing that he was so well able to communicate the physical heroism of the role. He was not an athlete and his drinking had already begun to undermine his health. But he had flair and style, and if he believed in a part he was able, with a talent unknown to most of us, to assume youthfulness and strength. He was a strange man, gifted with sensitivity and artistry, and yet something of a lost soul. His father ended up insane and perhaps Barrymore also had a touch of madness. Whatever it was, it was an extra dimension in the art of the actor, something that enabled him to understand Shakespeare's spiritually tormented Hamlet and wickedly possessed Richard III, Melville's Captain Ahab and Byron's Don Juan. Despite his talent he seemed to get little satisfaction from being an actor and claimed he did it because it was the family trade and his only way to make money. He probably would never have become successful had it not been for the prodding and the support of his friends. One of them was the great English actress Constance Collier, who persuaded him to take acting seriously and to tackle *Peter Ibbetson* in 1917, and later goaded him to become *Hamlet*. She once said, "He was the greatest of all actors I ever saw. He had a wild soul and no one could discipline him. He had something in his eye, an almost mystic light, that only men of genius have."

12

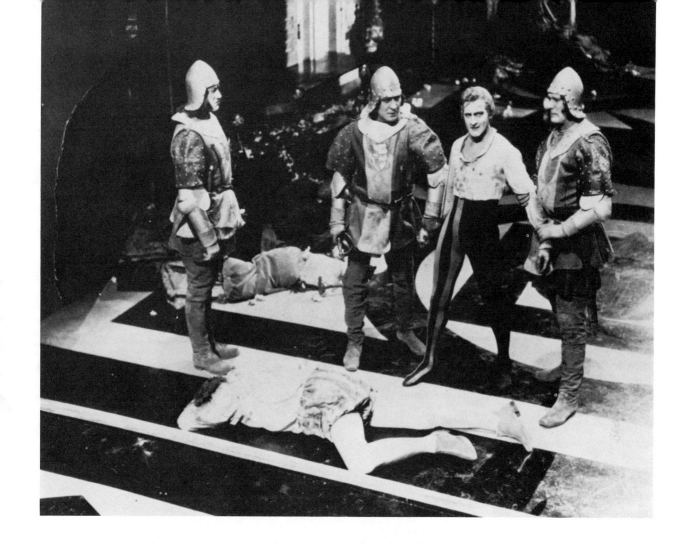

Juan to the rescue.

The General

1926

A United Artists Picture. Produced by Joseph M. Schenck. Directed by Buster Keaton and Clyde Bruckman. Screenplay by Al Boasberg and Charles Smith. Photographed by Bert Haines and J. D. Jennings. Running time: 82 minutes.

CAST

Johnny Gray, Buster Keaton; *Annabelle Lee,* Marion Mack; *Her Father,* Charles Smith; *Her Brother,* Frank Barnes; *Captain Anderson,* Glen Cavender; *General Thatcher,* Jim Farley; *Confederate General,* Frederick Vroom; *Recruiting Officer,* Frank Hagney.

The General is such a comedy classic of the silent screen that its inclusion in a listing of great adventure films may at first raise eyebrows. The eyebrows will lower quickly with a little thought. Buster Keaton's marvelous Civil War caper is not slapstick; it is a comedy drama with much movement and a respectable evocation of period. And it is interesting to consider that Keaton's film is almost as close to the Civil War in terms of time as we now are to the film. Moreover, it is based on a factual adventure. It came to Keaton's attention when he read the book *The Great Locomotive Chase* by William Pittenger, a firsthand account of a party of Union soldiers, dressed as Confederates, stealing a locomotive near Atlanta, Georgia, and driving it back to Union lines, destroying Southern railway lines, telegraph installations and bridges en route. The same book was the source material for Walt Disney's *The Great Locomotive Chase* in 1956, although it was the Keaton film that inspired Disney to do it. Pittenger's book, published in 1868, told of the 300-mile trek through Southern territory,

with Confederate troops in pursuit, and the recapture of the train, with the dash back to Atlanta and Union soldiers in pursuit. This immediately appealed to Keaton, who was looking for something a little different, something more substantial than the light fantasies in which he had made his name.

Keaton was anxious to make *The General* a genuine Civil War picture and not a farce. Initially he had wanted to film it on actual locations in Georgia and Tennessee but was constrained through cost and the problem of finding genuine period trains. He discovered two in Georgia. The picture was shot in Oregon because it was the only place Keaton could find sufficient narrow-gauge rails for his train, and he enlisted the entire Oregon State Guard to play his soldiers. These men also proved useful when sparks from the train caused a forest fire, joining Keaton and his crew in putting it out. Keaton, who outlined the story and co-directed it with Clyde Bruckman, saw to it that the uniforms were accurate and that the picture conveyed the activity of war—the movement of troops, horses, supply wagons and artillery. It is this sense of movement that makes *The General* an interesting

Laying tracks the hard way.

Keaton's method of checking cannons.

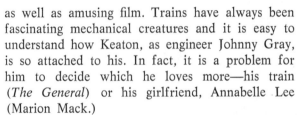

How to find out what the other side is up to.

as well as amusing film. Trains have always been fascinating mechanical creatures and it is easy to understand how Keaton, as engineer Johnny Gray, is so attached to his. In fact, it is a problem for him to decide which he loves more—his train (*The General*) or his girlfriend, Annabelle Lee (Marion Mack.)

Johnny Gray is a glum-faced little fellow, seemingly content with his job with the railroad, but when war is declared he rushes to join the colors. In this he is unlucky. His boss points out to the recruiting officer that he is far more valuable as an engineer than he would be in the army. One day a group of strangers enters the yards at Marietta, Georgia, and steals *The General,* just after Annabelle has climbed aboard. Johnny runs after the train, yelling for others to follow. After a while he stops and looks behind to find he is the only one in pursuit. Undeterred, he tries to pursue with a handcar and when that flies off the track he next picks up a bicycle. He gets to the Union camp after he comes across a Confederate train called *The Texas,* and he instructs the southern soldiers to climb on the cars and join in his campaign—but

when he drives the engine away he finds it is not connected to the cars. This does not cool his determination. He is spotted by Union soldiers and they give chase, with Johnny outmaneuvering them at every point. At the Union camp he looks for Annabelle and finds her tied up in the officer's quarters. In hiding under a table he overhears the Union staff outlining their campaign and once he and Annabelle make their escape he sees it as his duty to get back to his own side and relay the information.

Johnny steals into his beloved train and drives away, with Annabelle as his assistant, although the not very bright girl is more a hindrance than a help—sweeping wood chips out of the cab when he desperately needs all the fuel he can get. The Union forces again pursue the brave little man and again he outfoxes them, dumping things from his train onto the tracks, throwing out cases and barrels, pulling down telegraph posts, throwing switches and bending rails and finally setting fire to a wooden bridge the Yankees are about to cross. Their commander orders the train over and then gives a disgusted snort when he sees it collapse into the river. Coming across the Southern army Johnny conveys the information about the approaching Union soldiers and joins the Confederate ranks. Despite his clumsiness—tripping over his own saber—and miraculously surviving shot and shell, he proves to be the key to victory. He mans a cannon and more by chance than design hits a dam, which bursts and scatters the Yankees. Having recovered both his train and his girl, and having saved the day for the Confederates, the confused Johnny is rewarded with the rank of lieutenant.

Keaton's Johnny Gray was just one of the many portraits he created of the stoical little man, plain, undistinguished, unsung, innocent and somehow

Buster and his not very helpful girl (Marian Mack).

overcoming all of life's hazards and cruelties. The characterization was probably better etched in *The General* than in his other films because this one is so well constructed and dramatically interesting. It is not only funny, it is intriguing in its suspense and excitement—all of which makes it not only a great adventure film but a great film of any kind. It is also to the credit of Buster Keaton that he made one of the best of all Civil War films, a category far from overcrowded. The epic conflict between the North and the South has produced mountains of literature but few movies of note, mostly because Hollywood has had to steer clear of offending the descendants of either cause. *The General,* with its impressive lines of infantry, cavalry and artillery, gives a sense of what it was all about, and only a humorless Northerner could object to seeing courageous little Johnny Gray getting the better of the Yankees.

Taking care of another kind of General.

The Keaton solution for taking care of two duties simultaneously.

Wings

1927

A Paramount Picture. Produced by Lucien Hubbard. Directed by William Wellman. Screenplay by Hope Loring and Louis D. Lighton, based on a story by John Monk Saunders. Photographed by Harry Perry, with aerial photography by multiple cameramen. Musical score by John S. Zemecnik. Running time: 13 reels (approx. 120 minutes).

CAST

Mary Preston, Clara Bow; *Jack Powell,* Charles "Buddy" Rogers; *David Armstrong,* Richard Arlen; *Sylvia Lewis,* Jobyna Ralston; *Cadet White,* Gary Cooper; *Celeste,* Arlette Marchal; *Herman Schwimpf,* El Brendel; *Sergeant,* "Gunboat" Smith; *Air Commander,* Richard Tucker; *Mrs. Armstrong,* Julia Swayne Gordon; *Mr. Armstrong,* Henry B. Walthall; *Mr. Powell,* George Irving; *Mrs. Powell,* Hedda Hopper; *Peasant,* Nigel De Brulier; *Lt. Cameron,* Roscoe Karns; *MP,* James Pierce; *German Officer,* Carl Von Haartman.

It was the most dangerous of all sports and the most fascinating. It got into the blood like wine. It aged men forty years in forty days. It ruined nervous systems forever in an hour . . .

So wrote aviation ace Elliott White Springs in his book *Above the Bright Blue Sky,* which clearly spells out the glamour-horror of aerial combat in the First World War. Writing from his own experiences Springs claimed that a fighter pilot in that war had a service span of about three months, if he lived that long. The war had begun with enthusiasm, with regiments marching off to the sound of cheering crowds and martial music, but within a few months it had sunk in a quagmire of stinking mud. Military romanticism died in the trenches, and Europe was robbed of millions of young men. Famous cavalry brigades made their last charges as machinery gradually took over the science of warfare. Fighting became increasingly tedious and degrading as the four long years wore on. It was no longer a game for gentlemen—except in the air. There, at least in the beginning, knighthood had its last fling. The aristocrats of Britain, France and Germany took to jousting in the sky, saluting each other and sometimes breaking off the engagement when the other fellow signaled he had run out of ammunition. But by the time the Americans arrived, that kind of gallantry had gone, along with thousands of sons from Europe's finest families. By 1917 the planes were better and the dogfighting in deadly earnest.

With the signing of the armistice, Hollywood turned its back on the war. As a subject it was considered ugly and passé, but in 1924 Maxwell Anderson and Lawrence Stalling wrote a play, *What Price Glory?,* which won approval with its realistic

views of men in war. It was later made into a movie and with its success—and that of *The Big Parade*—the producers sensed that films about the war could find a market. The first to deal with World War I aviation was *Wings,* which came about when writer John Monk Saunders, who had served as a pilot, took a story to Paramount's Jesse L. Lasky. It captured Lasky's imagination and the decision was made to produce a movie of epic proportions, with a big budget and the unstinting aid of the U. S. War Department. Lasky retained Saunders as an advisor and hired William Wellman to direct. Wellman, then thirty, was the only Hollywood director to have seen active service as a pilot, having joined the Lafayette Flying Corps in 1916 and later transferred to the U.S. Army Air Service. Richard Arlen had also been a pilot in the last year of the war, as had a number of men who would be involved in the production of *Wings.*

The plot is thin, and viewed today an original print of this long silent picture hangs heavy—except for its extraordinary action sequences. The story

concerns Jack Powell (Charles "Buddy" Rogers) and David Armstrong (Arlen), who join the air service when America enters the war. Jack is loved by Mary Preston (Clara Bow), but he loves Sylvia Lewis (Jobyna Ralston), who is in love with David. The romantic complications cause friction between the two spirited young flyers but events while at a training camp draw them closer together and in France they become the best of friends. Mary joins a medical corps and is sent to France, where she sacrifices her job one night in Paris to save the drunk and disorderly Jack from being court-martialed for his behavior. The two friends, now both decorated for their bravery in combat, still bicker over Sylvia but an order arrives to attack and destroy German observation balloons. After successfully completing the mission, David is shot down and crash-lands behind German lines. He escapes capture and comes across an airfield, where he climbs into a Fokker and flies off. In the meantime, Jack is told that David has been killed in action. He takes to the sky in a rage of revenge, shooting down planes and strafing ground forces. Then he spots a lone

Charles "Buddy" Rogers, Clara Bow and Richard Arlen.

Roscoe Karns, Richard Tucker, Arlen and Rogers.

Arlen and Gary Cooper.

Fokker and attacks. David recognizes Jack's plane and waves to him to stop firing—but it is too late. David crashes into a large farmhouse and French soldiers lift him from the wreckage. Jack lands nearby to claim his trophy—the Iron Cross insignia, cut from the tail of the Fokker—and discovers his tragic mistake. He comforts the dying David and take his body back to the American base. Later, in America, Jack realizes his love for Mary.

The plot and the playing in *Wings* is dated, but not the aerial sequences. The chief photographer was Harry Perry, who had already won a reputation for shooting aerial footage, and who spent a year on *Wings,* heading up a team of twenty cameramen. The film contains no trick photography and no process footage. Camera mounts were welded over engines and behind pilots, and the photographers flew with the action. A few single cockpit planes had another cockpit cut into them for the cameramen. What they captured on film has never been surpassed—the swooping, banking, rolling, diving shots, the low sweeps over land and the covering of action incidents from all angles. The footage was at least equaled in *Hell's Angels* (1930) but it was the work of the same man—Harry Perry. In all the aviation films that followed, no one came up with any better ideas on how to photograph this kind of material.

Most of *Wings* was shot in Texas around San Antonio, where the government supplied personnel and facilities, including the use of Kelly Field and almost all the Army Air Service units then available. The Second Infantry Division, Army Engineers,

21

constructed a replica of the battlefield of St. Mihiel, at a cost to Paramount of more than a quarter of a million dollars, and five thousand men of the Second Division were made available, along with artillery and tanks, to reenact the decisive battle. *Wings* is a valuable film because of its aerial sequences but it also contains some of the best land fighting scenes done for a commercial picture. Acres of ground were used to depict the miles of trenches, barbed wire, shell holes, mud and sundry wreckage of this ghastly piece of warfare. It was filmed over an area of five square miles, using twenty-one cameras, half of them in airplanes and the others either shooting from a high tower or being tracked along the ground.

A few vintage planes were used in *Wings,* some Spads and Fokkers, but most were slightly disguised Army Air Service craft of 1926. They were flown by officers and cadets, with civilian stunt-pilots assigned to perform the daredevil sequences. One of them was the renowned Dick Grace, who fractured his neck crashing a Fokker. *Wings* was in production for over a year and ended up costing Paramount the then staggering sum of two million dollars. The time and effort paid off handsomely, with the picture receiving both public and critical approval, and triggering off other movie accounts of adventures in the First World War. *Hell's Angels* proved a worthy rival but most of the films made about aviation in that war failed to make any greater comment or impact. Warners did *The Dawn Patrol* in 1930, a much better story than *Wings* but containing less action, and improved upon it eight years later with the Errol Flynn remake. *Wings* elevated William Wellman to major directorial status and he did similar pictures like *Legion of the Condemned* (1928) and *Young Eagles* (1930), neither of which came within shooting distance of *Wings.* In 1956 he finally realized his ambition to do a film based on his own experiences as a World War I aviator but *Lafayette Escadrille* was lack-luster, with Wellman failing to make the picture the way he wanted. His arguments with Jack L. Warner were so bitter he turned his back on the film industry and retired. Perhaps Wellman had said all there was to say about being an aerial cavalier with *Wings.*

Rogers discovers the pilot of the German plane he has just shot down to be his friend Arlen.

Treasure Island

1934

An MGM Picture. Produced by Hunt Stromberg. Directed by Victor Fleming. Screenplay by John Lee Mahin, based on the novel by Robert Louis Stevenson. Photographed by Ray June and Clyde DeVinna. Music by Herbert Stothart. Running time: 95 minutes.

CAST

Long John Silver, Wallace Beery; *Jim Hawkins,* Jackie Cooper; *Billy Bones,* Lionel Barrymore; *Doctor Livesey,* Otto Kruger; *Captain Smollett,* Lewis Stone; *Squire Trelawney,* Nigel Bruce; *Ben Gunn,* Charles "Chic" Sale; *Pew,* William V. Mong; *Black Dog,* Charles McNaughton; *Mrs. Hawkins,* Dorothy Peterson.

The roster of adventure films would be considerably poorer were it not for the stories of Robert Louis Stevenson, as would a number of producers who have made booty from multiple versions of *Treasure Island, Dr. Jekyll and Mr. Hyde,* and *Kidnapped.* There have so far been three major productions of each of those novels, in addition to which there have been good pictures made from *The Black Arrow* (1948), a War of the Roses swashbuckler with Louis Hayward, and *The Master of Ballantrae* (1953), the last of Errol Flynn's top-notch action epics. *Ballantrae* had the advantage of being color photographed in Scotland, as did the 1971 version of *Kidnapped,* in which Michael Caine gave a performance that several critics considered quite Flynn-like. Stevenson himself was a Scot with an adventurous spirit, although cursed with poor health. This did not stop him from trying to live adventurously. His first book, *An Island Voyage*

(1878), written when he was twenty-eight, tells of his travels through Europe. It was on that trip that he met an American woman, Fanny Osbourne, and followed her to California, where they were married in 1880. For a while they lived in a mining camp, which produced his *The Silverado Squatters,* and they returned to Scotland in 1883, the year he wrote *Treasure Island.*

Treasure Island was Stevenson's first real success and came into being as an amusement for his stepson Lloyd, then thirteen and the obvious inspiration for Jim Hawkins. Stevenson one day sketched a map of an island and told the boy it was the hiding place of pirate swag. It was pure invention but it was so intriguing that Stevenson had to make up yarns to satisfy his son. The author soon realized the idea for a full book—one which came to be the primary item on almost any boy's list of adventure stories. *Treasure Island* and the books that followed enabled Stevenson to fulfill his desire to live in the South Seas, and he settled with his family in Samoa in 1890. He was then forty but ailing, and only four years remained for him. His funeral was of the kind he might well have invented for one of

The good ship *Hispaniola*.

his books; the Samoans, who treated him as if he were a king and called him Tusitala (Teller of Tales), carried his body to a high peak overlooking the ocean and buried him there. His tomb bears his own famous lines: "Home is the sailor, home from the sea, and the hunter home from the hill."

Choosing the MGM version of *Treasure Island* over the Disney version made in 1950, in which Robert Newton played Long John Silver, is a matter of personal preference and largely dictated by feelings of nostalgia. Newton played Silver in a very ripe fashion and did it so well it inspired a sequel, *Long John Silver* (1954) and a television series. Wallace Beery, a major attraction in 1934, similarly indulged himself in a hammy, growling performance as the treacherous but endearing pirate, strutting around on a wooden leg and a crutch, with a parrot on his shoulder screeching about "Pieces o' eight!"

This version of *Treasure Island* is a straightforward and robust account, thanks to the firm hand of director Victor Fleming, who was a charter member of the drinking-hunting-fishing en-

clave at MGM, along with Clark Gable and Spencer Tracy. Jackie Cooper was not exactly an ideal choice for an English lad, but at thirteen he was certainly the right age and his personality helped conceal his Hollywood aura. On the other hand Otto Kruger as Doctor Livesey, Lewis Stone as Captain Smollett, Nigel Bruce as Squire Trelawney and Lionel Barrymore as Billy Bones would doubtless have pleased Robert Louis Stevenson himself. It is their performances that give this picture much of its value.

The story is too familiar to need detailing. It begins at the Admiral Benbow Inn in an English port and has young Jim Hawkins becoming aware that rum-soaked old Captain Billy Bones has a secret, one that causes several shady characters to appear at the Inn and soon causes Billy's death. The secret is a map of an island in the Caribbean, where the late Captain Flint stashed his plunder. Jim gains possession of the map and his friends Squire Trelawney and Doctor Livesey outfit an expedition and hire the good ship *Hispaniola*, under the command of Captain Smollett. The crew turn out to be mostly ex-comrades of Flint and bound

Wallace Beery and Jackie Cooper check the original source.

Cooper, Otto Kruger and Dorothy Peterson.

Young Jim hears about the treasure from old Billy Bones (Lionel Barrymore).

Long John introduces Jim to his parrot, forever screeching about "Pieces o' eight, pieces o' eight!"

The Squire (Nigel Bruce), the Captain (Lewis Stone) and Jim await the pirate attack on the stockade.

Crazy old Ben Gunn (Charles 'Chic' Sale) advises the Squire not to make any deals with Long John.

for his treasure. Their leader is Long John Silver, who befriends Jim but violates the young boy's trust when he turns mutineer. Once on the island Smollett instructs Livesey, Trelawney, Jim and the loyal sailors to construct a stockade to defend themselves. But things don't go well for Silver and his pirates, who, among other things, can't locate the treasure. The reason for this is a strange, half-mad old man named Ben Gunn, who has long since dug up the treasure and hidden it in a cave. Ben, marooned years before by Flint, befriends Jim and helps his friends defeat the pirates. Smollett claps Long John in irons as they sail back to England with the wealth but the wily old seaman works his charm on Jim and manages to make his escape.

Treasure Island is such a perfectly constructed and appealing yarn that it defies doing badly. The 1934 version creaks a little with age but provided one is not repelled by Beery's somewhat rancid playing of Long John the picture still casts a spell. But whether it is this one or some other telling of *Treasure Island,* it has caused countless lads to stride around with wooden cutlasses in hand chanting:

> Fifteen men on the dead man's chest—
> Yo-ho-ho and a bottle of rum!
> Drink and the devil had done for the rest—
> Yo-ho-ho and a bottle of rum!

Long John captures Jim but uses him just to persuade the other side to lead him to the treasure.

The Scarlet Pimpernel

1934

A London Film. Produced by Alexander Korda. Directed by Harold Young. Screenplay by Lajos Biros, S. N. Behrman, Robert Sherwood and Arthur Wimperis, based on the novel by Baroness Orczy. Photographed by Harold Rossen. Music by Arthur Benjamin. Running time: 95 minutes.

CAST

Sir Percy Blakeney, Leslie Howard; *Lady Blakeney,* Merle Oberon; *Chauvelin,* Raymond Massey; *Prince of Wales,* Nigel Bruce; *Priest,* Bramwell Fletcher; *Sir Andrew Ffoulkes,* Anthony Bushell: *Suzanne de Tournay,* Joan Gardner; *Armand St. Just,* Walter Rilla; *Countess de Tournay,* Mabel Terry-Lewis; *Count de Tournay,* O. B. Clarence; *Robespierre,* Ernest Milton; *Colonel Winterbottom,* Edmond Breon; *Romney,* Melville Cooper; *Barber,* Gib McLaughlin; *Treadle,* Moreland Graham; *Jellyband,* John Turnbull; *Sally,* Gertrude Musgrove; *Lord Grenville,* Allan Jeayes.

> "We seek him here, we seek him there,
> Those Frenchies seek him everywhere.
> Is he in heaven? Is he in hell?
> That demmed, elusive Pimpernel."

Thus did Sir Percy Blakeney, with his foppish manner, his drawling, Mayfair accent, and his doggerel, amuse the members of London society in the 1790s as the French authorities strove to discover the brave Englishman rescuing aristocrats from the guillotine. Little did they realize that very man was Sir Percy himself.

The French Revolution, which officially began with the storming of the Bastille in 1789 but had been brewing for many years, has yet to find a definitive account on the screen. Mostly it has been the subject of adventure yarns, of which *The Scarlet Pimpernel* is the primary specimen, and romantic tragedies like Dickens' *A Tale of Two Cities* (filmed in 1917, 1926, 1935 and 1958) and the Thalberg production of *Marie Antoinette* (1938). *Reign of Terror* (1949), with Richard Hart as Robespierre, touched upon the vicious politics of the era but no film has fully caught the hideous frenzy of the revolution, with the oppressed masses exploding into a decade of bloody brutality and senselessly eradicating the entire aristocracy. The horror reached its peak in 1793 and '94, the period which came to be known as "The Reign of Terror," and it was this period in which Baroness Orczy set her celebrated story.

Emma Magdalena Rosalia Maria Josepha Barbara

Orczy understood the balance between peasantry and aristocracy. She was born of a noble family on an estate in Hungary in 1865, and her father was a member of Franz Josef's glittering court in Vienna. The family moved to England when she was fifteen, where they continued to move in high society, even though they had lost most of their wealth in the Hungarian agrarian troubles of the 1870s. In writing about the revolt of the French peasants, the young Baroness had only to use her imagination, since she had seen plenty of unrest —although no bloodshed—among the hungry, discontented peasants of Hungary. The Orczy family were also patrons of the arts, and in deciding on a career the Baroness studied art and became an accomplished painter. But while studying she married an illustrator of popular fiction, which led to her finding her talent as a writer. Emma Orczy first wrote short stories for magazines, but in 1905 she wrote a play about the French Revolution, calling it *The Scarlet Pimpernel*. While waiting for an available London theatre in which to stage it, she rewrote the material as a novel. No publisher showed any interest in the manuscript until the play proved to be a success. The Baroness always claimed that it was "God's will" that she wrote the novel that became a classic, but God was not so gracious about the dozen sequels she wrote about the adventures of the Pimpernel. They did well in their time but only the original story endures. However, she enjoyed success and lived a full, rich life, dying in 1947 at the age of eighty-two.

Alexander Korda's 1934 film captures the spirit of the Orczy novel, although why it took four scenarists to do it is somewhat mysterious. Korda tried again in 1950 with *The Elusive Pimpernel,* starring David Niven as Sir Percy, and failed to inject any excitment into it. Any mention of the film causes Niven to shudder. The glory of the 1934 version is the performance of Leslie Howard as Sir Percy, a perfect characterization of a laconic English fop—wealthy, bored and disdainful of almost everything. But it is all a mask for his endeavors as the leader of a league of gentlemen committed to rescue their peers in France. Nobody suspects Sir Percy, whose main interest appears to be fashion and who cultivates his friendship with the Prince of Wales (Nigel Bruce) by advising

Sir Percy Blakeney (Leslie Howard) at his club.

George Romney (Melville Cooper) paints the lovely Lady Blakeney (Merle Oberon).

him on his choice of clothes. His supercilious manners eventually prove a strain even for his wife, the lovely Marguerite (Merle Oberon). She is a French aristocrat but entirely in the dark as to the identity of the man who so gallantly and skillfully snatches her friends from under the very shadow of the guillotine. Sir Percy assumes many disguises, including those of an old hag sitting with others and enjoying the executions, and a country bumpkin driving an old cart. Sir Percy and his colleagues whisk the recued parties off to Calais and then across the Channel to safety in Dover. The situation grows ever more embarrassing for the French government, who send one of their most dedicated members, Chauvelin (Raymond Massey), to England as their ambassador.

Chauvelin minges with the English aristocrats in London, convinced that the Pimpernel must surely be one of their kind. He has no luck but when the French government informs him his life is forfeit unless he solves the mystery, Chauvelin decides to bear down on Lady Blakeney with a bargain—the life of her arrested brother in Paris in return for help in discovering the Pimpernel. The distraught Marguerite agrees and takes part in a maneuver in Calais which leads to Sir Percy's being trapped. And she is horribly surprised to find that the dashing Pimpernel is the meek man she has known as her husband. Sir Percy strikes a bargain with Chauvelin. In return for the release of his wife

Howard and Walter Rilla (as Armand St. Just).

The evil Chauvelin (Raymond Massey) coercing Lady Blakeney.

and her safe passage back to England he will surrender to Chauvelin, even though it means immediate death before a firing squad. Chauvelin's triumph is short-lived. He listens with intense satisfaction as he hears the rifles discharge but a few moments later he is aghast to see Sir Percy walk through the door—all the men of the firing squad are in the service of the Pimpernel—and the game goes on.

Leslie Howard was precisely the right man to play Sir Percy. His languid style of acting, the gentility masking strength and the slightly tongue-in-cheek attitude toward life all fitted the milieu of the part. Howard was one of those actors who best exemplified the old-fashioned concept of the English gentleman and yet he was actually of Hungarian blood. He was also a man of real courage and his services to England during the Second World War were considerable. Howard involved himself with making films of definite propagandistic value, beginning with *Pimpernel Smith,* a contemporary parallel with the Orczy novel, as a man helping people escape Nazi persecution. Then came his contribution to *49th Parallel, The Gentle Sex,* a salute to the Women's Territorial Service, *The Lamp Still Burns,* a tribute to nurses, and finally *The First of the Few,* in which Howard played R. J. Mitchell, the man who designed the Spitfire. He volunteered his services to the British government for use in any manner they might deem necessary and in early 1943 they sent him to Lisbon. He went there seemingly to lecture on the theatre and film business but he was really involved in seeking the goodwill of the Portuguese in the face of their possible siding with Germany. Shortly after leaving the airport at Lisbon, the plane carrying Leslie Howard was shot down in the Bay of Biscay. The Germans were under the impression Sir Winston Churchill, who had just left an allied conference in Algiers, was also on board. The personification of Sir Percy Blakeney thereby met his end.

Sir Percy bargains with Chauvelin.

The Count of Monte Cristo

1934

A Reliance Picture. Produced by Edward Small. Directed by Rowland V. Lee. Screenplay by Philip Dunne, Dan Totheroh and Rowland V. Lee, based on the novel by Alexandre Dumas. Photographed by Peverell J. Marley. Music by Alfred Newman. Running time: 113 minutes.

CAST

Edmond Dantes, Robert Donat; *Mercedes,* Elissa Landi; *De Villefort, Jr.,* Louis Calhern; *Mondego,* Sidney Blackmer; *Danglars,* Raymond Walburn; *Abbé Faria,* O. P. Heggie; *Captain Le Clere,* William Farnum; *Madame De Rosas,* Georgia Caine; *Morrel,* Walter Walker; *De Villefort, Sr.,* Lawrence Grant; *Jacopo,* Luis Alberni; *Valentine,* Irene Hervey; *Albert,* Douglas Walton; *Clothilde,* Juliette Compton; *Fouquet,* Clarence Wilson; *Haydee,* Eleanor Phelps; *Louis XVIII,* Ferninand Munier; *Judge,* Holmes Herbert; *Napoleon,* Paul Irving.

The Count of Monte Cristo was Robert Donat's only Hollywood picture. In 1933 this charming, handsome Englishman had cut a romantic figure as Thomas Culpeper, the lover of Catherine Howard, in *The Private Life of Henry VIII,* and producer Edward Small decided this was the ideal actor to play Edmond Dantes in his expensive movie of Dumas' classic tale of romance, intrigue and revenge in Napoleonic times. The film was a great success and Donat's strong performance elevated him to stardom. He returned to England but immediately entered into discussions with Warner Bros. about playing the lead in their proposed *Captain Blood.* Warners were so sure that Donat would be a hit as Sabatini's doctor-pirate that they even talked of thereafter giving him *Anthony Adverse* and possibly *Robin Hood.* But Donat changed his mind; he was asthmatic and any physical exertion was hard for him. (The affliction resulted in his death in 1958 at the age of fifty-three.) His decision caused worry for Warners but after much head-thumping they took a chance on a young Tasmanian on their payroll—Errol Flynn.

Prior to Small's production, *Monte Cristo* had been filmed several times in silent versions, of which the best was the one with John Gilbert in 1922. Despite the popularity of the Small film, no American producer touched the material again until 1974, when Norman Rosemont made an excellent version starring Richard Chamberlain and having the great advantage of being color photographed in some of the actual locations of the Dumas story: the port of Marseilles and the nearby islands of If and Monte

The Count breaks DeVillefort.

Cristo. The Rosemont film was shown only on television in the United States but released theatrically in Europe. In between there had been French versions in 1954 and 1961, the latter with Louis Jourdan as Dantes (Jourdan played De Villefort in the Rosemont production). And in Hollywood there had been some peculiar spin-offs: *The Son of Monte Cristo* (1940), *The Return of Monte Cristo* (1946), *The Wife of Monte Cristo* (1946), *The Sword of Monte Cristo* (1951), and most ridiculous of all, Sonja Henie's *The Countess of Monte Cristo* (1948).

The Donat film is faithful to the spirit of Dumas but simplifies the story somewhat and concocts a happy ending. Edmond Dantes is a young sailor, happy with his new promotion to officer and with his imminent marriage to Mercedes (Elissa Landi). Suddenly he is arrested, charged with being a supporter of the deposed Napoleon and thrown into prison at the Chateau d'If, without trial and with no prospects of release. Years drag by and young Dantes ages in the filthy cell and dreams of revenge. He realizes he is the victim of a plot and that his enemies are De Villefort (Louis Calhern), a high ranking civic official whose father is a Napoleonic sympathizer and to whom Dantes was unwittingly carrying a message from Napoleon; Montego, a soldier who has coveted, and soon marries, Mercedes; and Danglars, an envious fellow naval officer. All benefit from the banishing of Dantes and all fulfill their ambitions to reach points of wealth and power.

In prison Dantes one day hears tapping from a wall and is amazed to later see a large brick pushed out and an old man emerge from the hole. He is the Abbé Faria (O. P. Heggie), who has spent years digging a tunnel from his cell in the hope of reaching an outer wall. The erudite Abbé teaches Dantes about science, philosophy and languages as they dig together, but the old man dies. His body is sewn in a sack to be slung into the sea, but Dantes removes the body, places it in his own cell and sews himself into the sack. Once free, he makes his way to the island of Monte Cristo, where the Abbé has informed him of an immense repository of wealth. He finds the story to be true and soon establishes himself as the wealthiest man in Europe, the distinguished, cultured Count of Monte Cristo.

Some twenty years have passed since the plot

Young Edmond Dantes (Robert Donat) and his bride-to-be (Elissa Landi).

Edmond and the Abbe (O. P. Heggie).

The treasure in the caves of Monte Cristo.

and Dantes takes up residence in Paris, where he courts the interests of De Villefort, now a powerful government minister, Mondego, a famous general, and Danglars, now a prominent banker. None recognizes him and all seek to be of service. Dantes exposes Mondego's scandalous life, causing him to commit suicide; he inveigles Danglars into financial speculations which lead to bankruptcy and insanity; and he manages to get himself put on trial, with DeVillefort as his accuser, but producing evidence of great corruption which results in DeVillefort's arrest. Expunged of revenge, he then turns to the faithful Mercedes and they begin a life together— an ending at variance with the Dumas book, in which the lovers realize too much has happened to make a reconciliation possible.

Fascinating though Edmond Dantes is as a fictional figure, he is not as colorful as the man who invented him. Alexandre Dumas (1802–1870) was larger than life, with a forceful personality, an astonishing creativity and a craving for success, in which he compromised himself by quickly churning out hack material for magazines and the theatre, and by filching from other writers. Even the authorship of *The Three Musketeers* is questionable. It was done, with some of his other historical novels, in collaboration with Auguste Maquet, and it has never been determined as to who did what. Dumas' name appeared on almost three hundred books and copious quantities of articles and plays. He was a social carouser and a political liberal, and in 1860 he had a fling at real adventure with Garibaldi's campaign in Italy.

The Count of Monte Cristo was published in 1845 and it is probably entirely Dumas' work. Three years before, while visiting Marseilles, he had become intrigued with the islands of Elba, If and Monte Cristo, which lie within sight of the city. He hired a boatman to take him on a trip, in the course of which the boatman told him about the legend of

Young Mondego (Douglas Walton) challenges the Count.

Settling the score with Mondego.

Monte Cristo, a bleak, rocky island never visited because of the supposed presence of malaria-carrying mosquitoes. Dumas learned that the island was said to be the resting place of stores of pirate treasures, buried in the ruins of a long-deserted monastery. After peering at the island and visiting the Chateau D'If, and musing upon Napoleon's exile on Elba, Dumas concocted his story. He was already a popular writer, having pleased the Parisians with his plays and *The Three Musketeers,* and *Monte Cristo* first appeared as a magazine serial, the installments of which kept Paris in suspense, much as a popular television series would do today. Controversial though Dumas may have been, he wrote with flair and his inventions of plots and characters were exciting. He may well be regarded as the principal architect of the "cloak and dagger"

school of fiction. Those who were to specialize in historical romance in years to come—people like Baroness Orczy, Anthony Hope, A. E. W. Mason, P. C. Wren and Rafael Sabatini—obviously studied Dumas.

When Dumas was on his deathbed, his playwright-son Alexandre fils read some of his books to him, since the old man claimed he had never had time to read his own works and had forgotten their plots. It is said that the last one he heard was *The Count of Monte Cristo* and that he was only halfway through it when he realized his time had come. He whispered to his son, "I have only one regret. I wish I knew how it comes out," and lapsed into unconsciousness. Only a soulless scholar could doubt such an anecdote.

The re-union of the lovers, something Dumas never had in mind.

Tarzan and His Mate

1934

An MGM Picture. Produced by Bernard H. Hyman. Directed by Jack Conway (attributed to Cedric Gibbons). Screenplay by James Kevin McGuinness, adapted from the characters of Edgar Rice Burroughs by Howard Emmett Rogers and Leon Gordon. Photographed by Charles Clarke and Clyde De Vinna. Running time: 105 minutes.

CAST

Tarzan, Johnny Weissmuller; *Jane Parker,* Maureen O'Sullivan; *Harry Holt,* Neil Hamilton; *Martin Arlington,* Paul Cavanagh; *Bramish,* Forrester Harvey; *Saidi,* Nathan Curry; *Pierce,* William Stark; *Vanness,* Desmond Roberts.

In the minds of most film enthusiasts the personification of Tarzan will always be Johnny Weissmuller, the Olympic swimming champ who assumed the guise in 1932 and played the noble Ape Man over the following sixteen years. However, his was not the image Tarzan's creator, Edgar Rice Burroughs (1875–1950), had in mind when he began writing the stories in 1912. Burroughs wrote Tarzan as an English aristocrat lost in the African jungle as a child and brought up by apes after the death of his parents. He taught himself to read and later traveled the world before returning to Africa, where he married an American girl named Jane Porter. His was a split-level life—a gentleman whenever he wished to be and a jungle primitive in the

place he considered his home. This concept was adhered to when *Tarzan* was first filmed in 1918 with Elmo Lincoln in the role, wearing, as per Burroughs, a lion-skin tunic and a headband. Lincoln made two more films as Tarzan and so did some other actors. MGM's decision to get into the Tarzan business came about as the result of their filming *Trader Horn* in Africa, beginning in 1929 and taking the better part of two years to turn it into an acceptable picture. Director W. S. Van Dyke and his crew had come back from this first Hollywood safari into the Dark Continent with miles of footage but not much excitement and the studio added locally shot sequences to make it more interesting. It did, however, provide them with plenty of stock shots for their library and it would be put to good use in their Tarzan pictures.

The idea to do the series came from MGM's brilliant young head of production, Irving Thalberg, who felt that a new concept of Tarzan was needed. Burroughs made little objection to the changes and had nothing to do with writing the screenplays, other than collecting royalties. Thalberg accepted Weissmuller, who had no prior experience in films

40

Tarzan and his lovely mate.

but who had greatly distinguished himself as an aquatic athlete, having won five Olympic championships in 1924 and 1928 and numerous national events in swimming. The new Tarzan became a gentle brute, an illiterate and appealingly simple man attired only in a loincloth, and the love of his life became an English gentlewoman, stranded in the jungle after the death of her trader father. Weissmuller was to make six Tarzan pictures for MGM, with the refined Irish beauty Maureen O'Sullivan as his Jane, and the best of them is the second, *Tarzan and His Mate*.

An appreciation of *Tarzan and His Mate* requires a little knowledge of the first film, *Tarzan, the Ape Man*, since it is veritably a continuation. It concerns a safari to the fabled Mutia Escarpment (fictional), the place of the elephants' burial grounds and a vast repository of ivory. The escarpment is remote and exceedingly difficult to reach, involving thick jungles, steep cliffs, savage animals and fierce natives. The trek ends with the death of Jane's father, the leader of the safari, and Jane's rescue from a band of savage dwarfs by Tarzan, whom she at first fears but soon comes to love for his

tender, protective and childlike nature. Her suitor, Harry Holt (Neil Hamilton), the second in command of the safari, recognizes romantic defeat and returns to England. The picture was directed by W. S. Van Dyke, who spotted it with shots from his *Trader Horn*. In producing the first few of their Tarzan pictures MGM spared no expense or effort in order to make them major attractions. More than a year was spent on each of the first five and they were intricately edited with process and trick shots, action sequences, location shooting and difficult-to-film animal scenes. Most of the exteriors involving the actors were shot around Lake Sherwood and the Malibu hills about twenty miles north of Los Angeles.

With *Tarzan, the Ape Man* a box-office bonanza MGM set about making a sequel and assigned their prestigious art director Cedric Gibbons to direct it. It was his first and last stab at directing and he was taken off the project after a few weeks of shooting, apparently unable to handle actors or action. His name remained on the credit titles but *Tarzan and His Mate* was actually directed by the veteran Jack Conway. Despite a running time of

41

Tarzan and His Mate is rich with adventures and pictorial interest, not the least of which is the briefly attired Maureen O'Sullivan, before the Production Code called for a more conservative costume. The beautiful actress was locked into a firm MGM contract and despite her protests was required to play Jane in four more productions—*Tarzan Escapes, Tarzan Finds a Son, Tarzan's Secret Treasure,* and *Tarzan's New York Adventure.* Many more Tarzan pictures would follow, some with Weissmuller and some with other actors but those made at MGM in the 1930s were the best.

Film historian Rudy Behlmer covered the subject thoroughly in his article "The MGM Tarzans" for the magazine *Screen Facts* (No. 15, 1967). Referring to *Tarzan and His Mate,* Behlmer writes: "The production values and trick photography, together with the remarkable wealth of incident and imaginative contriving surpassed anything like it before or since in a jungle melodrama. [It] had a superabundance of everything: Jungle battles occurred every few moments—including a magnificently photographed fight between Tarzan and a giant crocodile. A veritable trapeze act involving Tarzan, Jane and Cheeta was carried on throughout the film; a native attack on a safari near the opening was so spectacular and elaborated upon, it would serve nicely as climax to any other jungle opus; and the actual finale was a deluge of killing, torturing, writhing, screaming, stampeding, trumpeting—a cacophonic nightmare involving Jane, the safari-unfriendly natives, lions, and Tarzan with his apes and elephants to the rescue . . . *Tarzan and His Mate* represents the quintessence of a combination Circus Maximus and sideshow. Succeeding jungle pictures never again dealt so profusely with the violence and carnage found in *Mate.* An underwater sequence with Tarzan and a brassiereless Jane (doubled), along with a good deal of other material, was cut from the film after the initial playdates. At that time the film was pruned from eleven reels to nine."

Censorship changed the course of the Tarzan pictures after 1934. Various bodies, notably the Catholic Legion of Decency, demanded reforms regarding violence and sexual references, especially for films such as these, so obviously designed for the younger market. Two years later The Society for the Prevention of Cruelty to Animals was able to bring considerable legislation to bear in the handling of animals in filming. Admirable though these moves were, they made it difficult for producers to make jungle movies with the excitement and the earthiness of *Tarzan and His Mate.*

almost two hours the film has little plot. It begins with Harry Holt (Neil Hamilton again) returning to Africa as a guide for ivory-hungry Martin Arlington (Paul Cavanagh), a none too scrupulous gentleman. The trip to the Mutia Escarpment proves brutal and the two Englishmen lose most of their bearers to attacking natives and animals. On reaching Tarzan they find him reluctant to reveal the burial grounds of his beloved elephants and to Harry's regret he finds Jane totally happy and content with her Ape Man. Arlington, on learning that a wounded elephant will always make his way to the burial grounds, deliberately wounds one and then shoots Tarzan. He leaves him for dead but various animals rescue Tarzan and he recovers. Jane and the hunters reach the prized burial grounds but the plans to haul away ivory are ended by attacking natives and then by a band of lions, in the course of which both Holt and Arlington are killed, with Jane being rescued in the nick of time by Tarzan, his apes and his elephants.

Neil Hamilton, Maureen O'Sullivan, Johnny Weissmuller and Paul Cavanagh.

Tarzan being introduced to the mysteries of recorded music and cocktail dresses.

That way to the elephants' graveyard.

So this is it?

Was the elephant's name Yorick?

The Lives of a Bengal Lancer

1935

A Paramount Picture. Produced by Louis D. Lighton. Directed by Henry Hathaway. Screenplay by Waldemar Young, John L. Balderston and Achmed Abdullah, based on the book by Major Francis Yeats-Brown, adapted by Grover Jones and William Slavens McNutt. Photographed by Charles Lang. Music by Milan Roder. Running time: 109 minutes.

CAST

Lieutenant McGregor, Gary Cooper; *Lieutenant Fortesque,* Franchot Tone; *Lieutenant Stone,* Richard Cromwell; *Colonel Stone,* Sir Guy Standing; *Major Hamilton,* C. Aubrey Smith; *Hamzulia Khan,* Monte Blue; *Tania Volkanskaya,* Kathleen Burke; *Lieutenant Barrett,* Colin Tapley; *Mohammed Khan,* Douglas Dumbrille; *Emir,* Akim Tamiroff; *Hendrickson,* Jameson Thomas; *Ram Singh,* Noble Johnson; *Major General Woodley,* Lumsden Hare; *Grand Vizier,* J. Carroll Naish; *The Ghazi,* Rollo Lloyd; *Snake Charmer,* Leonid Kinskey.

Whatever else may be said of British rule in India, it produced a Niagara of literature, both factual and romantic, and it provided the Indian Army with long chronicles of campaigns in trying to control the ever-conflicting elements of a most fractious country. Even today its hundreds of languages and dozens of religions, often bitterly opposed to each other, make it difficult to govern, and in the two centuries of British administration, India was an ever-seething cauldron of problems. Among the regiments that gained distinction in these years was the Bengal Lancers, who had served in the Afghan and Sikh wars prior to the Indian Mutiny of 1857 and who were instrumental in putting down the mutiny. The Lancers were prominent as defenders of India's northwest frontier, notably the Khyber Pass, with its rebellious tribesmen. In 1930 Paramount bought Major Francis Yeats-Brown's book *The Lives of a Bengal Lancer* and sent a team to India to study the settings of the story and shoot background footage. By the time the studio came to make the picture, very little of the footage or the book had survived the production. However, what did get on the screen was just about the best of all the many British and American movies about military adventures in India.

The story is brimming over with what is now rather snidely referred to in some quarters as male machismo. The only woman is a beautiful Russian spy, and it is interesting to note that Russia, as in

44

The Charge of the Light Brigade, is viewed in a villainous light because of its eyes on India. The whole history of India's northern boundaries is one of perpetual skirmishing with covetous neighbors, who, as this film has it, sponsored schemes of ambitious tribal chieftains to overthrow the British. The villain of the piece is the cultured, Oxford-educated Mohammed Khan (Douglas Dumbrille), who entertains British officers while plotting against them. New to the scene is young Lieutenant Stone (Richard Cromwell), fresh from England and eager to serve under his father, the colonel of the regiment (Sir Guy Standing). The young man is chilled to find his father greeting him impersonally, as just another junior officer, but he is befriended by Captain McGregor (Gary Cooper) and flippant Lieutenant Forsythe (Franchot Tone). Under their tutelage he soon learns about native customs, such as the Hindu horror of pigs. He watches with amazement as the veteran McGregor pries information out of a captured rebel by threatening to sew him up in a pigskin. The brave rebel is willing to endure any torture short of that.

McGregor is assigned to head a detail to discover what has happened to Lieutenant Barrett (Colin Tapley), sent weeks previously to gather information about the suspected plans for rebellion. They find Barrett and learn that Mohammed Khan is urging unity among local tribesmen and that he has promised to supply them with vast amounts of ammunition. Upon reporting the findings to Colonel Stone he learns that the ammunition has been delivered to the friendly Emir of Gopal (Akim Tamiroff). Stone, McGregor, Forsythe and young Stone then visit the Emir for a week of hunting, in the course of which young Stone is captured by the Khan's men. The capture is effected by the beautiful Russian spy and Stone is whisked away to the Khan's mountain fortress. McGregor and Forsythe disguise themselves as natives and enter the fortress, where they are soon captured and thrown into the same cell with Stone. Each of the officers is tortured in order to learn the whereabouts of the ammunition (in British hands). One of the devices is the sticking of wooden slivers under fingernails, with the slivers being set afire. McGregor and Forsythe withstand the torture but young Stone breaks down and reveals what the rebels want to know. Not only is the pain

Captain McGregor (Gary Cooper).

too much for him but he now resents his father and looks to harm him.

The Khan successfully locates the ammunition and brings it to his fortress, where he boasts to the British officers that the Bengal Lancers will be liquidated when they attack. McGregor, Forsythe and Stone manage to break out of their cell and make their way to the armory as the Lancers advance on the Khan's fortress. They seize machine guns and mow down the insurgents. Young Stone finds his courage and tackles the Khan, whom he kills, as McGregor blows up the stores of ammunition, which costs him his life. The Lancers then take care of the remainder of the battle. Later, on the parade ground of the 41st Regiment of the Bengal Lancers, Colonel Stone pins medals on the chests of his son and Forsythe, and attaches the Victoria Cross to the saddle of McGregor's horse.

The Lives of a Bengal Lancer is a glittering product of Hollywood's Golden Age, when companies like Paramount had a veritable army of artisans on their payrolls, and when the costs of hiring large numbers of actors and extras and moving them to a distant location were quite reasonable when balanced with the probable returns of a box-office winner in the assured block-booking circuits. Much of the picture

was shot in the spectacular Sierra Nevada range, around Bishop and Lone Pine, three hundred miles north of Los Angeles. The forty years that have passed since the making of *Bengal Lancer* have drastically altered views about military glory and made archaic such themes as "the honor of the regiment" and "the proper conduct of an officer and gentleman." The film must be seen in the proper perspective. There was a time when such themes were basic views and it is worthy of note that two of the actors playing officers, Sir Guy Standing and Sir C. Aubrey Smith, were themselves very much of this "old school." The fact that the three leading officers were played by Americans did not seem to worry even British moviegoers; in fact, the film received one of its best reviews from the London *Daily Telegraph*: ". . . the best army picture ever made." It was nominated for an Oscar as the best film of 1935, which it did not win, but Clem Beauchamp and Paul Winz deservedly picked up Oscars for their direction of the action sequences. The action, the handsomely uniformed Lancers and their ranks of fine horses, and the spirited playing made this a milestone in the art of making adventure films.

46

McGregor threatens a rebel with the sacrilege of being wrapped in a pig skin—and gets the information he needs. Lt. Fortesque (Franchot Tone) understands.

McGregor locates the missing men and reports to his colonel (Sir Guy Standing).

Kathleen Burke, Cooper, Douglas Dumbrille, Franchot Tone and Richard Cromwell.

Lt. Stone (Cromwell) joins his colleagues in jail.

47

The Call of the Wild

1935

A Twentieth Century Picture. Produced by Darryl F. Zanuck. Directed by William Wellman. Screenplay by Gene Fowler and Leonard Praskins, based on the novel by Jack London. Photographed by Charles Rosher. Music by Alfred Newman. Running time: 95 minutes.

CAST

Jack Thornton, Clark Gable; *Claire Blake,* Loretta Young; *Shorty Hoolihan,* Jack Oakie; *Smith,* Reginald Owen; *John Blake,* Frank Conroy; *Marie,* Katherine DeMille; *Groggin,* Sidney Toler; *Ole,* James Burke; *Francois,* Charles Stevens; *Kali,* Lalos Encinas; *Frank,* Duke Green; *Hilda,* Marie Wells.

In 1943 the late Michael O'Shea appeared in the title role of *Jack London* and while it was not a very deep account of London's life, it did convey the message that he was not simply a man who sat down and wrote stories. He lived them. The O'Shea picture related some of the adventures of the globe-trotting London (1876–1916), showing him as a sailor under canvas, as a war correspondent, and as a curious observer of life in rough and remote places. It did not touch upon his rather troubled spirit, his profound belief in socialism or the fact that he took his own life at the age of forty. That he wrote so vividly about firsthand adventures made him a popular author and a magnet for the film

business. Movies were made of his stories years before he died and his best books were made into pictures several times—there are, so far, half a dozen versions of *The Sea Wolf,* of which the finest is the Edward G. Robinson edition in 1941. Almost on the same level is *The Adventures of Martin Eden* (1942), with Glenn Ford as a writer sailing on a terror of a ship, clearly material derived from London's own adventures.

London gained his widest success with his stories of the wild northlands, the Yukon, Alaska, the gold-crazed prospectors in the Klondike, and most particularly, the dogs that were as much a part of these men's lives as the horse to the cowboy. His *White Fang* is the dog story *par excellence,* with *The Call of the Wild,* written in 1903, trailing not far behind. The hero of that book is Buck, a stout-hearted and faithful canine, but when Darryl Zanuck made *The Call of the Wild* as a Clark Gable vehicle, the dog's role was somewhat diminished, although the dog used, a huge and handsome St. Bernard, made it difficult for the actors to dominate the scenes. Other than that, the screenplay stuck fairly closely to London's novel. Jack Thornton (Gable) is an ad-

venturous young prospector, who strikes it lucky but then quickly fritters away his gold on the gambling tables of Skagway. Consoling himself at the bar, he comes across an old friend, Shorty (Jack Oakie), just out of jail and in possession of knowledge of a gold find. He and Thornton set out to locate it and in choosing a team of dogs, they come across Buck, a ferocious brute just about to be bought by an imperious Englishman named Smith (Reginald Owen). The dog bites Smith, who is then willing to pay any price for him just for the pleasure of killing the dog. Thornton is intrigued by the animal, buys him to stop Smith from getting him, and soon has Buck docile and devoted.

In making their way to the distant location of the gold cache, Thornton and Shorty come across Claire Blake (Loretta Young), adrift in the woods after losing her husband. The husband turns out to be the man with the real claim to the gold, and his wife is at first suspicious of her rescuers. They take her to Dawson and there make a partnership to locate the gold, since Claire is now convinced her husband is dead. But they need money in order to purchase equipment and supplies. Thornton is broke

but Smith, still adamant to get Buck and kill him, bets a thousand dollars that the dog cannot pull a thousand-pound weight over the course of a hundred yards. Buck seems to sense the urgency and comes through with a mighty effort that gets Thornton the money. After a long and arduous trek through the woods and mountains they locate the cabin which marks the site of the gold find. Shorty returns to Dawson to file the claim, and Thornton and Claire, who have gradually been falling in love, surrender to their feelings. So does Buck, who has a girlfriend in the woods, a she-wolf whose bays draw Buck away from the cabin—the call of the wild. But all is far from well. Smith and his cohorts have also been on the trail of the gold find and in order to find it they have escorted Blake (Frank Conroy), the husband believed to be dead, to his property. In sight of the cabin Smith orders his two men to kill Blake, after which they proceed to hold up Thornton, load their jackets with sacks of gold dust, and strap money belts containing it around themselves. Their victory is short-lived—Smith and his men are tipped out of their canoe in the rapids and because they are weighed down with gold they drown.

Jack Oakie, Clark Gable and the owner of the joint.

The idyll of Thornton and Claire is also short-lived. Blake is not dead. Buck finds the badly wounded man and leads Thornton to him. Claire now faces a choice and to Thornton's dismay she chooses to stay with her husband, although assuring Thornton that her love for him is genuine. Shorty arrives back, having filed the claim, now a joint ownership with the Blakes. Thornton has lost Claire but at least he has the loyal Buck, his friend Shorty and a considerable fortune.

The Call of the Wild has lost little of its appeal with the passing years, although it can be argued that it has an aura of romanticism that is at variance with the kind of harsh reality London wrote about in his tales of prospecting in the north. On the other hand, the film truly conveys the rigors of the climate and the grandeur of snowy wastelands, dark forests and mountain peaks. It comes to life vividly in the recreations of the wild towns of Skagway and Dawson, with their muddy main streets, high prices, raucous saloons and hordes of hard-drinking, gambling, grubby men. Much of the exterior filming was done in the state of Washington, on the slopes of Mount Baker at an elevation of five thousand feet.

The winter shooting proved much tougher than the cast and crew had expected. The company, about a hundred strong, had to use snowplows every day to get to their locations and back to their camp. The production was hit by blizzards, with the result that the shooting schedule was doubled. Those who worked on the location claim that there were times when they ran out of food and had to trek to nearby communities, and that with temperatures below zero the cameras became inoperable. However, the effort was worth it because the scenes of the actors making their way through the snowy mountains have a gripping reality to them. Making the picture proved almost as arduous as some of the adventures depicted in the screenplay, and probably caused Jack London to chuckle—somewhere up there in the great snowy beyond.

William Wellman's firm directorial hand and Charles Rosher's sharp black-and-white photography give *The Call of the Wild* its style, but the major asset is Clark Gable. Very much the man's man and a little embarrassed about making a living as an actor, he was perfectly at home in the role of Jack Thornton. It required little in the way of acting

And Buck.

and as an avid hunter-fisherman-outdoors type Gable enjoyed the assignment. And it was the picture that finally set him in the heroic mold, after a string of crime and gangster roles and knockabout comedies. Then came *China Seas, Mutiny on the Bounty, San Francisco, Test Pilot* and, in 1939, his spiritual cornerstone, Rhett Butler in *Gone With the Wind*. Gable did some real adventuring as a gunner with the U.S. Army Air Corps in Europe and even though he never fully regained his pre-war popularity, he remained an American original—the pleasingly gruff he-man with a twinkle in his eye, who refused to take his fame as a movie idol seriously and persisted in looking upon it all as one part talent and nine parts luck.

Gable, Loretta Young and Oakie.

A man and his dog.

Buck and his friends.

52

Mr. Smith (Reginald Owen) and his hirelings appropriate the gold.

53

The Crusades

1935

A Paramount Picture. Produced and directed by Cecil B. DeMille. Screenplay by Harold Lamb, Waldemar Young and Dudley Nichols, based on Lamb's book *The Crusades: Iron Men and Saints.* Photographed by Victor Milner. Music by Rudolph Kopp. Running time: 123 minutes.

CAST

Berengaria, Loretta Young; *Richard, the Lion Hearted,* Henry Wilcoxon; *Saladin,* Ian Keith; *The Hermit,* C. Aubrey Smith; *Alice of France,* Katherine DeMille; *Conrad of Montferrat,* Joseph Schildkraut; *Blondel,* Alan Hale; *Philip of France,* C. Henry Gordon; *Sancho, King of Navarre,* George Barbier; *The Blacksmith,* Montagu Love; *Robert, Earl of Leicester,* William Farnum; *Frederick, Duke of the Germans,* Hobart Bosworth; *Karakush,* Pedro de Cordoba; *John, Prince of England,* Ramsay Hill; *Monk,* Mischa Auer; *Alan, Richard's Squire,* Maurice Murphy; *Amir,* Jason Robards; *Arab Slave Seller,* J. Carroll Naish.

When the urbane George Sanders, never an actor to partake of conventional publicity, played Richard the Lion Hearted in *King Richard and the Crusaders* (1954) he made the point that the fabled king was actually a vainglorious fool who spent little of his reign (1189–1199) in England and twice bankrupted his country by financing crusades that proved little beyond his own bravery and love of fighting. Sanders also said that since he was close to fifty he was really too old for the part because Richard was forty-two when he died in battle in France, fighting his lifelong enemy King

Philip. The Sanders film, a tedious account and short on action, was based on Sir Walter Scott's *The Talisman,* which is so complicated as to defy turning into a screenplay. Cecil B. DeMille was luckier in 1935 when he tackled the adventures of King Richard I. He purchased Harold Lamb's *The Crusade: Iron Men and Saints* and hired Lamb as the chief scenarist. However, this did not result in an historically accurate picture. Lamb found that he was required with the help of Waldemar Young and Dudley Nichols, to whip up a lot of romantic nonsense to perpetuate the image of Richard as a dashing and chivalrous warrior.

DeMille's film deals with the third set of crusades—there were nine in all—and begins in Jerusalem in 1187 as the Saracens conquer and pillage the city. When their leader, Saladin (Ian Keith), parades through the streets he is confronted by a venerable Holy Man, cross in hand, known as The Hermit (C. Aubrey Smith). Saladin spares his life and makes no attempt to stop the Hermit in his vow to march through all the kingdoms of Christendom to rouse them in a crusade against the infidel invaders of the Holy Land. Saladin believes

The Holy Man (C. Aubrey Smith) enlists England in the Crusades.

that any such venture is doomed to failure. The Hermit's first major recruit is Philip of France (C. Henry Gordon), whose chief worry is the warlike Richard of England (Henry Wilcoxon). The vain Philip is inspired with the idea of leading the Crusade and becoming the foremost king in Europe. He proceeds to England to wed his sister Alice (Katherine DeMille) to Richard, as agreed when Richard and Alice were children, and thus unite the thrones and forestall any possible English invasion of France in his absence. He finds the lusty Richard quite uninterested in marriage, and when Richard hears The Hermit promising that a pledge to the Cross will supersede all other pledges, Richard decides to join the crusade. He characteristically assumes leadership of the entire enterprise, to the chagrin of Philip.

In Marseille, prior to sailing for the Holy Land, Richard finds himself short of supplies and his men in immediate need of food. The wily King of Navarre (George Barbier) promises to provide all Richard needs if he will marry his daughter Berengaria (Loretta Young). The irritated Richard agrees, having never seen the beautiful girl, and

sends his sword to the ceremony as a token. Berengaria is offended but when Richard sees her the next day he falls in love with her and commands his unwilling bride to accompany him on his campaign. Things do not go well in the plan to wrest Palestine from the Saracens. The Christians find their adversaries much better soldiers than they had imagined and in meeting Saladin, Richard discovers his enemy to be a cultured and civilized gentleman. Dissension spreads among the European monarchs, mostly between Richard and Philip, and they fail to conquer the infidels. Berengaria is captured by Saladin, who professes his love to her but does not force himself upon her when he realizes she loves Richard. The distraught and furious Richard engages the Saracens in battle in his attempt to reclaim his wife but fails to beat them. While walking the corpse-strewn battlefield at night Richard is approached by the enemy, who offer to take him to Saladin. He is then told that the weary Christians will be allowed to view the shrines they have fought so hard to defend and that all Christian prisoners will be released. Saladin makes one condition—that Richard himself will not

55

Blondell (Alan Hale) admires the new sword of his king (Henry Wilcoxon).

Richard greets Alice of France (Katherine DeMille) as Conrad (Joseph Schildkraut) and Prince John (Ramsay Hill) look on in hopes of a marriage.

be allowed inside the gates of Jerusalem. This humiliation is, however, made bearable for Richard when Berengaria joins him as he watches his men enter the Holy City and affirms her devotion to him.

Like all of Cecil B. DeMille's historical and biblical pictures, *The Crusades* is a piece of entertainment and not a lecture. In dealing with Richard's love life it is pure fiction and in dealing with facts it is a composite of several crusades. The Hermit, for example, was the man who inspired the First Crusade in 1095. The Third Crusade was instigated by Frederick, the Emperor of the Germans, relegated to a minor role in this film. But it was Richard, in fact, whose bravery and integrity won from Saladin a treaty granting access to the Holy City. The best things about DeMille's account are the visuals—the extensive sets and fine costumes, the pageantry involving masses of extras, and the admirable battle sequences. The siege of the city of Acre is impressively staged and furiously fought, as is a later battle between the cavalry forces of Richard and Saladin, with the two forces charging directly at each other and colliding with a terrifying impact.

At thirty Henry Wilcoxon was just about the right age to play Richard. He was an actor with a very limited range but his masculine good looks and fine physique, and his British "old school tie" manner, made him a perfect storybook hero. Just prior to this he had played Mark Antony in DeMille's *Cleopatra* and actually looked at ease in Roman garb and capable of leading a legion in battle. But he lacked warmth and charm, and after *The Crusades* Wilcoxon never again received top billing. He afterwards dropped to supporting roles, most often in splendid military uniforms, and worked in every film made by Cecil B. DeMille, for whom he eventually became an executive.

Alice is offended to find that Richard has chosen Berengaria (Loretta Young) for his queen.

When DeMille took ill while preparing the remake of *The Buccaneer* in 1958, Wilcoxon took over as producer.

The Crusades suffers, as do all the DeMille films, from a certain ponderous quality. He was afflicted with a sense of self-importance that robbed his action films of true excitement and cause them to bog down with posturing attitudes. Were it not for this he would deserve wider coverage in any book dealing with adventure films. Both versions of *The Buccaneer* have good passages but both fall short of relating the exploits of Jean Lafitte, the French pirate who helped the Americans win the battle of New Orleans in 1815. DeMille could have done better by both mighty subjects in *Union Pacific* and *North West Mounted Police,* and a director like Michael Curtiz could have pumped more adrenalin into the adventures of *Reap the Wild Wind* and *Unconquered.* On the other hand, DeMille had a rare talent for mounting spectacle and handling massive and splendid scenes, and that talent is very much evident in *The Crusades.*

The King of France (C. Henry Gordon) tries to assume command of the Crusades . . .

. . . until Richard re-appears with his bride which does nothing for Anglo-French unity.

Richard about to lose the day.

The Last of
the Mohicans

1936

A United Artists Picture. Produced by Edward Small and Harry M. Goetz. Directed by George B. Seitz. Screenplay by Philip Dunne, based on the book by James Fenimore Cooper. Photographed by Robert Planck. Music by Roy Webb. Running time: 91 minutes.

CAST

Hawkeye, Randolph Scott; *Alice Munro,* Binnie Barnes; *Cora Munro,* Heather Angel; *Colonel Munro,* Hugh Buckler; *Major Duncan Hayward,* Henry Wilcoxon; *Magua,* Bruce Cabot; *Chingachgook,* Robert Barrat; *Uncas,* Philip Reed; *Captain Winthrop,* Willard Robertson; *David Gamut,* Frank McGlynne, Sr.; *Jenkins,* Will Stanton.

By contemporary standards the novels of James Fenimore Cooper (1789–1851) make for difficult reading, with their long-winded prose and drawn-out plots, but they stand firm as a treasure trove of insight into Colonial life in America. What Sir Walter Scott did for British history, Cooper did for American, and it was his novels that whetted many European appetites for adventures in the New World. Cooper wrote florid accounts of the vast wilderness, with its forests and rushing rivers, of the battles between the British and French armies, of the scouts and trappers, and particularly of the Indians, whom he, more than any other writer,

caused to be viewed as "the noble savages." His books helped shape the world's notions of America, and it is interesting that the first film version of *The Last of the Mohicans* (1922) was directed by a Frenchman, Maurice Tourneur. The film was made in California but no American director could have given it greater excitement or imbued it with more affection for classic Americana. In some ways —pictorially and in the ferocity of its action sequences—it is superior to the 1936 version, although that version is a smoother treatment of the Cooper plot, with a good script and appealing characterizations.

Cooper himself had a taste for adventure. He was brought up on his father's estate at Otsego Lake, New York—now known as Cooperstown—and saw a great deal of frontier life. He hunted the plentiful game, trod the old Indian trails and listened to the accounts of early settlers about their skirmishes with the savages. He was expelled from Yale for his pranks and afterwards went to sea as an apprentice officer. Since he also had a fondness for writing he used his experiences as background. At the age of thirty he settled down to life as a gentle-

Col. Munroe (Hugh Buckler) puts his daughter Alice (Binnie Barnes) in the hands of Major Heyward (Henry Wilcoxon) for the trip to Fort William Henry.

man farmer and writer in New York's Westchester County. He won approval with his sea novel *The Pilot* but it was with his Leatherstocking tales that he created his claim to immortality. The best of them emerged in 1826, *The Last of the Mohicans,* and it was the one whose plot made it the easiest to film. Later novels like *the Pathfinder* and *The Deerslayer* would also find their way to the screen but in lackluster productions. Generally speaking, Hollywood has been remiss in covering the early periods of American history, preferring to churn out fictional concoctions about the far West in the latter part of the nineteenth century—few of which have any historical value at all.

The screenplay of the 1936 *Mohicans* adheres to the basic outlines of the Cooper novel, with Randolph Scott making Hawkeye a little more gentlemanly than the original. Hawkeye is a Colonial scout attached to the British army but unimpressed with military protocol or the British administration of America. His true love is the land and his allegiance is to his fellow Americans, which includes many Indians. However, no one knows better than he that certain tribes are treacherous and that those

in the employ of the French are dangerous. The British and the French are engaged in bitter conflict for the control of America, and the defense of the British fort—Fort William Henry, on Lake George in upper New York State—is the pivotal point of the film. The year is 1756 and French General Montcalm is waging a successful campaign against the British, although unable to control his fierce Indians. The Hurons are particularly hard to handle and one of them, Magua (Bruce Cabot) is a spy in British lines. Hawkeye and British Major Heyward (Henry Wilcoxon) are required by Colonel Munro (Hugh Buckler) to escort his two daughters, Alice (Binnie Barnes) and Cora (Heather Angel), to Fort William Henry. Alice loves Hawkeye, to the chagrin of the martinet major who would prefer that she loved him, and Cora falls in love with a handsome young Mohican, Uncas (Philip Reed), when he and his father, Chingachgook (Robert Barrat) joined the party on their dangerous trek. The Hurons, now joined by Magua, chase, harass and attack them all the way—along swift rivers in canoes, through the thick forests and over rugged hills. Magua yearns for Cora as his

The treacherous Magua (Bruce Cabot) points the way for Cora (Heather Angel), Alice and Heyward.

Uncas (Philip Reed), Chingachgook (Robert Barrat) and Hawkeye (Randolph Scott) are the men to trust.

Hawkeye knows the way better than the major.

squaw, a situation that results in tragedy. Magua traps the girl on a high, rocky peak and rather than submit to him she flings herself on the rocks below. The Mohicans put an end to Magua but Uncas falls to his own death, and with their dying breaths the lovers clasp hands.

The survivors reach the fort but only because Hawkeye makes it possible by holding off the Hurons, which resultes in his capture. The fort falls to the French but the chivalrous Montcalm negotiates generous terms and Hawkeye is rescued just before imminent death at the burning stake of the Hurons. The whole film is a flow of excitement and movement, with an intelligent script by Philip Dunne, crisp direction by George Seitz, and sharp photography by Robert Planck, with the handsome exteriors shot in the California Sierras. *The Last of the Mohicans* is picture-making of the old romantic-heroic school, and the lack of anything like it in contemporary Hollywood is regrettable.

For Randolph Scott *Mohicans* was a firm step up the movie ladder. He established himself in 1933 with *Wild Horse Mesa,* the first of nine Paramount westerns, all based on Zane Grey stories. After pictures of all kinds he eventually settled for making a fine line of westerns, taking his place alongside Gary Cooper and John Wayne as a distinctly American figure—cool, quiet and steadfast. With his dignified bearing and his soft Virginian voice, Scott cut a truly heroic figure. And it was an image he did well by, enabling him to retire a millionaire. He behaved well during his thirty-four years in the business and apparently made no enemies—an unusual record. Michael Curtiz once said of him, "Randy Scott is a complete anachronism. He's a gentleman. And so far he's the only one I've met in this business full of self-promoting sons-of-bitches."

The attentive Uncas, falling in love with Cora.

61

Mutiny on the Bounty

1935

An MGM Picture. Produced by Irving Thalberg. Directed by Frank Lloyd. Screenplay by Talbot Jennings, Jules Furthman and Carey Wilson, based on the book by Charles Nordhoff and James Norman Hall. Photographed by Arthur Edeson. Music by Herbert Stothart. Running time: 132 minutes.

CAST

Captain Bligh, Charles Laughton; *Fletcher Christian,* Clark Gable; *Byam,* Franchot Tone; *Smith,* Herbert Mundin; *Ellison,* Eddie Quillan; *Bacchus,* Dudley Diggs; *Berkitt,* Donald Crisp; *Sir Joseph Banks,* Henry Stephenson; *Captain Nelson,* Francis Lister; *Mrs. Byam,* Spring Byington; *Tehani,* Movita; *Maimiti,* Mamo; *Maggs,* Ian Wolfe; *Morgan,* Ivan Simpson; *Fryer,* De Witt Jennings; *Marspratt,* Stanley Fields; *Morrison,* Wallace Clark.

The mutiny on the H.M.S. *Bounty* in 1788 was a major factor in reforming attitudes toward the treatment of sailors in the British Navy, although the change from brutality to a modicum of compassion was not as immediate as the 1935 film probably led people to believe. The recruitment of crews by press ganging, the primitive living conditions and the floggings went on for many more years but the situation did gradually improve after the trial of the *Bounty* mutineers. *Mutiny on the Bounty* remains the best of the nautical adventure films and

Captain Bligh (Charles Laughton) and his officers— first of whom is Fletcher Christian (Clark Gable).

serves the double-barreled purposes of being vastly entertaining and being educational. It sticks closely to the historical facts but stretches a point for the sake of drama in making Captain William Bligh a more malevolent man than he actually was. It was a role that made Charles Laughton a major figure in film history, with his scowls and sneers, his nasty petulance and his biting harangues of Fletcher Christian. Laughton's Bligh became a favorite of impressionists, who always picked on his curse to Christian, "I'll live to see you hang from the highest yardarm in the British fleet."

This was not the first film to tackle the story of the mutiny. In 1932 Australian producer Charles Chauvel made *In the Wake of the Bounty* and gave twenty-three-year-old Errol Flynn his first job as an actor, playing Fletcher Christian. The Chauvel picture was a semi-documentary made on a small budget, but included footage he shot on Pitcairn Island, the final home of the *Bounty* mutineers. His most interesting shot was an underwater look at the scant remains of the famous ship. MGM acquired the rights to the Chauvel picture soon after its completion, partly to keep it off the American market but also to use some of its footage in short films to help promote their own feature, which wound up costing two million dollars, a hefty budget for its

H. M. S. *Bounty*.

day. The studio had purchased the trilogy by Charles Nordhoff and James Norman Hall (*Mutiny on the Bounty, Men Against the Sea,* and *Pitcairn Island*) and used material from the first two books to assemble the screenplay. The scenarists also drew upon the actual log of Captain Bligh. Production lasted the better part of two years and involved great efforts and occasional hardships for the cast and crew. One cameraman lost his life in filming a storm sequence. In Frank Lloyd the company had a director who loved the project with a passion. He had been responsible for another great nautical picture, the Milton Sills version of *The Sea Hawk* in 1924, and his *Bounty* is rich with authenticity, action, emotion and masculine qualities.

The film begins with the preparations for the departure of the *Bounty* from Portsmouth in December of 1787, its mission being to transport breadfruit from Tahiti to the West Indies as a cheap food for plantation slaves. Master's Mate (first officer to the Captain) Fletcher Christian (Clark Gable) reports to Captain Bligh for their third voyage together. Bligh advises him that if they are to serve together effectively Christian will have to follow orders and mind his own business. The tough but compassionate Christian knowingly agrees. New on board is flippant, aristocratic Midshipman Roger Byam (Franchot Tone), who quickly becomes appalled by Bligh's contempt for his men and his belief that they must be treated with brutality in order to be unquestioningly obedient. The voyage to Tahiti is terribly long and arduous and marked by conflicts between Bligh and Christian as to conditions of punishment and privations levied against the crew. Only the sighting of Tahiti avoids a serious confrontation. The months spent on the beauti-

ful island prove to be an idyll to the sailors as they enjoy the balmy climate and the hospitality of the natives. Both Christian and Byam marry local girls, as do some of the other men, and their departure from Tahiti is reluctant.

The *Bounty* is not long at sea before trouble again rears up as Bligh continues to abuse his crew. Several sailors who had attempted to desert on the island are ordered flogged and Bligh demands that the deathly ill ship's doctor (Dudley Digges) be present on deck. The effort to meet the order causes the doctor to die. The men are confined to irons and denied proper care and food, at which Christian finally rebels and takes command of the ship. He saves Bligh from death at the hands of the mutineers and sets him adrift in an open boat with those who prefer to remain loyal. Byam and several others who choose not to be a part of the mutiny have to remain on board for lack of room in the boat. Christian and his men then head back to their island paradise and Bligh completes an incredible feat of seamanship by taking his small boat 3,618 miles to the island of Timor in the Dutch East Indies without the loss of a single life.

Time passes and a British warship one day appears in Tahitian waters. Christian and most of his men, with their families, make haste to leave the island on the *Bounty* but Byam and a few others welcome the chance to return to England. The ship is the *Pandora,* under the command of Captain Bligh, who is obsessed with vengeance for Christian. He refuses to accept Byam's protestations of loyalty and imprisons him and the others in the hold. Such is Bligh's intense and hateful search for Christian that he sails the *Pandora* in dangerously shallow waters and wrecks the ship on a reef, causing yet another trip in an open boat—a trip that ends in England with Byam court-martialed as a mutineer. He and the few who remained loyal to him are all found guilty, but in accepting the death sentence Byam makes an eloquent statement on the need for greater understanding of seamen and for more leniency in commanding them. Bligh smiles with satisfaction at the trial but finds himself being politely snubbed by his superiors. Byam's plea does not go unheard and by royal decree he is reprieved and returned to duty. Meanwhile on the other side of the world, Christian and his followers settle down to life on Pitcairn, having burned and sunk the *Bounty* to destroy evidence of their presence and to make any change of mind on their part impossible.

The 1962 version of *Mutiny on the Bounty,* with Marlon Brando as Christian and Trevor Howard

The incident of the stolen food.

Christian and his Tahitian love Miamiti (Mamo).

The mutiny. Christian restrains the vengeful sailors.

as Bligh, has the advantage of color and some hand-some production values but it lacks the salty sting of the Frank Lloyd picture. The Brando version is more interesting in only one respect—that it re-veals the death of Christian, whose mutiny had weighed heavily on his mind and whose followers did not find happiness. Neither film shows just how miserable was the fate of the *Bounty* mutineers, who quarreled among themselves. Several drank themselves to death and others were murdered by natives. When the H.M.S. *Briton* visited Pitcairn in 1812 it found only one survivor, John Adams, and he was allowed to live out his life on the is-land.

Those moviegoers who were inspired by *Mutiny on the Bounty* to study the story further were prob-ably disappointed to find that Bligh was not quite the beast portrayed by Charles Laughton. He cer-tainly was hard, ill-tempered and merciless but not exceptionally so for a Royal Navy captain of the time. His naval career continued and he made an-other, more successful voyage to Tahiti to collect breadfruit plants. He finally rose to the rank of Vice Admiral and in 1805 he was appointed gov-ernor of New South Wales, Australia, where, ironi-cally, he was the subject of another mutiny, a mili-tary protest against his severity. Again the mu-tineers were pronounced guilty and again Bligh was exonerated. When he died in 1817, age sixty-three, he was buried in the churchyard of London's Lam-beth Palace but thanks to Charles Laughton none of us miss him very much.

The court-martial of Midshipman Byam (Franchot Tone).

The Prisoner of Zenda

1937

A Selznick-International Picture. Produced by David O. Selznick. Directed by John Cromwell. Screenplay by John Balderston, adapted by Wells Root from the novel by Anthony Hope, with additional dialogue by Donald Ogden Stewart. Photographed by James Wong Howe. Music by Alfred Newman. Running time: 100 minutes.

CAST

Rudolf Rassendyll, King Rudolf V, Ronald Colman; *Princess Flavia,* Madeleine Carroll; *Rupert of Hentzau,* Douglas Fairbanks, Jr.; *Antoinette de Mauban,* Mary Astor; *Colonel Zapt,* C. Aubrey Smith; *Black Michael,* Raymond Massey; *Fritz Von Tarlenheim,* David Niven; *Marshall Strakenez,* Lawrence Grant; *Cardinal,* Ian McLaren; *Johann,* Brian Foulger; *Josef,* Howard Lang; *Bersonin,* Ralph Faulkner; *Detchard,* Montagu Love; *Krafstein,* William von Brincken; *Lauengram,* Philip Sleeman; *DeGautet,* Alexander D'Arcy.

No story has epitomized the genre of romantic, costumed adventure better than Anthony Hope's classic novel, *The Prisoner of Zenda.* It has all the ingredients: men of honor versus men of avarice, political ambition and royal intrigue, gallantry, swordplay, handsome gentlemen in magnificent uniforms dancing with lovely ladies at court balls, and all of it set in the mythical, picturesque little kingdom of Ruritania. The time: a decade or so before the First World War swept it all under the carpet forever. Anthony Hope (1863–1933) was a barrister who took to writing as an outlet for his imagination. *Zenda,* published in 1894, proved to be his only lasting contribution to literature, although a sequel, *Rupert of Hentzau,* in 1898, makes for an interesting continuation, with Rudolf Rassendyll returning to Ruritania some years later and again becoming enmeshed in a plot to seize the throne. *Zenda* was first filmed in Hollywood in 1912, with a British version done three years later. MGM gave the story its first major treatment in 1922, with Lewis Stone as Rassendyll and Ramón Novarro as Rupert. David O. Selznick decided to do it his way in 1937, admitting that the royal hubbub caused by the Duke and Duchess of Windsor had a lot to do with his decision to revive an old-fashioned story of the love between a commoner and princess. His colleagues advised him he was making a mistake, but as was almost always the case with Selznick, he was not.

Selznick later revealed that he would not have made *Zenda* if Ronald Colman had refused to play

Rudolf Rassendyll (Colman) ponders the scheme of Fritz Von Tarlenheim (David Niven) and Col. Zapt (C. Aubrey Smith).

the part of Rudolf Rassendyll. He felt, as did everyone, that Colman was the very personification of an English gentleman, with his beautifully modulated voice and his courtly manners, his good looks, his charm and his dignity. Besides those qualities, he was a spellbinding actor. He was, however, not an athletic man and those roles in which he played the hero were achieved more by suggestion than physical effort. Colman made an excellent *Clive of India,* a believable Sydney Carton in *A Tale of Two Cities,* a roguish François Villon in *If I Were King,* and the quintessential Robert Conway in *Lost Horizon.* But a swordsman he was not, and the duel with Rupert (played with stylish gusto by Douglas Fairbanks, Jr.) works only because it was heavily doubled and because of the bantering dialogue between the two.

Selznick, in one of his many shrewd deals, later sold his rights to *Zenda* to MGM, who did it again in 1952 with Stewart Granger as Rudolf, James Mason as Rupert, and Deborah Kerr as Princess Flavia. It was an almost shot-for-shot refilming, and went so far as to reuse Alfred Newman's 1937 musical score. It was good but much lacking the

spirit of the Colman version—except in the Rudolf–Rupert duel, which was far superior, thanks to Granger's swashbuckling manner and the skill of his teacher and double, Jean Heremans.

The story begins with Rudolf Rassendyll arriving in Ruritania on vacation and being unaware that he is an exact double of the man about to be crowned king. Neither does he know that the king has bitter enemies, who want to keep him from the throne. Chief among them is his half-brother, Black Michael (Raymond Massey) and the ambitious young Rupert of Hentzau (Fairbanks). Two of the king's staunchest supporters, Colonel Zapt (C. Aubrey Smith) and Lieutenant Fritz Von Tarlenheim (David Niven), persuade Rassendyll to pose as the king at the coronation when the king is drugged and kidnapped. Rassendyll, who is a distant relative of the king, grudgingly agrees and soon finds himself caught in great danger and tensions. Part of his grief comes when he meets Princess Flavia (Madeleine Carroll), betrothed to the king. He falls in love with her, and she with him—to her surprise since she has known the king to this point only as a cold and indifferent man. Eventually she comes to

Rudolf meets Princess Flavia (Madeleine Carroll).

realize that he is another man, as does Rupert, who tauntingly refers to Rassendyll as "play-actor." The schemes of Black Michael and Rupert almost cost Rassendyll his life, and almost succeed in upsetting the kingdom, but Michael's mistress, Antoinette (Mary Astor), fearful that Michael's plans will cost him his life, as indeed they do, sides with the royalists and reveals information that enables them to squelch the plot.

Finally it is a matter of Rassendyll and Rupert *vis-à-vis*. Rassendyll not only fights for his life in the saber duel, but needs to inch his way to the rope holding the drawbridge and allow Zapt and his men to enter the castle. As they thrust, parry and swing with their swords they jest:

RUPERT: Your golden-haired goddess will look well in black, Rassendyll. I'll console her for you. Kiss away her tears. What, no quotations?

RASSENDYLL: Yes. "A barking dog never bites."

RUPERT: You'd be a sensation in a circus. I can't understand it, where did you learn such roller-skating?

RASSENDYLL: Coldstream Guards, my boy. Come on, when does the fencing lesson begin?

And so on, until Rupert realizes the game is up. He tosses his saber at Rassendyll, misses, dashes to a window and leaps into the moat, saying "This is getting too hot for me. Au revoir, play-actor!" Afterwards, Rassendyll bids a fond but sad farewell to the princess who cannot be his. Colonel Zapt and Von Tarlenheim escort him to the border, regretfully since they have come to like him:

RASSENDYLL: We'll meet again, Fritz.

VON TARLENHEIM: Fate doesn't always make the right men kings.

RASSENDYLL: Goodbye, Colonel. We're run a good course together.

ZAPT: Goodbye, Englishman. You're the finest Elphberg of them all.

Ronald Colman, Madeleine Carroll, Douglas Fairbanks, Jr., Mary Astor, Raymond Massey, C. Aubrey Smith, David Niven—the cast could hardly be better. The intelligent script, with Donald Ogden Stewart's witty dialogue, John Cromwell's crisp and tidy direction, the romantic music of Alfred Newman and the photography of the marvelous James Wong Howe make the Selznick film the archetypical romance of mythical kingdoms and palace plots.

Black Michael (Raymond Massey) urges his lady love Antoinette (Mary Astor) to join with him and Rupert in their plan.

The plot thickens when Rudolf and Zapt find the king's valet (Howard Lang) murdered.

Rupert of Hentzau (Douglas Fairbanks, Jr.) states his intention to plot against the throne.

The Prisoner of Zenda is perhaps best appreciated by those who were young and impressionable when it was first released. Madeleine Carroll, one of the most patrician actresses ever to grace a Hollywood sound stage, claims Princess Flavia as her favorite role. She spent much of the Second World War working as a nurse with the Red Cross and she says, "I was on a hospital train in France, wearing khaki trousers and shirt, my face smudged with dirt, my hair just any way. A wounded soldier on the train stopped me and said, 'You know, it's pretty nice to be waited on by Princess Flavia.'"

Rassendyll assumes the crown as Zapt and Fritz look on apprehensively.

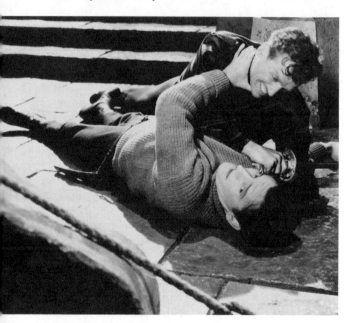

Antoinette comforts the imprisoned king as Rupert stands by confidantly.

Rupert meets his match.

Rassendyll bids goodbye to the woman who can never be his.

73

The Adventures of Robin Hood

1938

A Warner Bros. Picture. Produced by Hal B. Wallis. Directed by Michael Curtiz and William Keighley. Screenplay by Norman Reilly Raine and Seton I. Miller. Photographed in Technicolor by Tony Gaudio and Sol Polito. Music by Erich Wolfgang Korngold. Running time: 102 minutes.

CAST

Sir Robin of Locksley, Errol Flynn; *Maid Marian,* Olivia de Havilland; *Sir Guy of Gisbourne,* Basil Rathbone; *Prince John,* Claude Rains; *Will Scarlet,* Patric Knowles; *Friar Tuck,* Eugene Pallette; *Little John,* Alan Hale; *Sheriff of Nottingham,* Melville Cooper; *King Richard,* Ian Hunter; *Bess,* Una O'Connor; *Much the Miller's Son,* Herbert Mundin; *Bishop of the Black Canons,* Montagu Love; *Sir Essex,* Leonard Wiley; *Sir Ralf,* Robert Noble; *Sir Mortimer,* Kenneth Hunter; *Sir Geoffrey,* Robert Warwick; *Sir Baldwin,* Colin Kenny; *Sir Ivor,* Lester Matthews; *Dickon Malbete,* Harry Cording.

A good case can be made for claiming *The Adventures of Robin Hood* as the most glorious of all adventures movies. Admittedly the choice has something to do with nostalgia. To have first seen the film as an impressionable youngster in 1938 and to have kept it in mind over the years gives the picture an aura of romantic fantasy and vicarious involvement. But it continues to have similar affects on many young people seeing it now—and it is a

film that bears close study as just about the finest of its kind. The screenplay by Norman Reilly Raine and Seton I. Miller is literate and witty, and Michael Curtiz' direction (with portions done by William Keighley) gives it buoyancy and precise pacing. The costumes of Milo Anderson and the sets of Carl Jules Weyl (for which he won an Oscar) fairly glow in the Technicolor photography of Sol Polito and Tony Gaudio, the two Trojan cameramen at Warners for many years. They used the then new three-color process, which allowed for the most exact reproduction of rich colors. It made the filming more difficult, with cumbersome equipment and the demands of intense lighting and extra makeup, and by the mid-1950s it was obsolete. But little photography today can match the luster of *Robin Hood.* Yet another of the film's major assets is the musical score of Erich Korngold, one of the most perfect blends of sight and sound so far achieved on the screen.

Robin Hood is also one of those rare films in which the casting is faultless. Errol Flynn might very well have been Robin Hood in another life. He frequently said he felt at odds with the twentieth

74

Robin (Flynn) invites himself to Prince John's banquet.

century and offered continual evidence with his Regency-rake lifestyle. By the time he was forty his lusty carousing had given him the cardiac condition of a doomed man but at the time of filming *Robin Hood,* Flynn was twenty-eight and in fine athletic form. His vitality, his humor and his charm made him a unique Hollywood figure. Warners had long planned on doing *Robin Hood* but with possibly James Cagney in the lead. However, once Flynn had established himself with *Captain Blood* there was no contest. As Maid Marian, Olivia de Havilland looks as if she has stepped out of a storybook, making the perfect romantic match for Flynn. Basil Rathbone's arrogant Sir Guy of Gisbourne, with eloquent, biting diction, is a masterpiece of screen villainy, as is Claude Rains' sly, epicene Prince John. Alan Hale as Little John (he had played the same role in Fairbanks' *Robin Hood* in 1922), Eugene Pallette as Friar Tuck, Patric Knowles as Will Scarlet, Melville Cooper as the High Sheriff of Nottingham and Ian Hunter as King Richard—all are fondly memorable figures.

The script draws mostly from legend and its historical value is slight. Raine and Miller incor-

porated several of the celebrated incidents in the Robin Hood tales, such as his first meeting with Little John in Sherwood Forest and his being bested by him in a quarterstaff fight, his recruiting of the rotund cleric Friar Tuck by beating him in a swordfight and then offering him all the food he can ever eat, his prowess as an archer and his defense of Saxon England against Norman ambitions. The story begins with a town crier making an announcement that King Richard has been captured on his way home from the Crusades and is being held prisoner for ransom by Leopold of Austria. The news is welcomed by Prince John and his chief conspirator, Sir Guy of Gisbourne. Intent on becoming King, the Prince declares himself Regent of England in the absence of his brother and orders his Norman knights to exact even higher taxes from the Saxons, already oppressed by Norman thefts and brutalities. Prince John holds a banquet for his barons at Nottingham Castle and Robin Hood invites himself, giving the Prince a chance to meet the man about whom he has heard "precious little else since I've been here." He is impressed with Robin's charming impudence and asks him if he

75

. . . and after a few heated words, fights his way out.

feels the Saxons are overtaxed. Replies Robin, "Overtaxed, overworked and paid off with a knife, a club or a rope." When the Prince asks him what he intends doing about it, Robin states a bold case: "I'll organize revolt. Exact a death for a death and I'll never rest until every Saxon in this shire can stand up, free men, and strike a blow for Richard and England. From this night on I'll use every means in my power to fight you!" With that the Normans attempt to seize him but the agile Robin outfights them and escapes.

Robin and his Sherwood Forest outlaws ambush the Norman columns headed by Sir Guy and the High Sheriff as they begin to make their way back to London with the collected ransom funds. Lady Marian is also with them after her visit to Nottingham. She has been appalled by Robin's apparent campaign against Prince John but at the banquet following the defeat of the Normans she comes to realize his cause is just and his intentions to support Richard sincere. Sir Guy and the Sheriff are allowed to return to Nottingham, to report to the furious Prince, who vows that Robin must be captured. A means occurs to the Sheriff, who has noticed Marian's warm regard for Robin. An archery tournament will be held, with the winner to receive a prize directly from Maid Marian. Since Robin is the finest archer in England, the results are obvious. But Robin oversteps his confidence and he is captured. Sentenced to be hung in public, he escapes through the help of Marian, who has warned his men so that they can station themselves to facilitate the escape.

King Richard and a group of his knights arrive back in England disguised as monks. They overhear

With the encouragement of Will Scarlett (Patric Knowles), Robin decides to tackle Little John (Alan Hale) on the log.

After trouncing the Norman party, Robin invites Maid Marian (Olivia de Havilland) to join him for a meal, along with Friar Tuck (Eugene Pallette) and Sir Guy of Gisbourne (Basil Rathbone).

tales of Prince John's treachery and oppression, and contrive to meet Robin. In union, the King and the outlaw make their plan to stop Prince John's rise to power. Lady Marian is arrested for her part in helping Robin, and condemned to death. She advises him that only a king can pass sentence on a royal ward and he smilingly informs that it shall be so—he is about to become King of England, having declared Richard dead. At the coronation, a large body of monks enter the castle, all of them Robin's men, supported by Richard's knights. Just as Prince John is about to assume the monarchy, Richard makes his presence known. Sir Guy claims it is a trick and urges his men to seize the outlaws. The furious melee results in a victory for Richard and his banishment of Prince John and his followers from England—all except Sir Guy, who dies after a long and vicious duel with Robin. King Richard declares an end to oppression and justice for all in his realm.

The Adventures of Robin Hood began production in September of 1937 when Warners sent the company to Chico, California (a hundred miles north of Sacramento) to film exteriors in the attractive grounds of Bidwell Park. William Keighley was assigned as director and among the sequences shot there was the fight between Robin and Little John. Looking at this and the rest of Keighley's footage, Warners decided his approach was too lyrical and that what was needed was a more exciting and more driving direction. In short, what was needed was Michael Curtiz, who had already proved his skill with action epics with Flynn's *Captain Blood* and *The Charge of the Light Brigade*. And it is more than likely that Curtiz was miffed at not being given *Robin Hood* in the first place. Keighley was a fine director and the picture would probably have been good if made entirely

by him, but there is no denying the supercharge that the tough Curtiz was able to inject in his action sequences. In this endeavor he was greatly aided by second unit director B. Reeves Eason, a master at staging battles and stunts. In addition to the scenery of Chico, the film also reveals the past splendor of the long gone Busch Gardens in Pasadena, where the archery tournament was shot. Other exteriors were done at Lake Sherwood, northwest of San Fernando Valley, and on the backlot at Warners.

The glories of *The Adventures of Robin Hood* are many but to all those with an ear for music, mention must be made of the score by Korngold. About two-thirds of the running time of the picture is supported by his music and it is practically

The Archery Tournament.

Robin on the way to the gallows.

an opera minus a libretto. Korngold had achieved fame with his operas in Vienna and his approach to film scoring was operatic. All the major characters have themes, as well as musical descriptions of settings, battles and period. He later made a concert suite from the score and it is probably the most popular of all his work in Hollywood. However, it was a film that he did not really want to score, feeling that it was so full of action the music would never be noticed. Leo Forbstein insisted that Korngold was the only man to do it—by then Korngold had set the style for historical romance with his music to *Captain Blood* and *Anthony Adverse*—and he kept on until the composer agreed to take the assignment. The results won Korngold an Oscar but the real irony is that if he had not taken the job he would have returned to Vienna where he would certainly have run afoul of the Nazis, who had declared him *non grata*. Korngold often joked that Robin Hood had saved his life.

But above all *Robin Hood* is Errol Flynn's finest moment in Hollywood history. He was still flushed with the success of two years previous that had rocketed him from his obscurity as an adventurous drifter to a matinee idol of major proportions. In time he would grow weary of playing the swashbuckler, but in 1937 he enjoyed himself romping around in costumes playing the hero, swinging on ropes, leaping, vaulting, riding horses, flashing a sword and gallantly courting the exquisite Olivia de Havilland. No other actor was ever more beautifully heroic. Flynn in his prime had it all—the athletic gracefulness, the good looks, the physique and, most importantly, the twinkle in the eye that made the nonsense even more appealing.

Flynn's life ran tragically downhill in the last dozen years of his life and he burned himself out at the age of fifty. But no hero should be remembered in a way other than at a peak of glory—as in the closing scene of *Robin Hood*. With the Normans thoroughly trounced and the Merry Men of Sherwood grouped around their grateful king, he turns to Robin and asks, "Is there nothing England's King can grant the outlaw who showed him his duty to his country?" Replies Robin, "Yes, your majesty. A pardon for the men of Sherwood." Richard the Lion-Hearted agrees, "Granted with all my heart. But is there nothing for yourself?" "There's but one thing else, Sire," says Robin with his arm around Maid Marian. The king looks knowingly at his happy ward. "And do you too wish . . . ?" She beams, "More than anything else in the world." Commands Richard, "Kneel Robin Hood.

Arise Robin, Baron of Locksley, Earl of Sherwood and Nottingham, and Lord of all the lands and manors appertaining thereto. My first command to you, my Lord Earl, is to take in marriage the hand of the Lady Marian. What say you to that, Baron of Locksley?" Richard awaits his answer as the men of Sherwood cheer and gather around their leader, who slips away from them with Marian and heads for the massive doors of the Great Hall. There Robin turns and gives his answer, "May I obey all your commands with equal pleasure, Sire."

Exit Sir Guy.

And they lived happily ever after.

The Adventures of Tom Sawyer

1938

A Selznick-International Picture. Produced by David O. Selznick. Directed by Norman Taurog. Screenplay by John V. A. Weaver, based on the book by Mark Twain. Photographed in Technicolor by James Wong Howe. Music direction by Lou Forbes. Running time: 93 minutes.

CAST

Tom Sawyer, Tommy Kelly; *Huckleberry Finn,* Jackie Moran; *Becky Thatcher,* Ann Gillis; *Aunt Polly,* May Robson; *Muff Potter,* Walter Brennan; *Injun Joe,* Victor Jory; *Sid Sawyer,* David Holt; *Sheriff,* Victor Kilian; *Mrs. Thatcher,* Nana Bryant; *Schoolmaster,* Olin Howard; *Superintendent,* Donald Meek; *Judge Thatcher,* Charles Richman; *Mrs. Harper,* Margaret Hamilton; *Mary Sawyer,* Marcia Mae Jones; *Joe Harper,* Mickey Rentschier; *Amy Lawrence,* Cora Sue Collins; *Jim,* Philip Hurlie.

Mark Twain [Samuel Clemens (1835–1910)] published his *The Adventures of Tom Sawyer* in 1876 and immediately touched immortality. No writer has more warmly described the joys and trials of being a boy and living the good, old-fashioned life in the country. It was about a specific area of the American Midwest and yet it appealed to people in every part of the world, and left many of them feeling cheated that they had not been born in a little town on the banks of the Mississippi. In the foreword Twain wrote: "Most of the adventures recorded in this book really occurred; one or two were experiences of my own, the rest those of boys who were school-mates of mine. Huck Finn is drawn from life; Tom Sawyer also, but not from an individual—he is a combination of three boys I knew." Be that as it may, those who knew Twain claimed that Tom was very much like the author himself, and that the character of Aunt Polly was patterned after his mother.

The location of the adventures of Tom and his chums was a small Mississippi River town in the 1840s. This was an early period in the settlement of the Midwest, before the coming of the railroad, when rafts and steamboats plied the river and most local boys grew up with the idea of being riverboat captains. Young Sam Clemens was just such a boy. He became a riverboat man at the age of nineteen and wrote about it years later in his book *Life on the Mississippi.* The area around his home town, Hannibal, Missouri, offered a wonderful life to boys of his time. They had the river to play on, river life to observe, boats and rafts, swimming and fishing, a forest on the opposite shore, swamps to

Tom the supervisor.

hunt in and explore, an uninhabited island, and limestone caverns not far from the town. Such is the setting of *Tom Sawyer*.

The story is too familiar to need description here. Suffice to say that the screenplay by John V. A. Weaver in this fine Selznick version is faithful to the Twain plot, although necessarily truncating it. It contains most of the major incidents as the wildly imaginative Tom (Tommy Kelly) joins with his friend Huck (Jackie Moran) in their adventurous schemes, frequently bordering on mischief. Orphan Tom is the pride and despair of his warm-hearted guardian, Aunt Polly (May Robson). She tries to discipline him by getting him to whitewash the garden fence but the enterprising Tom inveigles other children to do the labor, to the admiration of his adoring but unappreciated girlfriend, Becky Thatcher (Ann Gillis). Even in school Tom gets by mostly on nerve. Asked to name the first two Apostles, he replies, "Adam and Eve." (In the book he says, "David and Goliath.") He and Huck immerse themselves in the far more important job of playing pirates, to the point of getting lost in the swamps. Missing for days, with items of their cloth-

ing picked up from the river, the townspeople assume them lost forever and conduct a memorial service. Tom and Huck return in time to attend it, resulting in a fair measure of wrath from those who have been grieving for them.

The two boys run into real danger when they creep through a graveyard and see Injun Joe (Victor Jory) kill a man. The village drunkard, Muff Potter (Walter Brennan), is put on trial and charged with murder, as Tom and Huck sit and watch, paralyzed by Injun Joe's threats of what will happen to them if they reveal the truth. Tom speaks up and Injun Joe escapes, but when Tom and Becky get lost in the caverns their lives hover on the brink as Injun Joe closes in on them. But just as Joe is about to strike, Tom lashes out with his foot and sends the villain hurtling to his death.

David O. Selznick approached *Tom Sawyer* with the same painstaking research and full resources he had brought to bear with his *David Copperfield*. The film beautifully recreates the period, with a little town built by such fine art directors as William Cameron Menzies, Lyle Wheeler and Casey Roberts. The main street, with its stores, homes and

83

Tom (Tommy Kelly) and his ever-exasperated Aunt Polly (May Robson).

The schoolmaster (Olin Howard) makes his point.

courthouse, was designed with accuracy, and photographed in Technicolor by James Wong Howe and Wilfred M. Cline. Rather than film in real caverns, Selznick had his company build an enormous set. Expense at this time in his career meant little to Selznick and the returns on *Tom Sawyer* proved, once more, than he knew precisely what he was doing. The visual quality of this picture is striking, with its river scenes, swamps, forests and dusty country roads, and yet it is the sequence in the studio-built caverns that most lingers in the memory. The sequence caused Selznick some concern because of the realism in portraying Becky's terror, the swooping bats and the approaching, fearsome Injun Joe. The huge cave, with its weird rock formations and the echoing cries of the lost children, tended to frighten the younger members of the audience, and Selznick instructed his editors to do a little trimming. This decision came only after he had thoroughly studied and digested the situation. No producer went to greater or more detailed lengths in making a film.

Selznick concerned himself with every step of the operations of all departments and frequently exhausted his employees with exacting suggestions and instructions. In preparing *Tom Sawyer* he decided that the roles of Tom and Huck should go to unknowns, preferably—in the tradition of Horatio Alger—to boys from an orphanage. His scouting in orphanages proved futile. In the case of Huck he had to settle on the professional Jackie Moran, but for Tom he insisted on a boy who would be totally fresh to moviegoers. He tested hundreds and finally gave the part to Tommy Kelly, a blue-eyed, freckle-faced lad from the Bronx, New York. His lack of experience made the production slower than it might have been but Selznick persisted and got the performance he needed, although it did not result in Kelly's becoming a star. After a few more parts he decided to quit the film world and take up teaching as a profession. However he could always prove to his students that he had once played the role of the world's most lovable scamp. And Norman Taurog could boast that he had survived the experience of being a Selznick director. H. C. Potter was the original director but after two weeks of Selznickian interference he walked off the picture.

Tom and Huck (Jackie Moran) in the graveyard at midnight.

Doc Robinson (Anthony Nace) directs Injun Joe (Victor Jory) and Muff Potter (Walter Brennan) in grave robbing.

Muff on trial for the murder committed by Injun Joe.

Aunt Polly advises Muff to keep away from the boys.

Tom and his adoring girl friend, Becky Thatcher (Ann Gillis)

Gunga Din

1939

An RKO Radio Picture. Produced by Pandro S. Berman. Directed by George Stevens. Screenplay by Joel Sayre and Fred Guiol, based on a story by Ben Hecht and Charles MacArthur, inspired by the poem of Rudyard Kipling. Photographed by Joseph August. Music by Alfred Newman. Running time: 117 minutes.

CAST

Cutter, Gary Grant; *MacChesney,* Victor McLaglen; *Ballantine,* Douglas Fairbanks, Jr.; *Gunga Din,* Sam Jaffe; *Guru,* Eduardo Ciannelli; *Emmy,* Joan Fontaine; *Colonel Weed,* Montagu Love; *Higginbotham,* Robert Coote; *Chota,* Abner Biberman; *Major Mitchell,* Lumsden Hare; *Mr. Stebbins,* Cecil Kellaway.

Ben Hecht and Charles MacArthur concocted a story, which Joel Sayre and Fred Guiol whipped up into a screenplay, about the adventures of the British Army in India, taking as their cue the poem by Rudyard Kipling about the water boy who yearned to be a soldier. It was pure invention on their part, although their guidelines were inspired by Kipling's *Soldiers Three.* However, the end result was more Dumas than Kipling, with Sergeants Cutter (Cary Grant), MacChesney (Victor Mc-Laglen) and Ballantine (Douglas Fairbanks, Jr.) romping around à la Athos, Porthos and Aramis, with Gunga Din (Sam Jaffe) timorously trailing behind as a sort of closet D'Artagnan. George Stevens directed this spectacular and rollicking yarn with gusto and humor, and it delighted movie-goers—all except Indians, who rightly criticized the ease with which three British cavaliers polished off hordes of their brethren. It also met with some American criticism, especially from isolationists who carped at Hollywood's waving of the Union Jack as the curtain rose on the Second World War.

Cutter, MacChesney and Ballantine are close friends, good soldiers but much given to carousing and brawling. When Ballantine announces his intention to resign and marry his Emmy (Joan Fontaine), the other two do all they can to dissuade him. The mischievous, fun-loving sergeants are occasionally called on the carpet for trouncing soldiers in other regiments but whenever their commanding officer needs men to carry out a dangerous mission he knows he can rely on Cutter, McChesney and Ballantine. Such a need arises when a band of natives wipe out a British station, killing everyone. The three sergeants proceed, taking with them a detachment of Indian soldiers and their water boy. Din has long pestered them with his desire to become a soldier but they only humor him, as they see him practicing drill, saluting and blowing an old bugle he has somehow acquired. But whenever there is action, Din is always there, right alongside them with his goatskin bag of water.

The sergeants search the seemingly deserted outpost but the fanatic insurgents, the Thuggees, are waiting to pounce on them. The Thuggees discover they have tackled a trio of whirling dervishes—the three Britons dash around with swords and pistols in hand, jump up walls, leap from rooftop to rooftop, and upon finding a cache of explosives, sling sticks of dynamite at the furious Thuggees. Their victory is temporary; now cut off from their regiment, the sergeants and the faithful Din make their way into the mountains where they come across a temple, the headquarters of the Thuggees. Upon creeping into it they overhear the leader, Guru (Eduardo Ciannelli), addressing his followers and outlining his plans to drive the British from India. The sergeants are discovered, taken prisoner, tortured, refuse to reveal information, and then overtake the band by grabbing the leader. With a knife at his throat they make their way to the roof of the temple, where the Guru proudly points to the advancing British troops and tells the sergeants their colleagues are marching into a trap. It is Din who saves the day. Although badly wounded he climbs to a pinnacle of the temple with his bugle and sounds the calls he has surreptitiously learned, calls

which warn the soldiers to change tactics. The ensuing battle puts an end to the Thuggee cause and Cutter, McChesney and Ballantine assure the dying Din that he is indeed a soldier. Din is given a funeral of full military honors and Rudyard Kipling (Reginald Sheffield), who happens to be visiting, writes a poem which the commandant reads over Din's grave:

". . . though I've belted you and flayed you,
By the living Gawd that made you,
You're a better man than I am, Gunga Din."

Gunga Din can be viewed *only* as entertainment. Interpretations about white supremacy and colonial domination lead only to distaste. As entertainment it is among the very best action epics, with Gary Grant, Victor McLaglen and Douglas Fairbanks, Jr., perfect as the swaggering Rover Boys, and Sam Jaffe memorable as the brave-hearted water carrier. It was RKO Radio's most prestigious and expensive production to that time, and to make it they set up a large location camp in the Alabama Range, near Lone Pine, California, some two hundred miles north of Los Angeles. Warners had used the same

McChesney and Cutter look on with disgust at Ballantine's tender regard for his fiancee Emmy (Joan Fontaine).

Sergeants Ballantine (Douglas Fairbanks, Jr.), McChesney (Victor McLaglen) and Cutter (Cary Grant).

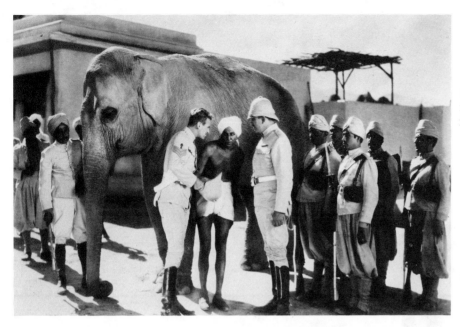

Gunga Din (Sam Jaffe), being reprimanded for taking his elephant friend for a walk.

The Rover Boys in action.

89

Ballantine restrains McChesney's loss of patience with Din.

area for *The Charge of the Light Brigade,* since it resembled the rugged northwest frontier of India. Six hundred people were encamped on the location and the sets constructed for the picture included a native town, a Hindu temple and a British Army post and parade ground. The impressively staged final battle was shot on the slopes of Mount Whitney and involved nine hundred extras.

Those who criticize *Gunga Din* on grounds of racism overlook the fact that Kipling (1865–1936), now glibly referred to in some quarters as a glorifier of British imperialism, wrote his poem as a sincere tribute to the *bhisti,* the native workers attached to the army. The *bhisti* were indispensable in the campaigns against the fiercely rebellious people of India's northern boundaries. Kipling, born in Bom-

90

bay, wrote his stories from firsthand observation as a newspaperman and was only twenty-three when he wrote *Soldiers Three*. He maintained that the soldiers, rough as they were in their treatment of natives, were not unappreciative of them and that many a *bhisti* bravely lost his life in the service. All of which is apparent in this film, despite the negative views of the cynical.

Hollywood did fairly well by Kipling, with good productions of *Captains Courageous* (1937), *Wee Willie Winkie* (1937—with Willie turned into a girl to accommodate Shirley Temple), *The Jungle Book* (1942) and *Kim* (1951). But when MGM tackled *Soldiers Three* in 1951, with Stewart Granger and David Niven, they turned it into a trite piece of bombastic slapstick—light-years removed from the fun and buoyancy of *Gunga Din*.

A better man than most.

The Four Feathers

1939

A London Film. Produced by Alexander Korda. Directed by Zoltan Korda. Screenplay by R. C. Sherriff, based on the novel by A. E. W. Mason. Photographed by Georges Perinel and Osmond Borradaile. Music by Miklos Rozsa. Running time: 130 minutes.

CAST

Harry Faversham, John Clements; *Captain John Durrance,* Ralph Richardson; *General Burroughs,* C. Aubrey Smith; *Ethne Burroughs,* June Duprez; *General Faversham,* Allan Jeayes; *Lieutenant Willoughby,* Jack Allen; *Peter Burroughs,* Donald Gray; *Dr. Sutton,* Frederick Culley; *Young Harry,* Clive Baxter; *Colonel,* Archibald Baxter; *Lieutenant Parker,* Derek Elphinstone; *Dr. Harraz,* Henry Oscar; *The Khalifa,* John Laurie; *Karaga Pasha,* Amid Taftazani.

A. E. W. Mason (1865–1948) wrote his *The Four Feathers* in 1902 and there has yet to appear a more entertaining analysis of cowardice and courage. Mason began his career as an actor but gave it up at the age of thirty to devote himself to writing, and although he turned out a large number of books and plays, it is only this one story that keeps his name alive. He traveled widely to observe life and in discussing *The Four Feathers* he said: "I took a little steamer from Suez down the Red Sea, disem-

barked at Suakin—there was no Port Sudan in those days and no railway—hired half a dozen camels with half a dozen Fuzzy Wuzzies, none of whom spoke any English whilst I spoke no Arabic, and pushed off into the eastern Sudan. In due time I arrived at Berber and Khartoum. Omdurman was still much as it had been during the life of Kalifa, and the "house of stone," his famous prison, still stood. I me Slatin Pasha and a good many of that distinguished group of officers who made the Sudan and its army famous and there was the setting for my story suggesting itself."

The Four Feathers had first been filmed in England in 1921 and in Hollywood, with Richard Arlen and Clive Brooks, seven years later. The best version is Alexander Korda's production in 1939, directed by his brother Zoltan and involving a great deal of color footage shot on the actual locations of Mason's story. The Kordas traveled more than a thousand miles up the Nile, through Egypt and the Sudan and proved that a British film company could equal what Hollywood producers had long been doing—glorifying the British Empire. Zoltan Korda tried to repeat his luck by remaking *The Four Feathers* in 1956,

Lt. Harry Faversham (John Clements) places his resignation.

calling it *Storm Over the Nile* and repeating a lot of the former action footage but it had little of the original flair. Anthony Steel played the leading role of Harry Faversham and fell short of the intensity John Clements gave the part in 1939. Faversham is a young army officer from a distinguished military family who resigns his commission on the eve of his regiment's departure for Sudan to support Lord Kitchener's campaign in 1898. Faversham has already disgusted his father, a general, by declaring no interest in a soldier's life and now that he is about to be married to his Ethne (June Duprez) daughter of General Burroughs (C. Aubrey Smith), he wants to settle down. All of his associates regard his sentiments as cowardice and three officers, John Durrance (Ralph Richardson), Ethne's brother Peter (Donald Gray) and Tom Willoughby (Jack Allen) hand him white feathers, the symbol of the coward. When he finds Ethne agrees with the officers, Faversham plucks another white feather from her fan. He then disappears.

Afraid he may really be a coward, Faversham consults the family doctor, who sympathizes and assures him he does not suffer from any abnormal condition. Faversham explains he wants to proceed to Egypt alone and the doctor gives him the address of a friend, Dr. Harraz (Henry Oscar). With the aid of Harraz, Faversham disguises himself as a native and in order to learn Arabic, assumes the identity of a Sangali, a tribe who have had their tongues cut out by their enemies. This involves Faversham being branded on the forehead with the letter S. He allows himself to be captured in the desert by Dervishes and dragged along as a laborer as they advance toward the British lines. Faversham observes his regiment being wiped out and he afterwards goes on the battlefield and finds the badly wounded Durrance. He cares for the officer, blinded by the sun, and guides him across the desert to a British outpost, without Durrance knowing the identity of the solicitous native. However, Faversham slips a white feather into Durrance's wallet.

Peter Burroughs and Tom Willoughby have been captured by the Dervishes and thrown into a packed and stinking prison. Faversham contrives to get himself arrested and put in the same compound, where he reveals himself to his former friends, who join him in a successful plan to overtake the captors

93

The accusations of cowardice, with which his fiancée
Ethne (June Duprez) sadly agrees.

and seize their fortification.. The prison is in Omdurman and as Kitchener attacks the city the
three Englishmen capture the arsenal, thereby helping to turn the British siege into a decisive victory.
Burroughs and Willoughby take back their white
feathers. At about the time the Omdurman victory
is announced in England, Durrance discovers the
feather in his wallet and realizes the native who
saved his life was actually Faversham. Durrance
has been Faversham's rival for Ethne's hand in marriage all along and now, with Ethne about to become his bride, he tells her he has changed his
mind. He knows Faversham has returned to England and that he still loves Ethne. On the evening
of Faversham's reunion with his family and with
Ethne, he performs one more act of bravery. Once
more a soldier, Faversham has the nerve to inter-

The attack of the Fuzzi Wuzzies.

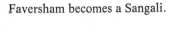

Faversham becomes a Sangali.

94

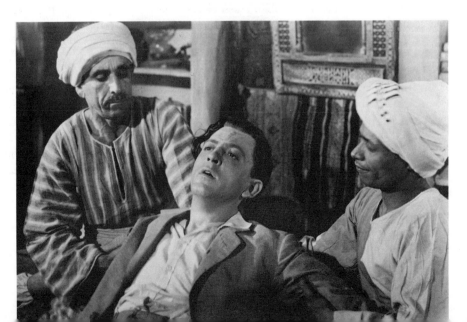

rupt General Burroughs, forever telling the same long-winded stories about his military campaigns, pointing out that his facts are not quite correct. The lamb has proved himself a lion and all is forgiven.

R. C. Sherriff's fine screenplay differs considerably from the Mason book and from the previous filmings, but as a great adventure film it stands firm. The story is solid and the playing by Clements, Richardson and the others make the characters entirely plausible. But what truly lingers in the memory about *The Four Feathers* are the stunning sequences filmed in the Sudan and the splendid staging of several battles, showing the then standard British tactics employed in holding off attackers—the forming of squares, with riflemen deployed in standing, kneeling and lying positions. These exciting scenes of combat and carnage were made impressive by the Kordas' hiring of thousands of natives, many of whom were—with a touch of irony—the descendants of the Fuzzy Wuzzies, the only enemies ever to have smashed through the famous British squares.

Faversham the native laborer.

Durrance begins to understand, as does Ethne and her father (C. Aubrey Smith), left.

95

Beau Geste

1939

A Paramount Picture. Produced and directed by William A. Wellman. Screenplay by Robert Carson, based on the novel by Percival Christopher Wren. Photographed by Theodor Sparkuhl and Archie Stout. Music by Alfred Newman. Running time: 120 minutes.

CAST

Beau Geste, Gary Cooper; *John Geste,* Ray Milland; *Digby Geste,* Robert Preston; *Sergeant Markoff,* Brian Donlevy; *Isobel Rivers,* Susan Hayward; *Rasinoff,* J. Carroll Naish; *Major Henri de Beaujolais,* James Stephenson; *Lady Patricia Brandon,* Heather Thatcher; *Augustus Brandon,* George P. Huntley, Jr.; *Lieutenant Martin,* Harvey Stephens; *Maris,* Stanley Andrews; *Renoir,* Harry Woods; *Dufour,* James Burke; *Schwartz,* Albert Dekker; *Hank Miller,* Broderick Crawford; *Buddy McMonigal,* Charles Barton; *Beau as a child,* Donald O'Connor; *John as a child,* Billy Cook; *Digby as a child,* Martin Spellman; *Isobel as a child,* Ann Gillis; *Augustus as a child,* David Holt.

The French Foreign Legion (actually an inaccurate reference to the *régiments étrangères* of the French Army) was founded in 1831 as a force to be used in colonial campaigns, particularly in French North Africa, where it became famous for its quelling of native insurrections. It also became one of the world's most romanticized military units, a curious twist of fate in view of its true reputation as a sort of voluntary penal colony. In order to get recruits to serve in remote and bleak outposts in brutal heat and continuous danger, the French

opened the legion to men of all nationalities on a no-questions-asked basis. As such it attracted adventurers, renegades, criminals and those who desired to retreat from ordinary life. And it was a magnet for novelists. One of them was Percival Christopher Wren (1885–1941), an English soldier-author who wrote *Beau Geste* in 1924, and followed its success with sequels about the legion, but neither the sequels nor any of his several dozen other adventure novels matched the appeal of this one story.

P. C. Wren traveled the world after graduating from Oxford University and spent years as a sailor, hunter, journalist and occasional laborer. He served in the British Army as a cavalry trooper and then signed on with the French Foreign Legion in Morocco. He later lived in Africa, where among other things he became a fencing champion, and with the outbreak of the First World War he joined the Indian Army. He distinguished himself in action and was invalided out of the service in 1917 with the rank of major. Impaired health curtailed his adventurous life and he thereafter settled down to a life of writing in England. Tales of the Foreign Legion had long been popular in pulp magazines

but his firsthand experiences enabled Wren to produce a story that captured the imaginations of millions. Within a year of the book's appearance it had been adapted into a stage play and in 1926 Paramount made a splendid movie out of it, with Ronald Colman as Beau, Neil Hamilton as Digby and Ralph Forbes as John. When Paramount remade it in 1939 they instructed director-producer William Wellman to duplicate the silent version as closely as possible, which he did, even shooting it on the same sand dunes near Yuma, Arizona, although it required the building of a new Fort Zinderneuf.

Beau Geste has one of the most fascinating opening sequences of any adventure film. A company of legionnaires under the command of Major Henri de Beaujolais (James Stephenson) turn up at Zinderneuf and receive no greeting, other than a single shot fired in their direction. Every parapet is manned by a legionnaire but closer inspection finds them all to be dead. The major dispatches a bugler, Digby Geste (Robert Preston), to scale the wall and open the gates. Inside, Digby finds the dead body of his brother Beau (Gary Cooper) and nearby the body

of a sergeant, Markoff (Brian Donlevy), with a French bayonet in his chest. When the bugler fails to return, the major himself enters the fort and is puzzled by the sight of the sergeant lying near a dead legionnaire with his arms folded peacefully across his chest. He examines the rest of the fort but then finds that the bodies of the sergeant and the legionnaire have vanished. The major opens the gates but as the column enters, shots ring out in the desert and they take cover. The mystery increases as the fort begins to go up in flames.

The story flashes back a dozen years or so to Brandon Abbey, the English estate of Lady Patricia Brandon, who lives with her son Augustus and her adopted children, the Geste brothers and Isobel. The brothers are devoted to each other and their favorite games are military, which includes climbing into the Abbey's suits of armor. It is while ensconced in one of the suits that Beau overhears his aunt, in need of money, sell her most precious diamond, the Blue Water. Years later, the grown-up children—Beau (Cooper), John (Ray Milland), Digby (Preston), Isobel (Susan Hayward) and Augustus (George P. Huntley, Jr.)—persuade their

aunt to show them the famous gem. She brings it
from a vault but as she shows it, the lights go out,
the gem disappears, and no amount of persuasion
brings its return. During the night Beau leaves,
with a note for John explaining that he took the
Blue Water and intends joining the Foreign Legion.
The next day, John leaves with the same purpose,
and followed later by Digby. The three brothers
are united at a training post in Morocco, where
they come under the command of the brutal martinet
Markoff. A weasel-like jewel thief named Rasinoff
(J. Carroll Naish) overhears the brothers talking
about the Blue Water and informs Markoff, who
sets his heart on getting it. He sends Digby off to a
remote outpost but takes Beau and John with him
to Zinderneuf.

Fort Zinderneuf is commanded by an ailing
lieutenant who soon dies, but not before warning
Markoff to ease up in his harsh treatment of the
men. With his death, Markoff assumes command
and sets about making his company tough. He tells
them, "I may kill half of you in training . . . but
the half that lives will be soldiers. I promise you!"
His regime proves too much for some of the men, a
few of whom have suffered under him before, and
they mutiny. A handful, including Beau and John,
remain loyal to the service and with their aid Markoff is able to contain the mutineers. He lines them
up and orders the Geste brothers to shoot the ring-
leaders. They refuse and as Markoff turns his pistol
on Beau and John, the fort is attacked by Arabs and
the company reassumes military stance to defend
itself. The attacks are forceful and prolonged, and
one by one the legionnaires die at their posts. Markoff, a skillful tactician, picks up every fallen body
and props it up in a parapet, ordering the survivors
to move from point to point and give the impression
of a large company. Beau voices his disgust to John
but admits, "He's the best soldier we'll ever see."

Markoff's methods eventually outsmart the Arabs
and they retreat. But by this time only Markoff and
John are left alive. The sergeant sends John for
coffee and sets about searching Beau's body for the
diamond. John interrupts him in the process and
Markoff draws his pistol. Beau is still alive and
with his last spurt of energy he pulls the sergeant
off balance, at which John runs a bayonet into him.
It is then that the relief column under Major de
Beaujolais arrives and John fires a shot to halt
them. John goes over the wall into the desert and
Digby enters the fort to find the bodies. He hides
when the major arrives and then takes both the
bodies of Beau and Markoff to the barracks where

Robert Preston, Ray Milland, Susan Hayward, Heather
Thatcher, George P. Huntley, Jr. and Gary Cooper.

Markoff (Brian Donlevy) puts down the mutiny.

Fort Zinderneuf under attack.

98

he prepares the Viking funeral that Beau had said he wanted when he was a boy—with a dead dog at his feet. Digby sets fire to the barracks and escapes the fort, where he finds John. Together they fire on the column to give the impression of an Arab attack and then make their way home. Digby is shot and killed by an Arab, leaving only John to turn up at Brandon Abbey with an explanation for Lady Patricia and for a union with his beloved Isobel. Lady Patricia reads a letter from Beau in which he confesses it was he who stole the Blue Water to spare her the humiliation of revealing its sale and the substitution of a fake to save face. She gratefully comments that the man was as good as his name, "Beau Geste—gallant gesture."

Beau Geste is pure romantic fiction, with story-book concepts of fraternal love, honesty and bravery, but done with such flair and flourish that it defies being measured by yardsticks of reality. To paraphrase Mae West's comment on goodness, "Reality had nothing to do with it."

John and Beau take a break. The other legionnaires don't need one—they're dead.

Having killed Markoff, John comforts the dying Beau.

Digby prepares the Viking funeral for Beau, with the dead dog, Markoff, at his feet.

99

Northwest Passage

1940

An MGM Picture. Produced by Hunt Stromberg. Directed by King Vidor. Screenplay by Laurence Stallings and Talbot Jennings, based on the novel by Kenneth Roberts. Photographed in Technicolor by Sidney Wagner and William V. Skall. Music by Herbert Stothart. Running time: 125 minutes.

CAST

Major Robert Rogers, Spencer Tracy; *Langdon Towne,* Robert Young; *Hunk Marriner,* Walter Brennan; *Elizabeth Browne,* Ruth Hussey; *Cap Huff,* Nat Pendleton; *Reverend Browne,* Louis Hector; *Humphrey Towne,* Robert Barrat; *Lord Amherst,* Lumsden Hare; *Sergeant McNott,* Donald McBride; *Jennie Colt,* Isabel Jewell; *Lieutenant Avery,* Douglas Walton; *Lieutenant Crofton,* Addison Richards; *Jesse Beacham,* Hugh Sothern; *Webster,* Regis Toomey; *Wiseman Clagett,* Montagu Love; *Sam Livermore,* Lester Matthews; *Captain Ogden,* Truman Bradley.

Kenneth Roberts (1885–1957) specialized in writing novels set in the backwaters of American history, most particularly pre-revolutionary New England. He was a meticulous researcher, quite intolerant of inaccuracy. He stated his case in regard to historical fiction: "I have a theory that history can be most effectively told in the form of fiction, because only in the writing of fiction that stands the test of truth do falsities come to the surface." His *Arundel, Rabble in Arms, Captain Caution, Oliver Wiswell, Northwest Passage* and *Lydia Bailey* proved him a man of his word, as well as a writer of great value. *Northwest Passage* first appeared as a serial in the *Saturday Evening Post,* and then as a book in 1937, the rights to which were purchased by MGM only three months after publication. By far the most popular of Roberts' novels, it relates the adventures of one of the most colorful warriors in American history, Robert Rogers (1717–1795), who organized a company of rangers in 1755 and distinguished himself in the French and Indian wars. The main dream of his life was to blaze a trail across unmapped America and find a route to the Pacific. He was never able to accomplish this but his estimates and proposals were employed by the Lewis and Clark expedition (1803–06), who found Rogers was perfectly reasonable as to the route and the time required. However, MGM's handsome movie does not touch on these aspects of his life, but focuses on his skill and bravery as an Indian fighter.

The film begins with Langdon Towne (Robert

The major briefs his men.

Young) arriving home in Portsmouth, New Hampshire, after having been expelled from Harvard University for the snide political comments contained in his cartoons. The year is 1759 and Towne, intent on being an artist, is among those critical of injustices in British rule. He fails to curb his tongue and takes to the woods to escape arrest, accompanied by his backwoods friend Hunk Marriner (Walter Brennan). At a tavern they meet Major Rogers (Spencer Tracy), who encourages them to drink with him. When the pair awaken they are in Crown Point, the headquarters of Rogers' Rangers, a company of colonial soldiers attached to the forces of British General Amherst (Lumsden Hare). Since Rogers needs a map maker and Towne is interested in sketching Indians, he agrees to join the Rangers, who are about to depart on a secret campaign. Once under way, Rogers tells his two hundred men that they are bound for St. Francis, the village of the Abenakis on the Canadian side of the border, to wipe it out. He offers to let any Ranger not sympathetic to the mission return, but none do. Most have lost relatives and friends to the brutal, marauding Indians, who have long been making fearful raids through the Ohio Valley, upstate New York and New England. Encouraged by the French, the Indians have also made British rule more difficult.

The trek to St. Francis is tough and made the more so by the presence of French forces on the lookout for Rogers. The Rangers proceed by boat up Lake Champlain and then, to avoid the French, they carry their heavy boats overland to other waterways, and eventually abandon the boats to make the remainder of the journey on foot, marching through swamps in order not to leave footprints. They arrive at St. Francis at a time when the Abenakis are engaged in a long ceremony, and Rogers tells his men that all is in their favor—the Indians will exhaust themselves with drink and the wind is in the opposite direction. "Even the dogs can't smell us," to which Marriner quips, "Lucky for the dogs." At dawn the next morning the Rangers infiltrate the village. Rogers and his group take over the small fort, with its cannon, and the rest advance from all directions with flaming torches. In the ensuing battle the Rangers lose sixteen men but the Abenakis are liquidated and their dozens of huts, shacks and tepees are razed.

Langdon Towne (Robert Young), Hunk Marriner (Walter Brennan) and Konkapot (Andrew Pena) awake from their hangover to find themselves at Crown Point, and so informed by Sergeant McNott (Donald McBride).

Major Rogers (Spencer Tracy), General Amherst (Lumsden Hare) and Sir William Johnson (Frederick Worlock) at the outset of Rogers' expedition.

Rogers checks his maps with Towne.

Now the hard part begins—the return, with almost no food and supplies. The men tire easily with only mouthfuls of corn to sustain them on their long trudge back to British lines. At Lake Memphremagog, where they expected to find a consignment of food, they find the French. They then head for Fort Wentworth to rendezvous with the British but when they arrive, the haggard survivors find it deserted and barren. Rogers sheds a tear in private but keeps up a brave front to try and inspire his men, who are too exhausted to be inspired. But it is at this moment that they hear the music of an advancing band. The British arrive and the Rangers are saved. Later, in Portsmouth, Rogers reads a royal citation to his recovered Rangers, about to depart on another mission. Rogers tells them that the previous trip will be a "duck hunt" compared to the rigors of the upcoming expedition. They will march to Fort Detroit and then westward and northward through uncharted territory to find a passage to the Pacific and a route to the Orient. Langdon Towne, no longer a Ranger but set to make his way as an artist, bids goodbye to Rogers, as does his fiancee Elizabeth Browne (Ruth Hussey). As they watch the Rangers march away, she asks Langdon if there really is a northwest passage. He says he doesn't know but philosophizes, "It's every man's dream to find a short route to his heart's desire."

Northwest Passage should rightly have been titled *Rogers' Rangers* since it deals only with Book One of Roberts' long novel and not with Rogers' attempts to raise support and funds for his obsession to travel northwest. The film is faithful for the most part to the spirit of Roberts' work and deviates wildly only at the end. Towne did not get to marry Elizabeth Browne—she married Rogers and went off to London with him after he had spent another five years in various campaigns against the French and the Indians. MGM planned to film Part Two of Roberts' book provided public response to *Northwest Passage* merited so doing. The film did well but the critics whipped it for delivering less than it promised, and the studio, apparently eager to avoid the trouble and expense involved in shooting this one, announced they would shelve the second half of the story. The wartime economies of 1940 gave them a good excuse. The pity was that it denied Spencer Tracy a vehicle of great potential. He was splendid as Rogers in *Northwest Passage,* a truly commanding and inspiring figure, but in Book Two he would have had magnificent material to work with, as Rogers butts his head about the Establishment in London, becomes alcoholic and difficult, court-martialed, thrown in a debtors'

prison, returns to America and gradually alienates himself from the American cause.

Visually *Northwest Passage* is remarkable. Director King Vidor tackled the project with a passion, although he found himself on location without a completed script. The scenarists had found the Roberts book extremely hard to translate exactly— another reason why MGM backed away from the sequel. The efforts that went into making the film were considerable, with seventy days of shooting in the wilds of Idaho and Vidor driving his men à la Rogers. Since the original locales of the story were too built up with roads and telephone poles, an MGM team searched for a remote area that would approximate the rugged hills and lakes of Vermont and upstate New York, and settled on the spectacular scenery around Idaho's Lake Payette. The company built a replica of the Crown Point fort on a peninsula jutting into the lake and on another location constructed the village of St. Francis, which required more than a hundred buildings. Three hundred Indians from local tribes were employed to play the Abenakis but their involvement in the film was not as grueling as that of the white actors

and extras. Vidor marched them through miles of swamps, had them pulling boats uphill and fording cold and swift rivers. Spencer Tracy, seldom a very tractable actor on location, admitted he rather liked the sense of physical well-being he gained from the weeks in Idaho and pointed out, "I don't care how good an actor you are, you can't speak lines while standing up to your neck in ice water, unless you're in good physical shape. That's what happened to all of us on *Northwest Passage*. It isn't exactly fun to work in bitter cold, and sloshing through mud all day."

Rogers questions the demented Crofton (Addison Richards), who carries an Indian head in his bag.

Leaving for his trek to find the Northwest Passage, Rogers bids goodbye to Towne and his fiancée (Ruth Hussey).

The attack on St. Francis.

105

The Sea Hawk

1940

A Warner Bros. Picture. Produced by Hal B. Wallis. Directed by Michael Curtiz. Screenplay by Howard Koch and Seton I. Miller. Photographed by Sol Polito. Music by Erich Wolfgang Korngold. Running time: 126 minutes.

CAST

Captain Geoffrey Thorpe, Errol Flynn; *Donna Maria*, Brenda Marshall; *Don José Alvarez de Cordoba*, Claude Rains; *Sir John Burleson*, Donald Crisp; *Queen Elizabeth*, Flora Robson; *Carl Pitt*, Alan Hale; *Lord Wolfingham*, Henry Daniell; *Miss Latham*, Una O'Connor; *Abbott*, James Stephenson; *Captain Lopez*, Gilbert Roland; *Danny Logan*, William Lundigan; *Oliver Scott*, Julien Marshall; *King Philip II*, Montagu Love; *Eli Matson*; J. M. Kerrigan; *Martin Burke*, David Bruce; *William Tuttle*, Clifford Brooke; *Walter Boggs*, Clyde Cook; *Inquisitor*, Fritz Leiber.

The Sea Hawk is a glorious specimen of Hollywood's so-called Golden Age, when talent, facilities and resources were plentiful, and when a huge and eager audience awaited an Errol Flynn swashbuckler. The circumstances can never be duplicated. Flynn, at thirty-one, was in the peak of condition, long before his hedonistic ways undermined his vitality, and Warners had on their roster the likes of director Michael Curtiz, composer Erich Wolfgang Korngold, cinematographer Sol Polito and any number of splendid character actors. The success of Flynn's *Captain Blood* made another pirate vehicle for him almost inevitable. Warners had instructed writer Delmer Daves to prepare a screenplay from Rafael Sabatini's *The Sea Hawk*, the rights to which they had acquired with the purchase of the First National Company, who had made a rousing movie of the book in 1924, starring Milton Sills. But by the time the Flynn version went into production it had been decided to dump the Daves–Sabatini material and make something that would bolster the British cause in the first year of the war with Hitler. Seton I. Miller had written a story called *Beggars of the Sea*, roughly based on the exploits of Sir Francis Drake and his fellow privateers in their plundering of Spanish booty, and Warners instructed Howard Koch to use this as the basis of the screenplay. The Sabatini title was retained bu the film itself bears no other similarity. Instead, it stresses the parallel between Philip of Spain's ambitions to conquer England and Hitler's expected invasion. *The Sea Hawk* could hardly have been more pro-British had it been made in London.

The picture begins with Philip (Montagu Love)

stating his warlike intentions to his cabinet and dispatching Don José Alvarez de Cordoba (Claude Rains) to England as his ambassador, to assure Queen Elizabeth (Flora Robson) of his love and goodwill. En route, the Spanish galleon carrying Don José and his beautiful niece Donna Maria (Brenda Marshall) is attacked and sunk by the *Albatross,* the warship commanded by Geoffrey Thorpe (Flynn). Thorpe and a half-dozen other captains, who call themselves "the sea hawks," are convinced that Spain will attack England, and they rob Spanish treasuries in the New World to build funds for the British fleet. The Queen officially disapproves but the charming Thorpe convinces her that defense is vital. At the court reception for the ambassador, Don José protests the sinking of his galleon but Thorpe points out that he freed twenty Englishmen used as galley slaves. Don José claims the men were duly tried and sentenced, but Thorpe speaks up, "I submit, your Highness, that the Court of the Inquisition is not qualified to pass fair judgment on English seamen or to subject them to the cruel indignities of the Spanish galleys." Lord Wolfingham (Henry Daniell), one of the Queen's

chief ministers, pleads the case of the Spanish ambassador and Thorpe is lightly reprimanded.

Donna Maria, at first appalled by Thorpe's behavior as a pirate, now sees him as a gallant gentleman and falls in love with him, and he with her. After leaving the palace, where he has convinced the Queen to allow him to make a mission to the Americas in search of more Spanish wealth, he spots Maria picking roses. He tells her that he must leave for a voyage but assures her of his love: "Maria, in the garden of a convent in Peru there's a beautiful statue. The Spanish nuns call it *Nuestra Señora de las Rosas.* This is how I'll remember you . . . as my Lady of the Roses." Later, she hears her uncle and Lord Wolfingham plotting against England and revealing their knowledge of Thorpe's intended attack on the garrisons at Panama. Maria rushes to Dover to warn Thorpe but his ship has already sailed.

In Panama, Thorpe and his men are ambushed as they march through the jungle, and most are killed in the fight. Thorpe and half a dozen others manage to make their way back to their ship, only to find it in Spanish hands. They are tried by the Inquisition and condemned to the galleys. After months of

Captain Thorpe (Flynn) addresses his crew, the freed slaves and the defeated Spanish soldiers.

being chained to oars, Thorpe leads his men in a successful escape and taking over a galleon they sail to England. Once inside the palace, Thorpe proceeds to the Queen but is halted by the treacherous Wolfingham, who sneeringly asks, "You have some papers for me?" Replies Thorpe, "I have some papers for the Queen." The papers to which they refer are the Spanish plans for an invasion, led by the Armada. The two draw swords and engage in a long, drawn-out duel—Wolfingham desperate to retrieve the papers and Thorpe eagerly edging in the direction of the Queen's chambers. Finally, Wolfingham lies dead and as the Queen approaches, Thorpe hands her the evidence she needs in order to build her fleet and declare war. In the final scene, on the deck of a new warship, she knights Sir Geoffrey Thorpe, as the faithful Maria smiles with pride.

The production of *The Sea Hawk* moved so well that Warners for a while considered issuing it as a special presentation, with an intermission—the intermission would have come just before Thorpe leaves for Panama. This plan was dropped and the film proceeded to do handsome business along the usual channels of release. When it was reissued in 1947 about ten minutes were trimmed from the original running time of 126 minutes, editing out some of the dialogue sequences and those portions which had obvious messages for the wartime British. In the final scene of the print now available, the Queen merely knights Flynn and he arises to the

cheers of his colleagues. In the original print she addresses the assembly: "When the ruthless ambitions of a man threaten to engulf the world, it becomes the solemn obligation of free men, whenever they may be, to affirm that the earth belongs not to one man, but to all men, and that freedom is the deed and title to the soil on which we exist. Firm in this faith, we shall now make ready to meet the great Armada." Standing alongside Flynn in this scene is Donald Crisp, in the role of Sir John Burleson, advisor to the Queen and friend of the hero. The fact that Crisp receives fourth billing is possibly a puzzle to those who know only the edited version. Quite a lot of Crisp's footage was lost in the 1947 editing, including a big scene in which he visits Thorpe in Dover and warns him to be careful in Panama, reducing his part to almost a bit.

Warners lavished $1,700,000 on the production, then a high figure, but it is difficult to calculate this in present terms since almost all the cast and crew were on the payroll of the studio. Large amounts of money were saved by using the beautiful sets and costumes that had been designed a year previously for *The Private Lives of Elizabeth and Essex.* A new sound stage was used for the first time in making *The Sea Hawk,* large enough to house two newly built, full-scale ships (one 165 feet long and the other 135 feet) sitting in water. The exciting battle between the *Albatross* and the Spanish galleon carrying the ambassador, rich with de-

Geoffrey Thorpe arrives at court—late.

Donna Maria (Brenda Marshall) receiving the courtly attention of the smitten Thorpe.

tail and brilliantly edited, used models for the long-shots, intercut with close action. Everything about the film rates merit—the fine script, with its intelligent dialogue, the costumes, the sets, the finely lit and shaded photography of Sol Polito, and the music of Korngold sweeping the whole enterprise along with a multitude of romantic and dramatic themes.

It did not seem to occur to many critics in 1940 just how good was the direction of Michael Curtiz. Time has brought evaluation for the difficult art of making action-costume epics—and time has proved that few, other than Curtiz, have been blessed with the talent for mounting spectacles and making them move convincingly. For Curtiz *The Sea Hawk* was just one of three large-scale adventures released in 1940. He preceded it with *Virginia City* and followed it with *Santa Fe Trail,* both of which also starred Flynn. Such productivity for a director is now unheard of. Ironically, though Flynn and Curtiz did some of their best work in each other's company, neither man cared much for the other. Curtiz had no use for actors in general. He was a work-obsessed taskmaster who thought little of an actor's safety and comfort in making physical sequences, something that Flynn finally rebelled against. Their last picture was *Dive Bomber* in 1941, which starred the actor in a purely passive role.

Flynn was in fine fettle for *The Sea Hawk,*

On trial in the court of the Inquisition.

Condemned to the galleys, and welcomed aboard by the captain (Pedro De Cordoba).

The traitorous Wolfingham (Henry Daniell) tries to stop Thorpe reaching the Queen.

The galley slaves escape.

swinging from ropes in battle ("Over the side, men!"), and yelling orders to his crew ("Aloft there! clear your leash lines!") and moving with athletic aplomb. His swordplay was adept and graceful but the duel with Wolfingham had to be extensively doubled due to Henry Daniell's inability to fence. Don Turner doubled for Flynn in the long shots and both Ralph Faulkner and Ned Davenport performed all but the close-ups for Daniell. The esteemed fencing masted Fred Cavens choreographed the duel, with rapid movements through rooms and corridors, down stairs, across tables, over fallen candelabra and against a background of columns and tapestries. The skill of the swordplay, the pacing, the photography and the music combined to make this a pinnacle in the roster of adventure films.

The court guards can't stop him either.

"... we shall now make ready to meet the great Armada."

49th Parallel

1941

An Ortus Film. Produced and directed by Michael Powell. Screenplay by Emeric Pressberger and Rodney Ackland. Photographed by Frederic Young. Music by Ralph Vaughan Williams. Running time: 123 minutes.

CAST

Philip Armstrong Scott, Leslie Howard; *Andy Brock,* Raymond Massey; *Johnnie,* Laurence Olivier; *Peter,* Anton Walbrook; *Anna,* Glynis Johns; *The Factor,* Finlay Currie; *Lieutenant Hirth,* Eric Portman; *Vogel,* Niall MacGinnis; *Nick,* Ley On; *Art,* Eric Clavering; *Andreas,* Charles Victor; *Lieutenant Kuhnecke,* Raymond Lovell; *Lohrmann,* John Chandos; *Jahner,* Basil Appleby.

Canada has yet to produce any major entertainment films depicting the scope of its epic geography and history. Such features are costly and the funds have never been sufficient within the country itself. Canada's reputation in the film world has come from the many fine shorts and documentaries produced by the National Film Board and the Canadian Broadcasting Corporation, but its production of features has been severely restricted by the control of its theatre circuits by American and British interests. The track record of the Canadian Film Development Corporation, a federally funded body created in 1968 to foster production, has so far been undistinguished and Canadian filmmakers, doubtless because of working with small budgets, have settled for dealing with minor, and very often shabby, aspects of the national life rather than the splendid.

Hollywood has always been aware of Canada, al-

The U-37 arrives in Canadian waters.

though it is an awareness mostly of the Royal Canadian Mounted Police. The Mounties, the world's most romanticized policemen, were the subjects of hundreds of B westerns, including eight serials, and occasionally a major production, such as Cecil B. DeMille's *North West Mounted Police* (1940), *Saskatchewan* (1954), starring Alan Ladd, and *The Canadians* (1961), with Robert Ryan. Other Hollywood forays into Canadiana include *Canadian Pacific* (1949), a conventional railroad yarn with Randolph Scott, and *Captain of the Clouds,* a tribute to the Royal Canadian Air Force, with James Cagney as a rambunctious bush pilot. All contained interesting footage shot in Canada—whereas most of Hollywood's Mountie pictures were done in the High Sierras of California—but some were quite good enough to deserve listing as great adventure films.

The adventure film which reveals the most about Canada's vastness is *49th Parallel,* a very calculated piece of British propaganda made in 1941 to bolster pride in the Empire and further contempt for the Nazis. Its sophistries about the decency of Democracy and the nastiness of National Socialism now seem rather ludicrous but the story, the acting and the direction retain their strengths. The grand title—referring to the line of latitude dividing much of Canada from the United States—is misleading since the film is not about American-Canadian relations, and the only point in which Americans are involved occurs at Niagara Falls, which is not on that latitude. In handling the film for American distribution Columbia changed the title to *The Invaders.*

49th Parallel was a prestige production. Laurence Olivier, Leslie Howard, Anton Walbrook and Raymond Massey were readily agreeable to playing small roles, the British government put up some of the financing and Ralph Vaughan Williams (then 69) was persuaded to make his debut as a film composer. The score is sparse and its main theme, a very stately melody, is heard over the credit titles, shown against a slow pan of the Canadian Rockies. The drama begins as a German submarine, the U-37, surfaces in the Gulf of St. Lawrence and a party of six men, under the command of Lieutenant Hirth (Eric Portman) are put ashore to forage for food and supplies. While ashore they watch with surprise as the U-37 is attacked by RCAF bombers and sunk, leaving them stranded in a bleak landscape. They make their way to a Hudson's Bay trading post, where the agent (Finlay Currie) is entertaining his friend Johnny (Olivier), a French

The trapper (Olivier) and the factor (Finlay Currie) meet their first Nazis (Raymond Lovell and Eric Portman).

The Hutterite leader (Anton Walbrook) entertains the Germans.

Canadian trapper. Johnny's saucy contempt for the Germans and his attempt to get a message out by radio costs him his life. The Germans than commandeer a seaplane but their combined weight makes it impossible to take off. An Eskimo marksman unwittingly helps them by picking off a German standing on one of the plane's pontoons. They fly west and eventually crash-land in a lake when their gas runs out, which costs another German life.

The four survivors next encounter Canadian life in the form of a Hutterite seltlement in Manitoba. They assume that because the Hutterites are of German blood they will be sympathetic to the Nazi cause. Hirth lectures his generous, pacifistic hosts but fails to move them. Instead their leader, Peter (Walbrook) gives a quiet but firm rebuttal. One of the German sailors, Vogel (Niall MacGinnis) the only decent one of the bunch, decides to stay with the Hutterites but Hirth passes judgment and Vogel is executed. The three Germans push on westward by foot, until they come across a traveling salesman changing a tire on his car. They turn up in Banff, Alberta, on the day of an Indian ceremonial parade and join the onlookers but news of their presence has been made known by broadcasts and one of the men is grabbed by the RCMP. Hirth and his one remaining comrade, Lohrmann (John Chandos), quickly head for the woods and after days of stumbling around they come across an elegant Englishman, Philip Armstrong Scott (Howard), an author and expert on Indian history, who offers them the hospitality of his camp. Their contempt for his apparently soft and decadent lifestyle results in an altercation, in which Lohrmann is shot and Hirth escapes.

The lonely Hirth manages to make his way back across the country by riding freight cars and pins his hope of escape on getting across the American border into a neutral country. As the train heads for Niagara Falls he is joined by an absent-without-leave Canadian soldier, Andy Brock (Massey), who gripes about the army and the government but who rises to the occasion when he realizes he has a Nazi at bay. Hirth takes Brock's revolver and his uniform but as the train comes to the border it is boarded by U. S. Customs officers. Brock persuades the Americans to send the car back to the Canadian side since both he and Hirth are unlisted on the manifest. The officers, having relieved Hirth of the revolver, make a phone call to their Canadian counterparts and complain about being sent unspecified items. The film ends with a gleam in Brock's eyes as he prepares to forcibly retrieve his

Vogel (Niall MacGinnis) falls for Anna (Glynis Johns), to the disgust of Hirth.

Hirth and Lohrmann (John Chandos) stagger through the Canadian Rockies.

Philip Armstrong Scott (Leslie Howard) has his hospitality abused by Hirth.

Hirth tries to get across the American border but Andy Brock (Raymond Massey) foils him.

uniform from Hirth—and a shot of the train shunting back across the bridge over the Niagara Gorge.

49th Parallel, even in the shortened version now shown on television, bogs down with outdated political sentiments but stills holds its interest as an adventure film. Its Germans were clearly set up as villains and yet such is the tenacity of their trekking through the Canadian wilds that they take on a certain aura of heroism, and the actor who emerged as the real star of the picture was Eric Portman, despite the presence of Olivier and Howard. His cold-blooded but dedicated Hirth was not a likable character but no one could fault him for lack of courage.

The film was begun in April of 1940 and took eighteen months to complete. More than two-thirds of it was shot in Canada and required a great deal of travel. The Canadian government assisted the company by giving facilities and loaning servicemen and policeman whenever necessary, but the Royal Canadian Navy declined to allow the use of a submarine in the role of the U-37 since the few they had were actively engaged in real warfare. The company solved their problem by commissioning a shipyard in Halifax, Nova Scotia, to build them a replica of a German U-boat.

The Jungle Book

1942

A Korda–United Artists Picture. Produced by Alexander Korda. Directed by Zoltan Korda. Screenplay by Laurence Stalling, based on the book by Rudyard Kipling. Photographed in Technicolor by Lee Garmes. Music by Miklos Rozsa. Running time: 115 minutes.

CAST

Mowgli, Sabu; *Buldeo,* Joseph Calleia; *The Barber,* John Qualen; *The Pundit,* Frank Puglia; *Messua,* Rosemary DeCamp; *Mahala,* Patricia O'Rourke; *Durga,* Ralph Byrd; *Rao,* John Mather; *English Girl,* Faith Brook; *Siku,* Noble Johnson.

Sabu (1924–1963) could almost have been a figment of Rudyard Kipling's imagination. He was a stable boy in Mysore, India, when he was noticed by director Robert Flaherty and given the title role in Alexander Korda's production of *Elephant Boy* in 1937—a screenplay derived from Kipling's *Toomai of the Elephants.* Korda signed him to a contract and took him to England, where he next used him in *The Drum* (titled *Drums* for the American release), yet another epic of the British Army in India. Sabu's boyish and exotic charm made him popular with moviegoers but a difficult actor to cast. Korda next placed him in *The Thief of Bagdad* (1940), a lavish fantasy which was begun in England and finished in Hollywood because war-

time restrictions proved confining. Then came *The Jungle Book,* the artistic high point in Sabu's career, and as Mowgli he would surely have pleased even Kipling. He thereafter signed a contract with Universal, with time out for service as a gunner with the U. S. Army Air Corps, and appeared in some popular but undistinguished jungle adventure pictures. A very limited actor, his appeal waned by the end of the Forties and his appearances on the screen thereafter were infrequent. At the time of his death from a heart attack at the age of thirty-nine, Sabu was a partner in a furniture store business.

The Jungle Book is a beautiful evocation of Kipling's stories about Mowgli and his animal friends in the Indian jungle. Lawrence Stalling's screenplay takes incidents from both *Jungle Books.* The adaptation is free-flowing but true to the spirit of the original and helps point up Kipling's considerable talents as a children's storyteller, rather than the tales of military glory with which his name is now mostly associated. The two books were published in 1894 and '95, and it is interesting to note that they were written in Brattleboro, Vermont. Kipling had married an American girl in 1892 and

116

Mowgli (Sabu) and some of his jungle friends.

spent a few years in New England before moving to Olde England, where he spent the remainder of his life. The genial quality of his *Jungle Books* might well have had something to do with distance lending enchantment to the view.

Mowgli, a name meaning The Little Frog and given him by the animals, is a boy reared in the jungle by a family of wolves, after wandering away from his village as an infant. A fierce Bengali tiger known as Shere Khan has attacked the village and killed Mowgli's father. In the Korda film the narrator is Buldeo (Joseph Calleia), now an old man but once the villain who tried to kill Mowgli. He tells of Mowgli's background and how one day the boy returned to the village, with no knowledge of the white man's ways or language. Mowgli meets his mother, Messua (Rosemary DeCamp), who gradually wins his confidence, as does Buldeo's pretty young daughter, Mahala (Patricia O'Rourke). Mowgli enchants her with tales of the jungle and his animal friends. Together they go into the jungle and come across the ruins of a once great city, containing vast stores of wealth. Mahala takes a gold coin and on her return to the village

tells her father about the treasure. Buldeo is filled with greed and when Mowgli, feeling that the secrets of the jungle must not be violated, refuses to reveal the location, Buldeo brands him as a demon. Sentenced to be burned to death, Mowgli escapes and heads for the ruins, but Buldeo and a band of gold-hungry villagers follow his tracks. Their avarice causes them to die, all except Buldeo, who lives to grow wiser and tell the tale.

The sub-plot of *The Jungle Book* is Mowgli's vow to find Shere Khan. All the animals in the jungle are his friends and all fear the arrogant tiger. They warn him of Shere Khan's movements and help Mowgli trap him, until finally the boy drives a dagger into the tiger's heart, avenging the death of his father.

The exteriors of the film were shot around Lake Sherwood, twenty miles north of Los Angeles, and the picturesque area was made more so by Korda's set designers, who dressed it up with added foliage and spray-paint colors. The superb color photography is the work of the veteran Lee Garmes, who was also the associate producer of the picture. Recalls Garmes, "It was one of the smoothest pic-

117

Mowgli introduces his mother (Rosemary De Camp) to his elephants.

tures I've ever worked on. The Kordas were highly professional, with Alex producing, Zoltan directing and Vincent in charge of the art direction. And Sabu was easy to work with. Much more than half of it was shot out at Lake Sherwood and the rest at the General Services Studio in Hollywood, where we built a tank for some of the water sequences and where we did most of the fire footage. The shooting was about eight weeks, longer than usual because of the use of animals, but even they were well organized. It was really a gem of a picture to do and I look back on it with fond memories."

A major asset of *The Jungle Book* is the score by Miklos Rozsa, which goes beyond the usual functions of film music and is virtually a symphonic accompaniment to the picture from beginning to end. Rozsa began his film career writing the score for Korda's *Knight Without Armor* in 1937 and wrote music for many of the producer's films for the next three years, including *The Four Feathers* and *The Thief of Bagdad*. Korda returned to London after *The Jungle Book* but Rozsa stayed in California and gradually became one of the industry's most deft and prestigious composers. His music for *The Jungle Book* is richly scored, with a central theme for the jungle, a lullaby for Mowgli's mother, leitmotifs for all the animals, music in the style of Indian ragas for the Hindu scenes, plus descriptive material for the dramatic incidents, most noticeably for the killing of Shere Khan and the terrible fire in the jungle that puts an end to the treasure-mad villagers. The themes for the animals—the elephants, wolves, the bear, the crocodile, the black panther, jackals, hyenas, the python, the cobra and the chattering monkeys—are all marked by instruments appropriate to the characters of the animals. Rozsa made a concert adaptation of the score soon after production and *The Jungle Book,* with narration spoken by Sabu, has the distinction of being the first Hollywood film score to emerge as a record album. Long deleted, although pirated, the recording was superseded in 1955 by another RCA Victor recording, again conducted by Rozsa but this time with Leo Genn telling the story. Whether on discs or on the sound track, the score is a masterpiece of musical fantasy.

Mahala (Patricia O'Rourke) and her father (Joseph Calleia) are puzzled by Mowgli's tales of the jungle.

Mowgli's mother begs for his life.

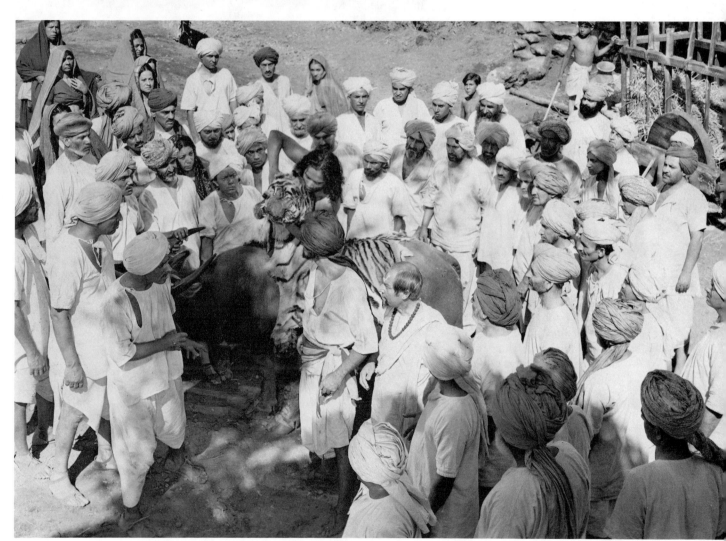

Mowgli brings the head of the dreaded Shere Khan to the relieved villagers.

Henry V

1944

A Two Cities Film. Produced and directed by Laurence Olivier. Based on the play by William Shakespeare, edited by Laurence Olivier and Alan Dent. Photographed in Technicolor by Robert Krasker and Jack Hildyard. Music by William Walton. Running time: 134 minutes.

CAST

King Henry V, Laurence Olivier; *Chorus*, Leslie Banks; *Pistol*, Robert Newton; *Princess Catherine*, Renee Asherson; *Fluellen*, Esmond Knight; *Constable of France*, Leo Genn; *Archbishop of Canterbury*, Felix Aylmer; *Mountjoy*, Ralph Truman; *King Charles VI of France*, Harcourt Williams; *Alice*, Ivy St. Heller; *Duke of Berri*, Ernest Thesiger; *The Dauphin*, Max Adrian; *Duke of Orleans*, Francis Lister; *Duke of Burgundy*, Valentine Dyall; *Duke of Bourbon*, Russell Thorndike; *Captain Gower*, Michael Shepley; *Sir Thomas Erpingham*, Morland Graham; *Earl of Westmoreland*, Gerald Case; *Queen Isabel of France*, Janet Burnell; *Duke of Exeter*, Nicholas Hannen; *Bishop of Ely*, Robert Helpmann; *Mistress Quickly*, Freda Jackson; *Williams*, Jimmy Hanley; *Captain Jamie*, John Laurie; *Captain MacMorris*, Niall MacGuinnes; *Sir John Falstaff*, George Robey; *Lieutenant Bardolph*, Roy Emerton; *Earl of Salisbury*, Griffith Jones; *Bates*, Arthur Hambling; *Corporal Nym*, Frederick Cooper; *Duke of Gloucester*, Michael Warre.

It is one of the great ironies of film history that the man who was responsible for the most proud and splendid British picture made during the Second World War was interned at the start of the war as an enemy alien. The main credit for *Henry V* belongs to Laurence Olivier but the man who thought of making the film and persuaded Olivier to be its producer-director was Filippo del Giudice, a lawyer who had fled the Mussolini regime and whose interest in films led him to set up Two Cities Films in London in 1937. Being interned for a short period on the Isle of Man did not sour del Giudice on the British; instead he made valuable contributions to the morale of his adopted country. It was del Giudice who talked Noel Coward into making a picture in praise of the Royal Navy (*In Which We Serve*) and raised the money to back it, and it was del Giudice who prevailed upon Olivier to do *Henry V*, despite the actor's feeling that Shakespeare's plays were not really suitable for the screen. He had made *As You Like It* in 1936 and

The magnificent miniatures of London, 1600.

the public response had been dismal, but del Giudice argued that Oliver's esteem with Shakespeare on the stage, plus his popularity in the movies, plus the heroic and exalting image of the British character contained in *Henry V* would combine for success. Olivier finally agreed, provided he would have total control over the project. Del Giudice astutely kept himself in the background and never even bothered Olivier with the fact that money was so much a problem during production that he had to sell a major block of shares to J. Arthur Rank in order to complete the film. The final cost was two million dollars, the most spent on a British picture at that time.

Laurence Olivier had appeared in British films all through the Thirties but it wasn't until he went to Hollywood in 1939 to do *Wuthering Heights* that he became a popular movie actor. He followed

it with *Rebecca, Pride and Prejudice,* and *Lady Hamilton* but then gave up this new-found plateau of wealth and fame, and returned to England to serve the cause. Admirable though this decision was, the truth is that Olivier was an undistinguished junior officer in the Royal Navy's Fleet Air Arm. He was a man out of his element, a problem to his superiors and denied duty as a pilot after cracking up several planes in training. He was shunted into a training camp as an instructor but twice released from service in order to appear in films in the national interest (*49th Parallel* and *The Demi Paradise*). He was finally released from the service in mid-1943 in order to make *Henry V,* and it was then that his real service to his country began. It was a timely film, clearly intended to boost British spirits as the Allies prepared for the inevitable invasion of Europe. By the time the picture was ready

Chorus (Leslie Banks) sets the scene.

for distribution, in December of 1944, the invasion was long past but it served to remind Britons that King Henry V had invaded France in 1415 and returned in triumph. However, the film did much more than that. It celebrated the British ethos. Prior to playing the role Olivier had sought advice from Charles Laughton on how Henry might be played. Said Laughton, "Be England!"

Olivier and Alan Dent edited the play and eliminated certain characters, mainly the plotters against the throne, in order to stress the visual aspects. In doing so the film simplifies the politics of the time, which had much to do with corruption and power plays between the Church and the landed gentry. Henry V, twenty-eight at the time of gaining the crown, had been a playboyish Prince of Wales and his advisors deemed it necessary for him to establish his leadership in battle in order to bind together a badly disorganized England. In early August of 1415 he set sail from a point near Portsmouth in a rather arbitrary campaign against the French, the traditional enemy, and took with him an army of thirty thousand men, eight thousand of

whom were archers. Henry swept through the northern provinces of France during the next two months, winning every encounter but at high cost. By the time he engaged the French at Agincourt on October 25 he had only twelve thousand men left—facing a force of sixty thousand. Despite the odds the British thoroughly trounced and routed the French. The highly mobile, unarmored British bowmen with their light, quick-shooting longbows proved disastrous to the heavily armored French cavalry. Losses were ten to one in the British favor and from the victory came the treaty at Rouen and Henry's courtship of the French princess Catherine.

Olivier's primary concern in making the picture was in bridging the gap between the verbal and the visual. In the opening speech of the play Chorus asks the audience to "piece out our imperfections with your thoughts," but with film Olivier was able to supply the images and the action. It occurred to him to begin and end the film with an actual performance of the play at London's Globe Theatre in 1600. The camera gradually moves toward the actors on stage and we become involved with their

The King (Olivier) receives the Archbishop of Canterbury (Felix Aylmer).

movements; then the artificial sets become more real and the performance is no longer that being done in a theatre. Finally the action moves into actual locations and we are with Henry on his campaign in France. Toward the end of the film the procedure reverses and Chorus gives his final lines on the stage. In the two hours between the audience has been taken on a dreamlike trip.

The making of *Henry V* was a bold experiment but it was also an adventure. The odds were all against it. Much of the picture was filmed at the Denham Studios, which had been damaged in air raids and every component needed to make the film was in short supply, including skilled technicians. Technicolor stock was particularly hard to come by and yet del Giudice somehow managed to find enough. Photographers Robert Krasker and Jack Hildyard then achieved the near-impossible by filming with only a twenty-five per cent wastage of stock, as against the usual ninety per cent in most major film productions. The more than one thousand costumes were devised from whatever scraps the company could gather, swords and lances were made

Departure for Calais.

from wood and then painted, knitted garments were sprayed with aluminum paint and turned into chain armor, cheap blankets were dyed and became splendid horse jackets, and crowns were fashioned from papier mâché. It is greatly to the credit of art directors Paul Sheriff and Roger Furse that none of this looks cheap and shoddy.

The problem of filming the battle of Agincourt was solved by moving the company to Ireland, where there was no likelihood of air raids. Olivier chose to film on the estate of Lord Powerscourt at Enniskerry, not far from Dublin, and five hundred men were loaned by the Eireann Home Guard to perform as medieval soldiers. Two hundred Irish horsemen were hired with their mounts to appear as the French cavalry and the participants were disappointed when the filming came to an end after several days. The staging of the battle is exciting and convincing. It may not be historically exact but Olivier was more concerned with poetry than

Henry rouses his tired soldiers.

reality. There was enough reality in the war news at the time. This was a visualization of storybook chivalry, the romantic concept of medieval pageantry, with hordes of archers and ranks of costumed cavalry choreographed over a luscious green landscape. The music of William Walton—one of the landmarks in film scoring—throbs and builds the excitement to that mighty moment when the English archers discharge a cloud of arrows into the charging Frenchmen. The loud swish is built right into the orchestration. Walton's music is, in fact, as much as part of this film as the photography. It is accompaniment rather than background and rightly so. *Henry V* is a glorious fantasy of valor and romance, and Walton provided an audio counterpart to the visual.

The battle sequence is what audiences remember most about *Henry V*, but the film merits attention at every point. It is valuable for a better understanding both of Shakespeare and of an ancient

Henry receives the French delegation.

European conflict. Olivier proved to himself that the Bard could be effectively adapted to the screen and he has admitted that making the picture was a maturing experience for him. He had previously looked upon filmmaking mainly as a means of income but with this film he developed a more serious attitude. But neither he nor anyone should forget Filippo del Giudice, who brought about this "little touch of Harry in the night," and allowed us to "entertain conjecture of a time." It was this Italian gentleman who enabled millions to become acquainted and thrilled by King Henry V and his soldiers:

"We few, we happy few, we band of brothers . . .
. . . That fought with us upon St. Crispin's Day!"

"Once more into the breach . . ."

Scott of the Antarctic

1948

An Eagle-Lion-Rank Picture. Produced by Michael Balcon. Directed by Charles Frend. Screenplay by Walter Meade and Ivor Montague. Photographed in Technicolor by Jack Cardiff, Osmond Borradaile and Geoffrey Unsworth. Music by Ralph Vaughan Williams. Running time: 109 minutes.

CAST

Robert Falcon Scott, John Mills; *Dr. E. A. Wilson,* Harold Warrender; *Capt. L. E. G. Oates,* Derek Bond; *Lt. H. R. Bowers,* Reginald Backwith; *Taff Evans,* James Robertson Justice; *Lt. E. J. R. Evans,* Kenneth More; *Chief Stoker Lashly,* Norman Williams; *Petty Officer Crean,* John Gregson; *Surgeon Atkinson,* James McKechnie; *Apsley Cherry Garrard,* Barry Letts; *Charles S. Wright,* Dennis Vance; *Petty Officer Keohane,* Larry Burns; *Dimitri,* Edward Lisak; *Cecil Meares,* Melville Crawford; *Bernard Day,* Christopher Lee; *Kathleen Scott,* Diana Churchill; *Oriana Wilson,* Anne Firth.

Robert Falcon Scott was forty-four when he met his death at the South Pole in January of 1912. By trade he was an officer of the Royal Navy but by instinct he was an explorer. In 1900 he was given the rank of commander and put in charge of the National Antarctic Expedition, the work of which spanned the next four years but never succeeded in reaching the South Pole. Reaching it became an obsession with him and when he finally did get there he faced a shattering disappointment—Norwegian Roald Amundsen and his party had planted their flag at the Pole just a few weeks earlier. Scott and his four partners all died soon after as they tried to make their way back through blizzards, and one of Scott's last entries in his diary reads: "I do not regret this journey; we took risks, we knew we took them, things have come out against us, therefore we have no cause for complaint."

Scott of the Antarctic is a faithful and accurate account of one of history's most epic misadventures, with an admirable performance from John Mills as Scott. Mills, an ideal film *persona* of quietly courageous middle-class Englishmen, has often played the hero in war pictures but he has done it with such dignity that he seldom comes to mind in any discussion of screen heroics. Some American critics, while giving *Scott* full marks for valor, could not help mentioning that the film suffered somewhat from a case of British stiff-upper-lipism, although in this case "frozen upper lip" would have been more apropos.

The film was difficult to make, not only because

it dealt with the severe conditions of the Antarctic—as difficult for cameramen as for explorers—but because it was about suffering and failure, and presented little in the way of histrionics. However, the acting, direction, scripting, photography and painstaking research in *Scott of the Antarctic* make in an almost perfect film of its kind. The story begins in 1910 with Scott trying to raise money to back his expedition to the South Pole and finding little interest. He manages to enlist the aid of a prominent scientist, Edward Wilson (Harold Warrender) and they receive a small grant from the government. The money is enough to outfit one ship, instead of the two Scott hoped for, and they take several tractors, ponies and dogs as their means of tracking the Antarctic wastes. In deciding on these means Scott flies in the face of advice from other explorers. At about the same time, a Norwegian party under the leadership of Amundsen sets out on a similar mission, although announcing that its object is the North Pole. Scott lands his ship at Cape Evans, where he and his men build a hut and then spend six months waiting for favorable conditions before starting on the 900-mile trek to the

Pole. The trek proves far more arduous than they had imagined; the tractors break down and have to be abandoned, the horses have to be shot and even the dogs have to be cut loose.

When the five men of the Scott party finally arrive at the Pole they find the Norwegian flag. The scene is heart-rending. As physically debilitated as disappointed, the men head back to their base but under conditions far worse than they expected. Two men die en route. Scott documents his trek in his log (which was discovered a year later) and he and his companions eventually succumb to exhaustion, defeated by the unrelenting blizzards. By this time they had also run out of supplies. Perhaps the cruelest irony of all is that they died only eleven miles from a supply depot.

Scott of the Antarctic was made with a fervent regard for accuracy. Producer Michael Balcon received the full cooperation of the British Museum, which provided the records of Scott's expedition and certain possessions used by him on his ill-fated trek. John Mills was able to wear Scott's own pocket watch, to use the actual tent and to play the gramophone Scott took with him. Balcon and

Dr. Wilson (Harold Warrender) says goodbye to his wife (Anne Firth).

The last Christmas party.

his art director, Arne Akermark, reproduced even the correct brand names of the products used by the Scott party, such as Peter Dawson's Whisky, Fry's Milk Chocolate and Huntley and Palmer's Biscuits. Particularly impressive in this film is the Technicolor photography, with the brilliant Jack Cardiff heading up the team. Footage was shot at Hope Bay in the Antarctic, at Finse, Norway and on the Aletsch Glacier in Switzerland. The scenes of ice floes, snowy landscapes and raging blizzards are awesome, and it is to the credit of director Charles Frend that Mills and the other actors are not swamped by the settings. It is essentially a film about men and about bravery.

The film employed several men who had been with Scott on his expeditions but perhaps the man who contributed the most valuable touch was the venerable Ralph Vaughan Williams. The picture cried out for a superior music score, something that would help the episodic story flow more evenly and act as an emotional current to the stunning but chilling visuals. Balcon and music director Ernest Irving decided to try for the very dean of British composers. Vaughan Williams was not immediately interested but the producer bombarded him with photographs of the Scott expedition and the composer was gradually hooked. Reveals his widow Ursula in *R.V.W.—A Biography of Ralph Vaughan Williams* (Oxford University Press, 1964): ". . . he was excited by the demands which the setting of the film made on his invention, to find musical equivalents for the physical sensations of ice, of wind, blowing over the great, uninhabited desolation, of stubborn and impassable ridges of black and ice-covered rock, and to suggest man's endeavor to overcome the rigors of this bleak land and to match mortal spirit against elements." Vaughan Williams' score for *Scott of the Antarctic* is one of the greatest achievements in film music. It transcends mere pictorialism and delves into the

mystery of man's compulsion to adventure in forbidding places. The composer was well aware of what he had accomplished and later reshaped his material into what would become his seventh symphony, *Sinfonia Antarctica*. To those familiar with the film, hearing the symphony easily conjures up all the images.

The final entries.

The Treasure of the Sierra Madre

1948

A Warner Bros. Picture. Produced by Henry Blanke. Directed by John Huston. Screenplay by Huston, based on the novel by B. Traven. Photographed by Ted McCord. Music by Max Steiner. Running time: 126 minutes.

CAST

Fred C. Dobbs, Humphrey Bogart; *Howard,* Walter Huston; *Curtin,* Tim Holt; *Cody,* Bruce Bennett; *McCormick,* Barton MacLane; *Gold Hat,* Alfonso Bedoya; *Presidente,* A. Soto Rangel; *El Jefe,* Manuel Donde; *Pablo,* Jose Torvay; *Pancho,* Margarito Luna; *Flashy Girl,* Jacqueline Dalya; *Mexican Boy,* Bobby Blake; *Man in the White Suit,* John Huston; *Flophouse Bum,* Jack Holt.

The Treasure of the Sierra Madre is very much a product of John Huston, one of the free spirits of the American cinema. It brought him two Oscars, for his script and his direction, but it did not bring him packed movie houses in 1948. The public at that time looked up it as long-winded and bitter, as did studio head Jack L. Warner, who was virtually coerced into making the picture by Huston and his sympathetic producer, Henry Blanke. Warner, who seldom bothered to fully read a script, was given to understand that it was a fairly conventional western in a Mexican setting and felt it should be shot on Warners' ranch at nearby Calabasas, where almost

all their westerns had been filmed. He finally agreed to the film being done in Mexico but he was justifiably concerned when the months slipped by and the costs reach the three million dollar mark, and he believed it was a mistake to have the star of the film, Humphrey Bogart, turn so nasty and be killed. Public response at first supported the astute Warner but with time *Sierra Madre* gradually assumed the rank of classic. It was a breakthrough picture for Hollywood and the beginning of a new wave of maturity in attitudes toward humankind. In Italy, Vittorio de Sica, Roberto Rossellini and Frederico Fellini had already established this fresh viewpoint about filmmaking but they would have had a much tougher time striking the same path in the confines of Hollywood.

John Huston first came across the novel *The Treasure of the Sierra Madre* in 1935 when he was making a living as a script writer. By this time he

132

Fred C. Dobbs (Bogart) puts the touch on a tourist (John Huston).

was already an enthusiast for Mexico, having spent some of his younger years as a cavalryman in the Mexican Army, and he became possessed of the idea of turning this novel into a film. Warners bought it and Huston begged them to hold it until he was free to do it. He went into the army in 1942, after making *The Maltese Falcon, Across the Pacific* and *In This Our Life* for Warners and he was away from Hollywood for almost five years. It was an important absence because Huston made a number of fine documentary films about the war and returned to Hollywood, as did others, with a sharper sense of reality. Once he had prepared his screenplay Huston sent a copy to the mysterious author of *Sierra Madre*, a man known only as B. Traven and living a reclusive life in Mexico. An agent got the script to Traven (real name Traven Torsven, Chicago-born and an avowed Marxist) and the author agreed to meet Huston in Mexico City.

Huston waited for days and was about to give up when he was approached by a man who called himself Hal Croves, claiming that he had been instructed by Traven to represent him and give Huston whatever help he needed. Croves was hired as technical advisor and proved greatly helpful all through the long filming. He afterwards vanished, never to be seen again by the film company, and Huston later learned, as he had suspected, that Croves was actually Traven.

Sierra Madre combines the adventure form with the morality tale and manages to get its message across without preaching. The message is basic— the desire for wealth can be destructive. The central figure is Fred C. Dobbs (Bogart), a rather mangy American drifter, down to panhandling, who teams up with another American, Curtin (Tim Holt), an ordinary but decent-minded type, in a plan to prospect for gold and get enough money to

133

Dobbs buys a lottery ticket from a young vendor (Bobby Blake).

Curtin (Tim Holt) and Dobbs ward off bandits.

go home. With their earnings as construction workers and with cash won by Dobbs in a lottery they buy the necessary equipment and take on another partner, a seemingly eccentric old prospector named Howard (Walter Huston), who knows the territory but warns them of the danger involved and of the corruptive effects that gold has on the character of men. Dobbs and Curtin dismiss the advice. En route by train from Tampico to Durango they are attacked by bandits, led by a man with a large gold-colored sombrero (Alfonso Bedoya), but with the aid of the soldiers on the train the bandits are driven away. After buying their supplies and burros in Durango the three men head into the hills, where the trek proves tougher than Dobbs has expected and where signs of his greed and viciousness begin to show up.

The partners find gold and pack it away in small sacks but as the trek progresses Dobbs becomes increasingly suspicious of Howard and Curtin and begins muttering irritably to himself about their probable treachery. When a lone American prospector, Cody (Bruce Bennett) enters their camp and asks to become a partner, the angry Dobbs urges the others to join in killing him. This becomes unnecessary when the group is attacked by Gold Hat and his bandits, and in fighting them off Cody is shot. Howard persuades his partners that the time has come to end the search and to return to civilization with their considerable haulings. On the way back they are approached by a large band of Mexicans, who turn out to be villagers in need of help to save a dying boy. Howard wisely decides to go with them and avoid the trouble a

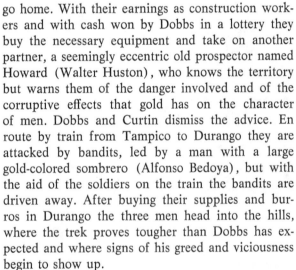

Curtin restrains the impatient Dobbs from hitting old Howard (Walter Huston).

refusal would cause. He saves the life of the boy and is then swamped with the hospitality of the villagers. Meanwhile, as Dobbs and Curtin make their way to Durango, tension mounts with Dobbs' fear of losing his wealth. He regards Curtin hatefully and one night decides to kill him and take the entire proceeds of the trip for himself.

Dobbs' shooting of Curtin does not prove fateful and the badly wounded younger man makes his way, with the help of Indians, to Howard. The two then ride out in search of Dobbs but they arrive too late. The now demented Dobbs has already met an appropriately shabby end. While stumbling across the desert pulling his burros, he is approached by three bandits as he feverishly drinks at a water hole. One of them is Gold Hat, who recognizes Dobbs and after taunting him savagely ends his life with a swipe of a machete. The bandits strip the body and take the burros, after dumping the sacks of gold and slashing them open. The gold means nothing to them. A windstorm rises and blows the gold over the desert, to the amusement of the philosophical Howard. The old man lapses into laughter as he points out to the dumbfounded Curtin, "It's a great joke, Curt. The gold has gone back to where we found it!"

The Treasure of the Sierra Madre will probably never lose its impact or its appeal. It was made the way a film should be made—with a passion. John Huston did it because he believed in it and had to do it. And he did it exactly as he wanted, despite the hardships and despite the protestations of his employers. He insisted on using actual locations, starting in Tampico and then going up into the mountains about a hundred miles west of Mexico City. This was country Huston had come to know when he served with the Mexican Army and this is one of the main reasons for his film being among the very best ever made about adventuring in Mexico. *Sierra Madre* stands up to the closest study. The acting is impeccable, as is the pacing, the editing and the starkly dramatic photography of Ted McCord. Max Steiner's score has been criticized for being more Spanish than Mexican and for being too loudly symphonic. The criticism is justified but assuming a fondness for Steiner it also has a tunefulness that helpfully lightens the darkly hued tale. And the main theme, the acutely accented melody that marks the spirit of the trek, is now so well associated with the picture that it is difficul to imagine *Sierra Madre* without it.

Doubt begins to creep in among the prospectors.

In years to come John Huston would compromise himself by making films in which he was not greatly interested but there is not a note of compromise in his *Sierra Madre*. He asked only one man to play the old prospector—his father, whom he persuaded to swallow his pride and do it minus his false teeth. Walter Huston came up with an indelible characterization of a man who seems a little balmy but who really has learned about life and its values. The director also had only one man in mind to play Fred C. Dobbs, a man whose lack of character causes him to disintegrate as the love of gold consumes him. Humphrey Bogart and John Huston had become friends while making the excellent *The Maltese Falcon* and there was no question about Bogey playing the part. The fact that Jack L. Warner didn't think it was right for him simply increased the iconoclastic actor's determination to do it. Bogart deprecated almost all his films but wherever *Sierra Madre* was mentioned he would sheepishly admit, "Yeah, that wasn't a bad one."

Doubt turns to dislike.

136

Dobbs and the man who ends his life, Gold Hat (Alfonso Bedoya).

Captain From Castile

1947

A 20th Century-Fox Picture. Produced by Lamar Trotti. Directed by Henry King. Screenplay by Lamar Trotti, based on the novel by Samuel Shellabarger. Photographed in Technicolor by Charles Clarke and Arthur E. Arling. Music by Alfred Newman. Running time: 140 minutes.

CAST

Pedro De Vargas, Tyrone Power; *Catana,* Jean Peters; *Cortez,* Cesar Romero; *Juan Garcia,* Lee J. Cobb; *Diego De Silva,* John Sutton; *Don Francisco,* Antonio Moreno; *Father Bartolome,* Thomas Gomez; *Botello,* Alan Mowbray; *Luisa,* Barbara Lawrence; *Marquis De Caravajal,* George Zucco; *Captain Alvarado,* Roy Roberts; *Corio,* Marc Lawrence; *Manuel,* Robert Karnes; *Soler,* Fred Libby; *Dona Maria,* Virginia Brissac; *Coatl,* Jay Silverheels; *Escudero,* Reed Hadley.

It would be most unreasonable to ignore Tyrone Power in any roster of Hollywood's adventure films and yet it is also difficult to place him because he was not a really robust and dashing figure. He was handsome and charming but his movements were not Fairbanksian and his grace with weapons was far from Flynnish. This did not stop 20th Century-Fox from starring Power in a number of good costume-action epics and skillfully creating a romantic-heroic aura about him. He wore costumes beautifully, as in *Lloyds of London* and *Marie Antoinette,* and in swashbucklers like *The*

Mark of Zorro, Blood and Sand, Son of Fury and *The Black Swan* his ability as an actor enabled him to convey heroism, while skillful doubles did the dangerous stuff. Power was a much better actor than the critics or his doting fans realized and toward the end of his short life he performed impressively on both the stage and screen. Prior to his war service (1943–1946) he had accepted whatever roles Fox assigned him in their plan to create a matinee idol, but with his return he pressed Darryl Zanuck for meatier material. Zanuck obliged with *The Razor's Edge,* which did well for the star and the studio, well enough for them to indulge Power in his wish to do *Nightmare Alley.* This darkly fascinating excursion into evil impressed the critics but not the fans and Fox decided it was time to put Tyrone Power back into doublet and hose.

Fox bought Samuel Shellabarger's *Captain from Castile* in 1944 even before it was published, paying the then whopping sum of $100,000. It had appeared in condensed form in the magazine *Cosmopolitan* and captured the imagination of a wide public with its romantic and bloodthirsty

tales of the Spanish Inquisition and Cortez' conquest of Mexico. Shellabarger (1888–1954) was not only a fine writer but a distinguished scholar and for a long time a professor of English at Princeton. His research was solid and his literary style was fluid, which made a translation to the screen almost inevitable, although, because of the scope of the story, problematic. Zanuck handed the assignment to Lamar Trotti, a veteran screen writer who had attained the rank of producer. There was little doubt about who would direct it—Henry King, the Fox equivalent of Warners' Michael Curtiz. King had already directed Ty Power in six pictures, including *The Black Swan,* and it was a job he relished because he loved scouting locations in faraway places, which he did in his own airplane.

The gentleman of the title is Pedro De Vargas (Power), the son of an aristocratic Castilian family who runs afoul of the controlling political parties, who function behind the mask of religion, who operate in the name of religion, chiefly Diego De Silva (John Sutton). De Silva covets the De Vargas estates and brands the family heretics. Pedro's

young sister dies under torture and he vows revenge. He manages to escape prison and takes to the hills, where he becomes acquainted with a beautiful peasant girl, Catana (Jean Peters), and a roistering soldier-of-fortune, Juan Garcia (Lee J. Cobb). After arranging for his parents to flee to Italy, Pedro is persuaded by Juan to leave Spain and try adventuring in the New World, and taking Catana with them. They land in Cuba and soon meet Hernando Cortez, the leader of an expedition bent on discovering the treasures of the Aztecs in Mexico. Pedro is given the rank of captain and learns that a great many of Cortez' men are escapees of the Inquisition. Catana is now Pedro's wife and together they proceed with the Cortez expedition. The route is fraught with problems, both physical and personal, as the men strain through the difficult Mexican landscape, with its jungles, mountains and resentful Indians. The situation for Pedro becomes complicated when De Silva turns up as the King's representative. A Mayan prince who was once a slave in Spain kills De Silva, and Pedro is accused of the murder, tried and convicted. But the Mayan speaks up at the last

moment and Pedro is free to continue the trek with Cortez.

Captain from Castile gives a good account of the Cortez conquest of Mexico, although putting it in an heroic light that contemporary historians find offensive. They point out that Cortez was little more than a self-motivated plunderer, shielding himself under the Spanish flag. The film glorifies the Cortez expedition but it also makes apparent that he blustered his way through Montezuma's empire against the wishes of the Aztecs, compromising them with a show of military power. The picture ends with a magnificent panoply—the Conquistadores in full array, hundreds of brightly uniformed soldiers, with breastplates and helmets, with horses, guns and carriages, moving off en masse toward their objective over the horizon—the storied wealth of the Aztecs.

Tyrone Power was everything the part needed, and with maturity he seemed more convincing as a hero. He certainly looked splendid in his costumes and his swordplay was better than it had been before. But the real surprise of the picture was Cesar Romero as Cortez. Formally a pleasing but lightweight performer, Romero here came up with a bold and commanding characterization, sporting a beard and a flashing but determined smile. The film met with mixed critiques, the main charge being that it was too long and sagged in places. This cannot be denied. As producer and scenarist the merits and demerits had to be laid at Lamar Trotti's feet. Perhaps he was too earnest in trying to keep in all the many episodes and incidents of Shellabarger's rich canvas. Novels of historical romance are the hardest kind to film. However, *Captain from Castile* has much to offer, including magnificent Technicolor photography of remote and almost surreal Mexican landscapes, and hordes of soldiers and Indians moving across them. And no intelligent mention of the film can be made without praising Alfred Newman's score. The incredibly busy Newman—as head of music for Fox he supervised everything, conducted every major score and somehow found time to compose for several pictures a year—here outdid himself. This is a major symphonic composition, richly scored to match the color of the story, and flowing with melodies. The suite from the score has several times been recorded and Newman's march for the Conquistadores, *Conquest,* is a masterpiece in itself. Few pieces of film music speak so eloquently about the spirit of adventure.

The De Vargas family brought to heel by the villainous Diego De Silva (John Sutton).

Pedro makes his escape from prison, wounding De Silva.

Cortez meets Diego's wife, Catana (Jean Peters). Juan Garcia (Lee J. Cobb) clearly shares the appreciation.

Hernando Cortez (Cesar Romero).

Pedro arrested on suspicion of having killed De Silva.

Cleared of the charges, Pedro resumes his rank as a captain of Conquistadores.

As Zanuck had expected, *Captain from Castile* pleased the Tyrone Power fans. Power was interested in advancing himself as a serious actor but he was locked into a Fox contract and the studio decided there was more money to be made in adventure films. In 1949 they starred him in another Shellabarger story, *Prince of Foxes,* beautifully filmed and a delight to the eyes of those interested in Renaissance Italy—but rather dull for whose who are not. Next came *The Black Rose,* a pedestrian filming of Thomas B. Costain's novel, for which Power was trotted around England, Europe and North Africa, but to little avail. He managed to conclude the contract in 1955, but not until after he had put in service as a Canadian mountie in *Pony Soldier,* a half-caste officer in *King of the Khyber Rifles* and a South African wagon master in *Untamed.* Power afterwards distinguished himself on the Broadway stage in *John Brown's Body* and *The Dark Is Light Enough,* and with his last completed film, *Witness for the Prosecution,* a few formerly fussy critics agreed he had become a considerable actor.

Tragically, it was the making of another costume-action epic that cost Power his life. He had developed a heart condition, apparently inherited (his actor father died of a heart attack while making a film), but he accepted the lead in *Solomon and Sheba.* Ironically, he left for Spain soon after appearing in a short film for the American Heart Association, in which he warned of the dangers of exertion and said, "time is the most precious thing we have." The role of Solomon required a good deal of physical exertion and Power was loath to let a double do his riding and swordplay. At Fox he had had no say in whether or not his action sequences were doubled. As an independent star he felt he should do almost everything the script required. On the afternoon of November 15, 1958, Power filmed a scene with George Sanders as the villain, in which the two duelled with broadswords. The scene was incomplete when Power asked to stop, complaining of pains in his arms and chest. He went to his dressing room to lie down and an hour or so later he was dead. Age: forty-four.

The Flame and the Arrow

1950

A Warner Bros. Picture. Produced by Harold Hecht and Frank Ross. Directed by Jacques Tourneur. Screenplay by Waldo Salt. Photographed in Technicolor by Ernest Haller. Music by Max Steiner. Running time: 89 minutes.

CAST

Dardo the Arrow, Burt Lancaster; *Anne,* Virginia Mayo; *Alessandro,* Robert Douglas; *Nonna Bartoli,* Aline MacMahon; *Ulrich,* Frank Allenby; *Piccolo,* Nick Cravat; *Francesca,* Lynne Baggett; *Rudi,* Gordon Gebert; *Troubadour,* Norman Lloyd; *Apothecary,* Victor Kilian; *Papa Pietro,* Francis Peiriot; *Skinner,* Robin Hughes.

The Flame and the Arrow looks as if it might have been tailored for Errol Flynn. Actually it wasn't, and by 1950 Flynn was no longer capable of sustaining physical derring-do, his hedonistic lifestyle having severely undermined his health. However, scenarist Waldo Salt must have been familiar with *The Adventures of Robin Hood* since the plot structure is similar, although his script has plenty of its own wit and zest. The parallel is heightened by the use of some of the *Robin Hood* sets and costumes, plus a few leftovers from Flynn's *Adventures of Don Juan.* But the major asset here is Burt Lancaster, brimming over with vim and verve. As a boy in New York Lancaster had idol-

ized Douglas Fairbanks and this is his handsome homage. Lancaster may have lacked the gentlemanly charm of Flynn but he had, at this stage in his career, a tremendous vitality—in addition to a shrewd sense of business. *The Flame and the Arrow* is a Hecht-Lancaster production and its star wisely decided to play it for high humor.

Lancaster knows something about adventure. As a schoolboy he had excelled in athletics and first thought of being a physical training instructor, but he became bored with study at New York University and took to a life as an acrobat. He and his friend Nick Cravat worked up an act and for ten years eked out a living in circuses and vaudeville companies. It wasn't until 1946 that he turned up in Hollywood, age thirty-two. He and his agent-partner Harold Hecht had their minds set on production even before they arrived in California and it took them only two years to get going, their first picture being the dismal melodrama *Kiss the Blood Off My Hands.* This failed to make much profit and they made a much more commercial choice for their second enterprise—*The Flame and the Arrow,* something that fully cashed in on Lancaster's phys-

ical abilities. Ever since becoming a film actor his publicity had played up his exploits in the circus world and now it was apparent that for once the publicity was valid. To make it even more valid Lancaster and Cravat did a short personal appearance tour, doing the stunts they performed in the picture.

Warner Bros. overstepped the mark in claiming that Lancaster did every stunt and never required a double. This brought a justified protest from the veteran Don Turner, who pointed out that he was involved in doubling for Lancaster in at least three fight sequences. But he wanted no credit for the purely acrobatic work, the aerial gymnastics, the balancing, the bar and pole tricks and the complicated tumbling. Only an expert like Lancaster could handle that sort of thing, and much of the joy of *The Flame and the Arrow* derives from that fact.

The story takes place in medieval Italy, in a small town in Lombardy occupied by Hessians. The local people resent the foreign domination but it takes a spirited mountaineer, Dardo the Arrow (Lancaster), to organize them in revolt. He and his

seven-year-old son (Gordon Gebert) wander into town the day Ulrich of Hesse (Frank Allenby) arrives back with a new contingent of German mercenaries. The situation is complicated by the fact that the boy's mother (Lynne Baggett) has thrown in her lot with Ulrich and wants her son. Ulrich obliges and sends a group of his soldiers to get the boy. Dardo is wounded in trying to thwart the plan but once he recovers he retaliates by abducting the lovely niece (Virginia Mayo) of Ulrich. She resents being dragged off to his forest hideaway but gradually changes her mind about him and comes to love him. In the meantime Ulrich announces he will hang hostages if Dardo does not return the girl and give himself up. This he does, and finds himself sentenced to be hanged. With the aid of friends in Ulrich's service, Dardo is hanged in an apparatus that spares his neck. The villains relax when they believe they have disposed of their main irritant. Then, one evening as they enjoy a banquet, a troupe of entertainers arrive at the castle and offer to perform for the Hessians. They are, of course, Dardo and his men, gaily bedecked in bright costumes, and they put on

145

Dardo and Anne (Virginia Mayo) held at bay.

Dardo (Lancaster) and his friends Papa Pietro (Francis Peiriot) and Nonna Bartoli (Aline MacMahon).

Piccolo (Nick Cravat) and Pardo taunt their pretty captive. Their friend Alessandro (Robert Douglas) is confused.

Dardo breaks his men out of jail—
the hard way.

a fine show of acrobatics before turning on their hosts and routing them.

The Flame and the Arrow is nothing much more than a fine show of acrobatics in itself—a fable for fun and a showcase for Lancaster. The trappings are beautiful, as is Max Steiner's pseudo-Italian score, with its lyrical main theme strummed by mandolins. In its finale the picture turns into a circus romp, as Lancaster and Cravat indulge themselves in long leaps and vaults, pirouetting in mid-air, swinging on tapestries and chandeliers, and baffling the comparatively spastic Hessians with their tricks. Jacques Tourneur is credited with directing all this but it would come as no surprise to find out that Ringling Brothers was responsible for the finale.

Burt Lancaster immediately inherited the crown as top swashbuckler, a position never at any time overpopulated, and consolidated his claim two years later with *The Crimson Pirate*. Among enthusiasts of this genre there are those who prefer his *Pirate* to his Dardo. Certainly it contains plenty of swaggering action and even bolder gymnastics but the mood is different. *The Flame and the Arrow* verges on spoof but stays within the framework of adventure yarns. *The Crimson Pirate* vigorously satirizes the traditions, to the point of fantasy, with the heroes employing primitive machine guns, tanks and balloon bombers to scourge the Spanish Main.

Ulrich and his guests are entertained by a troupe of fine acrobats . . .

Unfortunately, these two films represent Lancaster's entire contribution to costumed adventure. It was a field he could have had to himself but except for some adventures in the Foreign Legion *(Ten Tall Men)* and an occasional western he chose to take acting seriously. Dardo turned out to have a cerebral side to his nature.

147

. . . who turn out to be the invading forces of Dardo, who bring a quick end to Ulrich's career.

148

King Solomon's Mines

1950

An MGM Picture. Produced by Sam Zimbalist. Directed by Compton Bennett and Andrew Marton. Screenplay by Helen Deutsch, based on the novel by H. Rider Haggard. Photographed in Technicolor by Robert Surtees. Running time: 102 minutes.

CAST

Elizabeth Curtis, Deborah Kerr; *Allen Quartermain,* Stewart Granger; *John Good,* Richard Carlson; *Smith,* Hugo Haas; *District Officer,* Lowell Gilmore; and Kimursi of the Kipsigi Tribe, Siriaque, Sekaryongo and Bariga of the Watusi Tribe.

Twenty years after sending a company to Africa to film *Trader Horn,* MGM dispatched another group to shoot a mighty adventure in the wilds of the Dark Continent, which, fortunately, was a lot less dark than a few years previously. The *Trader Horn* crew took six weeks to get from Hollywood to their locations and underwent dreadful discomforts and sicknesses. The *King Solomon's Mines* crew, wisely limited to eleven Hollywood members and the rest of the team recruited locally, took only two days to reach their base of operations, Nairobi, and then used powerful trucks made to order by Chrysler, and airplanes, to cover the 14,000 miles necessary to get their footage. They also had medical supplies unheard of by their counterparts on *Trader Horn,* which, however, did not prevent some of the crew coming down with malaria and dysentery, or from tempers fraying during the five months of filming. But it could have been worse, as

crews on *The African Queen* and *The Roots of Heaven* would discover, and looking back on it director Compton Bennett says, "It was the best organized and best conducted trip I've ever been on."

Sir Henry Rider Haggard (1856–1925) spent some years in Africa as a government official and grew fascinated with the grandeur and mystery of the continent and its peoples. What he saw, heard and imagined colored his many books of African adventure, of which *King Solomon's Mines,* written in 1885, is the finest. Its hero, Allan Quartermain, is the ideal concept of The Great White Hunter— wise, brave, knowledgeable and stalwartly British. Cedric Hardwicke had played him in subdued fashion in a good English version in 1937, but for their expensive new account of the Haggard epic they signed Stewart Granger, a much bolder and more heroic figure. A swashbuckler by nature, Granger reveled in the role of Quartermain, taking after big game both on and off camera. He had played hero in a number of British pictures but this one set him off on a winning streak in Hollywood adventures.

John Good (Richard Carlson), the rather haughty Elizabeth (Deborah Kerr) and their guide Allain Quartermain (Stewart Granger).

The screenplay by Helen Deutsch scales down the plot of the Haggard novel and changes it to accommodate a love story. Here Quartermain, after fifteen years as a hunter and safari guide, talks of giving up his way of life and returning to England, weary with customers greedy for animal blood and disrespectful of nature. He is approached by a beautiful but rather imperious English lady, Elizabeth Curtin (Deborah Kerr), who wishes to hire him to lead her and her brother John (Richard Carlson) into uncharted territory to seek the fabled diamond mines of King Solomon. Her chief reason is to trace her husband, who has disappeared in his own search for the mines. Quartermain scoffs at the proposal but accepts when Elizabeth offers him five thousand pounds, many times his usual fee. Like all trips into the African wilds, this one proves much more hazardous and tiring than the employers had imagined. Elizabeth sets out proudly in fine attire but soon learns to be more casual and to respect the instructions of Quartermain.

The trek proceeds through all kinds of terrain— forests, swamps, desert sands, lush meadows and rugged mountains. They survive a gigantic animal stampede caused by a bush fire, and in visiting a village housing a renegade white who calls himself Smith (Hugo Haas) they barely escape with their lives. Smith confirms that Elizabeth's husband passed through the village a year ago. Quartermain senses that Smith wants his ferocious villagers to kill the group, so that he can never be traced by the authorities, so Quartermain holds a gun on him as he forces Smith to lead them out of the village. Smith then turns on Quartermain, who kills him. By this time, all Quartermain's native bearers have deserted for fear of the unknown and he, Elizabeth and John are left to struggle on by themselves. However, they are joined by a very tall and exotic-looking warrior who is headed in the same direction, and who offers to be a bearer for them. They at first fear him but he turns out to be their salvation. He is a Watusi king making his way to his people to claim the throne from a usurper, a treacherous man who greets the Quartermain party coolly. The Watusis, after a shot from Quartermain's rifle fells their vicious medicine man, agree to take the party to the caves containing the diamonds of King Solomon, where they also find the

A long way to go . . .

. . . with problems all the time.

152

Taking cover from the stampede.

A nasty man named Smith (Hugo ~~Hass~~) needs persuasion to help the party. *Haas*

Elizabeth, by now a lot less haughty and grateful for every drop of water.

skeleton of Elizabeth's husband. The Watusis try to seal the three whites in the cave but they make their way out through a passage. Back at the Watusi village they see the king engage the usurper in a death duel, which he wins. The king and the now friendly Watusis supply the Quartermain party with bearers and bid them goodbye as they make their way back to civilization. Quartermain and Elizabeth, antagonistic at the start, are now lovers and face the future together.

The plot of *King Solomon's Mines* is really a secondary factor, although as scripted by Helen Deutsch the characters are sound and the dialogue intelligent, with some rather trenchant stabs at human motivations in tackling danger and the unknown. What really mattered was how the picture was made—and it was made beautifully. Its greatest asset is the color photography of Robert Surtees, who justly received an Oscar for his work. He and his team shot miles of film. So much was left over that MGM devised a screenplay around it and made another picture, *Watusi,* starring George Montgomery. Surtees' landscapes are gorgeous—vista after vista of jungles, deserts and mountains, sunrises and sunsets. The *Mines* company fanned out from Nairobi into Kenya and the Belgian Congo, shooting at Lake Victoria, Mount Kenya, Murchison Falls, as far west as Stanleyville for the nearby river rapids, and up into the high ranges of the Watusi country north of Lake Tanganyika. The physical efforts were a strain on the company and director Compton Bennett exhausted himself. He offered no resistance when taken off the picture when the company returned to California, where the remaining scenes were shot by Andrew Marton, who had directed all the second unit footage in Africa. According to producer Sam Zimbalist, more than half of *King Solomon's Mines* can be attributed to Andrew Marton.

Richard Carlson, who wrote a series of articles for *Colliers* about his adventures making the picture, says, "The sun was our absolute master in Africa. It ruled our lives much more than in just a physical sense. Its presence or absence dictated whether, at the end of the day's work, elation or gloom pervaded our camp. For when you're using color film no outdoor work can be done without full, brilliant sunlight.* For this reason, people who see *King Solomon's Mines* will conclude, I suppose, that tropical Africa is a land of perpetual sun. It isn't."

There is a touch of irony in the fact that this

* No longer true.

154

splendid film, seemingly thoroughly masculine in appeal, was scripted by a woman. Early in the film Allan Quartermain snorts about having to go on a trek with a female, who surely won't be able to stand the pace and the rigors. The one person in the company who maintained the best health and optimism was Deborah Kerr. Richard Carlson recalls, "Her good nature always astonished crew and cast alike. We were all convinced that no other girl in the picture business would have taken the beating she had to take on this African safari."

Compton Bennett tells of one sequence shot at the top of Murchison Falls: "We had our camp at the foot of the falls. Every morning we spent nearly two hours crawling up to the top—a distance of some 500 feet. Then we'd work on a love scene between Deborah and Stewart Granger in 140-degree heat. We were using Technicolor film, so the reflectors had to be just twice as close to the principals. This threw more light and heat into their faces. It's a wonder they are not both blind."

Says photographer Surtees, "Sure it was tough. Many of us became ill—at one time we had just four members of the crew left behind the cameras, and 500 natives in front of it. All of us must have been homesick many times. But there was always Deborah, ready for whatever was next, with never a complaint of any sort. A man just couldn't gripe."

At the Watusi compound.

Finally, in the mines of King Solomon—but trapped.

155

Captain Horatio Hornblower

1951

A Warner Bros. Picture. Produced by Gerry Mitchell. Directed by Raoul Walsh. Screenplay by Ivan Goff, Ben Roberts and Aeneas MacKenzie, based on three novels by C. S. Forester. Photographed in Technicolor by Guy Green. Music by Robert Farnon. Running time: 117 minutes.

CAST

Horatio Hornblower, Gregory Peck; *Lady Barbara Wellesley,* Virginia Mayo; *Lt. William Bush,* Robert Beatty; *Lt. Girard,* Terence Morgan; *Lt. Crystal,* Moultrie Kelsall; *Quist,* James Robertson Justice; *Leighton,* Denis O'Dea; *Polwheal,* Richard Hearne; *Langley,* James Kenney; *Hebe,* Ingeborg Wells; *El Supremo,* Alex Mango; *Gundarson,* Michael Dolan; *Mr. Harrison,* Stanley Baker; *Seaman Garven,* Sam Kydd; *MacRae,* Richard Johnson; *Spanish Officer,* Christopher Lee.

Errol Flynn was the actor Warner Bros, had in mind when they negotiated with C. S. Forester to do a film based on the adventures of his noble nautical hero of Napoleonic times, Horatio Hornblower. But by the time the picture was ready for production, feelings between the actor and the studio had almost reached breaking point. Flynn had worked up a strong dislike for Warners, in addition to which his rapidly declining health made his casting as Hornblower less ideal than previously.

The decision was made to give the part to Gregory Peck, an actor with the proper heroic bearing although somewhat short on the air of flamboyance the role really required. The choice of director was fairly obvious—the virile Raoul Walsh, who had done so well with Flynn in half a dozen action epics. Making the picture in England was also an obvious choice, since it required a British cast and the days of the populous British colony in Hollywood had already started to fade away. Also there was the question of using accrued funds in England. A replica of Hornblower's ship *Lydia* was built on a London sound stage and pitched and rolled by hydraulic action—as well as by the forty members of Jock Easton's Stunt Team jumping all over the place.

The book titled *Captain Horatio Hornblower* is a grouping of the three earliest Hornblower stories —*Beat to Quarters, Ship of the Line* and *Flying Colours,* all written in 1937 and '38. The three novels cover Hornblower's adventures in the years 1808 to 1810. Forester himself did the adaptation of the material, which Ivan Goff, Ben Roberts and Aeneas MacKenzie whipped up into a screenplay.

Hornblower (Peck) and his two lieutenants, Bush (Robert Beatty) and Girard (Terrence Morgan).

Forester (1899–1966) could never account for the ease with which the Hornblower stories came to him. He had not intended to go beyond the first few but the success of each novel called for more. At the time of his death he was putting the finishes touches to *Hornblower During the Crisis;* the published book ends with his notes on the rounding out of the plot. It was the eleventh novel in the fictional saga of the stalwart British naval officer and as a body of work it is bound to keep Forester's name alive. The Egyptian-born Englishman also wrote a dozen other successful novels, many of them based on historical themes, and among his biographies of historical figures were those on Napoleon and Horatio Lord Nelson. He was a writer with a great fondness for the sea and he wrote in a realistic, straightforward style that made his work as easy to read as it was interesting. As a writer he had the Midas touch; Forester had planned on being a doctor but the success of his *Payment Deferred* at the age of twenty-four he laid aside the medical journals and spent the rest of his profitable life putting words on paper.

Captain Horatio Hornblower begins with the dashing young officer proceeding to deliver arms to a Central American dictator, El Supremo (Alex Mango), to aid him in his campaign against the Spanish. However, political winds change fast. Britain and Spain announce an alliance in the common fight against Napoleon and El Supremo suddenly becomes the enemy. He seizes a Spanish Galleon, the 50-gun *Natividad,* but Hornblower puts an end to his schemes with his nimble 36-gun frigate. Hornblower then rescues the Lady Barbara Wellesley (Virginia Mayo), the sister of the Duke of Wellington, from plague-ridden Panama City to take her home to England. But it turns out that the lovely lady has contracted malaria and it is the gallant Hornblower who nurses her through the sickness. This promotes a feeling of love between the two but since Lady Barbara is the intended wife of Admiral Leighton (Denis O'Dea), Hornblower realizes there is nothing to be done but say goodbye.

In England Hornblower is given a new command, to proceed against the French. He raids the port of La Teste, destroys four anchored French warships, and when his own vessel becomes too dam-

Paying heed to the lovely Lady Barbara (Virginia Mayo).

aged to navigate, he sinks it strategically to block the harbor. Hornblower and the surviving members of his crew are taken prisoner, with the British hero slated for a date with the guillotine in Paris. This can never be, so Hornblower organizes an escape, frees a batch of British prisoners and seizes a French warship in the port of Nantes. After more lusty fighting he arrives back in England, there to receive a promotion and even more happily to find that Lady Barbara is free to be his love.

The film is a rollicking adventure in pure storybook tradition, with well-mounted action sequences and furiously staged hand-to-hand fighting, in addition to broadsides and explosions. The firm hand of Raoul Walsh is apparent—he was never a director given to sentimentality—and romance is kept to a minimum. Virginia Mayo was a less than ideal choice for Lady Barbara, but she looks beautiful, and for most Hornblower buffs the hero's love life is simply something to be tolerated and not dwelt upon. Guy Green's Technicolor photography contributes to the aura of splendid adventure, as does the particularly fine score by Canadian composer Robert Farnon. The music is full of nautical gusto and romantic bravura, and it is a pity that Farnon has had so few chances to score other movies of this ilk.

Putting a Spanish officer (Christopher Lee) in his place.

The beaten enemy asks for clemency.

Gregory Peck suffered a back injury as a youth and it made athletic dexterity difficult for him in later years. But like Ronald Colman he was able to suggest heroism, with his fine figure and impressive face, and with a dignity that has become ever more rare in film actors Peck was a logical choice for Hornblower. His cultured American voice is close in tone to that of England's West Country (Somerset, Devon and Cornwall), the area that has long produced many of England's fabled seamen, and could well have been the home of the fictional Hornblower. Five years after this romp over the waves Peck tackled a much tougher salty tale—*Moby Dick*—and although it failed to find much acceptance with either the critics or the public, the consensus being that it was rather ponderous, it deserves further study as an interesting item in the very difficult business of transferring heroic sea sagas to the imagery of film.

Checking the damage.

Hornblower and his crew in the French prison, from which they escape, of course.

The African Queen

1951

An Horizon-Romulus Picture. Produced by Sam Spiegel. Directed by John Huston. Screenplay by James Agee and John Huston, based on the novel by C. S. Forester. Photographed in Technicolor by Jack Cardiff. Music by Alan Gray. Running time: 105 minutes.

CAST

Charlie Allnut, Humphrey Bogart; *Rose Sayer,* Katharine Hepburn; *Rev. Samuel Sayer,* Robert Morley; *Captain of the* LOUISA, Peter Bull; *First Officer* (LOUISA), Theodore Bikel; *Second Officer* (LOUISA), Walter Gotell; *Petty Officer* (LOUISA), Gerald Onn; *First Officer* (SHONA), Peter Swanwick; *Second Officer* (SHONA), Richard Marner.

C. S. Forester admitted to writing *The African Queen* as something of a spoof on adventure yarns but when he saw what John Huston had made of it as a film he realized the director and scenarist James Agee had actually added dimensions to his story. The film has Forester's tongue-in-cheek quality but the highly improbable adventure that is the core of the tale—a pair of middle-aged misfits taking an almost derelict motor launch down a wild river in Africa and sinking a German warship—comes close to being credible. Forester's pair of adventurers are about as unlikely a couple as has ever appeared on the screen. Charles Allnut is a product of a lower order, a gin-sodden drifter, grimy and uncouth and none too brave, a Canadian mechanic in Africa because of a job offer which has fallen through. Rose Sayer is a prim, innocent spinster, a missionary dedicated to converting the

heathens and equally dedicated to strict morality and temperance. Not only do Charlie and Rose pull off their grand adventure but they fall in love. That it happens so believably in this picture is due to another pair of remarkable characters—Humphrey Bogart and Katharine Hepburn.

The film opens in the German East Africa of 1914, just after the start of war, as a platoon of German soldiers arrive at the settlement in which Rose and her brother, the Reverend Samuel Sayers (Robert Morley), administer their services to the natives. The Germans drive away the natives and set fire to the buildings, including the church, and when the Reverend protests, an officer clouts him with a rifle butt. The blow causes the already rather addled minister to lose his mind and he dies a few days later. Charlie Allnut, who has previously visited the Sayers, returns when he spots the flames and he takes Rose with him on his battered old thirty-foot launch, grandly named *The African*

The Queen herself.

Queen. Charlie's plan is to sit out the war in the backwaters but Rose soon becomes possessed of a scheme to take action against the Germans. She badgers the drunken skipper to take the *Queen* down river to a lake dominated by the warship *Louisa* and attack her. Charlie's protestations do him no good but when thoroughly drunk he gets his true feelings off his chest: "You crazy psalm-singing, skinny old maid." Awakening from a drunken stupor he is horrified at her revenge—she calmly pours his dozens of bottles of gin into the river. Charlie submits to her plan and as the trip progresses their personalities undergo certain changes. He becomes more courageous in his sobriety and she becomes more warm toward him. As they shoot the precarious rapids of the Bora River she becomes exhilarated by the first real excitement in her life. And to the astonishment of both of them, they fall in love.

After various hazards, including passing unhurt under the guns of a German fort, they come to a weary halt in the still side waters of the lake. By this time they have fixed homemade torpedoes in the prow of the Queen, with the object of ramming the *Louisa.* They are about to abandon the scheme but they suddenly become aware they are near their enemy and they make steam to attack. A storm on the lake capsizes the *Queen* and the couple are picked up by the Germans, who interrogate them and sentence them to be hung as British spies. As the ropes are about to be placed around their necks Charlie asks the Captain (Peter Bull) to marry them. The flabbergasted officer does so but before the newlyweds can be hoisted, there is an explosion—the *Louisa* has run into the upturned prow of the partly submerged *Queen* with her torpedoes and the Germans sink. When last seen Charlie and Rose are in the water, joyously embracing at the success of their mission and presumably bound to enjoy a happily married life.

Miss Rose Sayer (Katharine Hepburn), the Rev. Samuel Sayer (Robert Morley) and crude old Charlie Allnut (Bogart).

Drunken Charlie, soon to be put in his place.

Keeping the old girl well oiled, the boat, that is.

Manufacturing torpedoes.

That *The African Queen* is so totally acceptable rests very largely on the marvelous performances of Humphrey Bogart and Katharine Hepburn, almost as unlikely a pairing as Charlie Allnut and Rose Sayer. This is veritably a two-character film and because of the superb playing it never flags. Bogart and Huston, both hard-drinking men, received lectures on temperance from Hepburn but once they became used to her firm views and decorous behavior they came to like her. Said Bogart, "I don't think she tries to be a character. I think she is one." The role of Charlie Allnut brought Bogart an Oscar and in accepting it he quipped to the audience at Hollywood's Pantages Theatre, "It's a long way from the Belgian Congo to the stage of the Pantages, but it's a lot nicer here." Only those who were with him on location could realize that he was not mouthing an idle jest.

The forty members of the cast and crew of *The African Queen* spent nine arduous weeks in the Congo. It was intended to film entirely on location but as the days went by individuals dropped out because of illness and had to be flown to London, where remaining scenes eventually had to be shot in studios. Huston scouted thousands of miles of Central Africa before picking on Ponthierville, on the Lulaba River, for his opening shots and then trekking fifteen hundred miles with the boat they had purchased for the title role to the confluence of the Victoria Nile and the Albert Nile in Uganda, in the lake country. The company labored through dirt, insects, extreme heat and discomforts. They found that unless their clothes were kept in cellophane bags they mildewed and turned moldy in a matter of days. Malaria hit several of the British crew and Huston claims that he had to order the men to stop working, that they wanted to continue their jobs even while shaking with fever fits.

The greatest hazard to the company was working in waters populated by crocodiles, leeches and quickly contracted diseases. The film called for many water shots and whenever the actors or the crew had to work in water, it was for short periods, after which they were quickly washed and dried. Another constant threat was the soldier ant, a tough beast about an inch long, moving in swarms and capable of devastating anything in its path. Says John Huston: "That's the way it was all the time we were shooting *The African Queen*. Not always dangerous but always exciting. And with everybody always coming up to what was expected of them, and often going beyond it. Bogie and Katie expanded as actors. They were both playing roles strictly against type, and for me they were a revelation. The spontaneity, the instinctive subtle interplay between them, the way they climbed inside of the people they were supposed to be—all of this made it better than we had written it, as human, as comprehending as we had any right to expect from any two actors."

Courageous Charlie and his admiring Rose, trying to explain their presence to the Germans . . .

. . . unsuccessfully. But triumph is just around the corner.

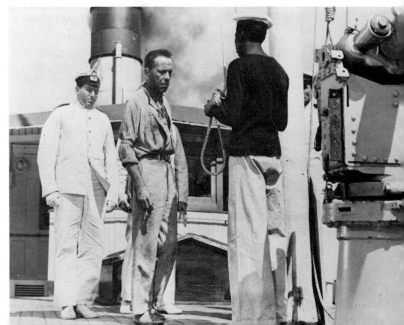

Ivanhoe

1952

An MGM Picture. Produced by Pandro S. Berman. Directed by Richard Thorpe. Screenplay by Noel Langley, adapted by Aeneas MacKenzie from the novel by Sir Walter Scott. Photographed in Technicolor by Frederick A. Young. Music by Miklos Rozsa. Running time: 106 minutes.

CAST

Ivanhoe, Robert Taylor; *Rebecca,* Elizabeth Taylor; *Rowena,* Joan Fontaine; *De Bois-Guilbert,* George Sanders; *Wamba,* Emlyn Williams; *Sir Hugh De Bracy,* Robert Douglas; *Cedric,* Finlay Currie; *Isaac,* Felix Aylmer; *Font De Boeuf,* Francis DeWolff; *Prince John,* Guy Rolfe; *King Richard,* Norman Wooland; *Waldemar Fitzurse,* Basil Sydney; *Locksley,* Harold Warrender; *Philip de Malvoisin,* Patrick Lovell; *Ralph de Vipont,* Roderick Lovell; *Clerk of Copmondurst,* Sebastian Cabot; *Hundebert,* John Reedclock; *Baldwin,* Michael Brennan.

When MGM announced its plans to produce *Ivanhoe* in England, with Robert Taylor in the title role and Americans directing and producing it, a good many Britons feared a Hollywood vulgarization of one of the noblest pieces of historical romance in British literature. Once the picture was shown, only severe purists could quibble. What producer Pandro Berman and director Richard Thorpe put on the screen is, so far, the finest of medieval swashbucklers, a truly spectacular picturization of the age of chivalry, with splendid scenery, castles, regal courts and halls, jousting tournaments and beautifully costumed knights and ladies.

A major part of MGM's decision to do the film in England lay in their London bank accounts. The studio had piled up fortunes from the British release of their pictures over the years and a portion of it was frozen by government decree—it had to be used in England. MGM certainly did not skimp on *Ivanhoe*.

The novels of Sir Walter Scott (1771–1832), the veritable cradle of historical fiction, are too complex and lengthy to allow for literal film treatment. *Ivanhoe*, published in 1819, is perhaps the easiest, although it required much work on the part of Aeneas MacKenzie to adapt the novel into screen terms and scope, from which Noel Langley then wrote his excellent screenplay. It was part of Scott's genius to be able to combine historical facts and legends with the people and situations of his own invention. Only one writer did this better than he —Shakespeare—and yet in actually describing the rich tapestries of his settings Scott had no equal. Much of that richness of detail and atmosphere is apparent in this film, with bushels of praise due Alfred Junge for his sets and Roger Furse for his costumes. And as is so often the case with the best

166

The battle of Torquilstone Castle.

of action epics, the photography and musical scoring are assets of the highest order. Britain's masterful Freddie Young was responsible for the glorious Technicolor camera work, and Miklos Rozsa, a musicologist as well as composer-conductor, spent time researching twelfth century music and used it to color his full-blooded score.

The screenplay follows the outlines of the Scott novel. It begins with Wilfred of Ivanhoe (Robert Taylor) making his way home to England after serving with King Richard in the Third Crusade. Richard has been held captive by the Austrians and Ivanhoe discovers in which castle the king is held. In England he vows to uphold Richard's cause in the face of a Norman plot to put his treacherous brother, Prince John (Guy Rolfe), on the throne. Ivanhoe has been disowned by his father Cedric (Finlay Currie) for adventuring with Richard instead of remaining in England and supporting the Saxon cause. He slips into Cedric's house and makes his return known to his love, Rowena (Joan Fontaine), who warns him that the Norman knights are confident of success in their plans to rule England. To raise money to ransom Richard, Ivanhoe

turns to a prominent Jewish patriarch, Isaac of York (Felix Aylmer), who believes in Richard as a just and unprejudiced monarch, and quite the opposite of John. Isaac's beautiful daughter, Rebecca (Elizabeth Taylor) falls in love with Ivanhoe, and he with her, although both know the difference in their religions makes the admission of their feelings impossible.

Upon hearing that the Jews are raising funds for the ransom, Prince John sends his foremost warrior, Sir Brian de Bois-Guilbert (George Sanders), to arrest the Saxon leader and crush the campaign. Sir Brian employs guile and treachery to do so, and manages to capture and imprison Ivanhoe, his family and followers. The Normans, ensconced in Torquilstone Castle, imagine the situation is settled. It is not. To the castle comes Locksley and his hordes of outlaws from the forests. Locksley demands the release of Ivanhoe. The Normans sneer but Ivanhoe shouts to the Saxons, "In the name of Richard, attack and wipe them out!" Immediately the air is full of waves of Saxon arrows and the siege begins. A platoon of Norman knights attempts to charge out of the castle but the archery is too

167

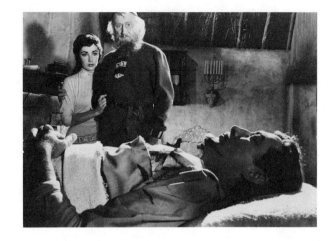

Rebecca (Elizabeth Taylor) and her father Isaac (Felix Aylmer), care for the wounded Ivanhoe.

Two imperious Normans, Sir Hugh de Bracy (Robert Douglas) and Sir Brian de Bois-Guilbert (George Sanders) question Ivanhoe.

much for them and they retreat. Ivanhoe breaks free of his bonds and starts a fire in the keep, which further confuses the now sagging Norman defense. Sir Brian, sensing that the game is up, grabs Rebecca and carries her off as he dashes from the castle.

Sir Brian, arrogant warrior though he may be, also has a heart, and it beats for the lovely Rebecca. This is of no concern to Prince John, who is persuaded by his advisors to try Rebecca as a sorceress, to be burned at the stake, in order to get the Jews to turn the money over to John. But the money is sent to Austria and Rebecca is condemned —until Ivanhoe appears and claims the right to defend her. As a nobleman he has this right to act as a challenger on the field of honor, at the risk of his life in tournament. Prince John instructs Sir Brian to defend the royal position. The resultant duel with chains, mace and broadswords is long and bloody, and Sir Brian loses. As he lies dying, a band of knights ride upon the field. It is the returned Richard and his crusaders. The politics are immediately settled—Ivanhoe bids farewell to Rebecca, as she and her father are guaranteed safe passage abroad, and he then turns to the waiting Rowena, to assume his place as a Saxon leader in a peaceful England.

Richard Thorpe's direction of *Ivanhoe* is as sure as the ticking of a reliable clock. It keeps the pageantry flowing smoothly and advances the story swiftly. The difficult scenes of crowds in furious action are especially well handled. The battle of Torquilstone Castle lasts for almost a quarter of an hour and is a non-stop montage of rapid scenes and quick cuts. Editor Frank Clarke deserves men-

tioning at this point. Thorpe, whose directorial career spanned forty years, was a solid craftsman but seldom an inspired one. *Ivanhoe* obviously brought out the best in him and when MGM decided to do *Knights of the Round Table* (1954) and *Quentin Durward* (1956), both with Robert Taylor, they assigned Thorpe. While both films were good swashbucklers, with moments of colorful action, neither managed to come shoulder-high to *Ivanhoe*. But in all of them, Taylor performed with dignity and with a really credible heroic bearing—his deep American voice lessening the medieval image just a little.

Ivanhoe was the biggest film production undertaken in England up to the time its cameras started to turn in July, 1951. Prior to that a vast amount of work had been done in research, with the aid of the British Museum, to be certain about sets and

The gallant Ivanhoe (Robert Taylor) and his lovely Rowena (Joan Fontaine).

Ivanhoe gets rid of Font De Boeuf (Francis DeWolff).

Ivanhoe surrenders to De Bois-Guilbert in the hope of saving his family.

costumes. It was shot at the 120-acre Boreham Wood Studios, outside London. The biggest single set was Torquilstone Castle, which was begun two years before the filming. It was a full-scale replica of a twelfth-century fortress, and the moat that was cut around it was twenty feet wide and ten feet deep. The set was later used for other films, including Errol Flynn's *The Warriors* in 1955. *Ivanhoe* also called for the making of an armory of medieval weapons and costumes, including thousands of arrows, hundreds of suits of chain-mail, swords, shields, saddles, crossbows, maces and a

recreation of the jousting fields of Ashby-de-la-Zouche, with its brightly decorated stands and pavilions, knightly tents and costumed horses. The efforts were considerable and the results are beautifully apparent in Freddie Young's photography.

The action sequences of *Ivanhoe* called for from five hundred to a thousand extras each day and the training required was nothing less than military. Dozens of men were drilled in the use of lances, spears and maces for the jousting scenes and squads of men were given instruction in the use of the longbow and crossbow. The filming also required one hundred suitably handsome and spirited horses, a requirement more difficult to fill than those unfamiliar with horses might imagine. Equine experts scouted England to find them and then spent time training them. The long filming provided the stunt men will a number of field days, with falls from horses and plunges from parapets into moats. The man in charge of the military aspects was Col. Linden White, who said at the time, "How any old-time knight fought for years without injury is a mystery. The chain-mail armor of Ivanhoe's time was like the mesh rings in a modern woman's purse. A pointed barb could go through. The twelve- and fifteen-foot lances were lethal weapons. We made them as replicas, but with hollow centers and rubber ends. We had to design special saddles so that a falling rider wouldn't be trampled by a horse, and we had one of the hardest jobs teaching players how to charge at full speed with a forty- to sixty-pound suit of armor. We had some accidents, but luckily nothing too serious."

170

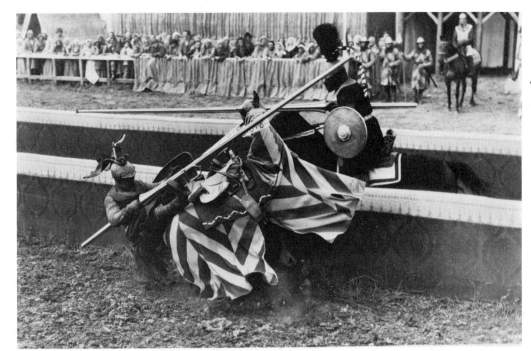

The tournaments at
Ashby-de-la-Zouche.

De Bois-Guilbert dies a noble death.

Scaramouche

1952

An MGM Picture. Produced by Carey Wilson. Directed by George Sidney. Screenplay by Ronald Millar and George Froeschel, based on the novel by Rafael Sabatini. Photographed in Technicolor by Charles Rosher. Music by Victor Young. Running time: 115 minutes.

CAST

Andre Moreau, Stewart Granger; *Lenore,* Eleanor Parker; *Aline de Gavrillac,* Janet Leigh; *Noel, Marquis de Maynes,* Mel Ferrer; *Chevalier de Chabrillaine,* Henry Wilcoxon; *Marie Antoinette,* Nina Foch; *Philippe de Valmorin,* Richard Anderson; *Gaston Binet,* Robert Coote; *Georges de Valmorin,* Lewis Stone; *Isabelle de Valmorin,* Elisabeth Risdon; *Michael Vanneau,* Howard Freeman; *Fabian,* Curtis Cooksey; *Doutreval,* John Dehner; *Doctor Dubuque,* John Litel; *Sergeant,* Jonathan Cott; *Pierrot,* Dan Foster; *Perigore,* Richard Hale.

"He was born with the gift of laughter and a sense that the world was mad."

These are the opening lines of Rafael Sabatini's *Scaramouche,* a delightful novel about the adventures of a dashing nobleman in the years of the French Revolution. Its theatrical qualities were so obvious that MGM purchased the screen rights soon after the book was published in 1921. Two years later the public flocked to see the spectacular movie version, with young Ramón Novarro as the hero and Lewis Stone as the villain. Thirty years later another generation lined up to see Stewart Granger and Mel Ferrer swashbuckling their way

172

through the merry saga, with Lewis Stone playing a minor role. The 1923 picture is closer to the book and shows more of the revolution—in 1952 it was just talked about. The latter also alters the relationship of the hero and the villain. In the original he villain turns out to be the father of the illegitimate hero. To make the Granger–Ferrer version more palatable they are set up as half-brothers.

Rafael Sabatini's contribution to the art of writing historical fiction is enormous. Sabatini (1875–1950) was born in Italy of an Italian father and an English mother, and took up residence in England as a young man. He was educated to be a businessman but his fascination with history and his ability to write soon led him away from the world of stocks and bonds, and into the imagery of knights, cavaliers and pirates. His first success was *The Tavern Knight* in 1904 and with *The Sea Hawk* in 1915 there was no doubt that Sabatini had found his niche in life. The success enabled him to delve even deeper into historical studies to turn out romantic fiction, which was the only kind of writing that interested him. *Scaramouche* became a best seller and he followed it with *Captain Blood,* filmed in 1924 with Milton Sills and in 1935 with Errol Flynn. His 1933 novel *The Black Swan* was the basis of Tyrone Power's swashbuckler of that name in 1942 and in 1950 Louis Hayward starred in *The Fortunes of Captain Blood,* which Sabatini wrote in 1936. Aside from these Hollywood productions there have also been European filmings of his work, such as the French *Adventures of Scaramouche* in 1964. All in all, the movies have done well with the imagination of Rafael Sabatini.

The 1952 screenplay by Ronald Millar and George Froeschel has the hero, Andre Moreau (Granger), as a lighthearted playboy, supported by the stipends of his unknown father. When the payments cease, Andre forces the intermediary lawyer to reveal the source and learns he is the son of the powerful Duc de Gavrillac. He proceeds to the duke's home and finds he has died. En route to the estate Andre falls in love with the beautiful Aline de Gavrillac (Janet Leigh) and is dismayed when he learns her name, assuming her to be his sister. Aline is impressed by Andre and confused when he does not continue his romancing. At the same time, Aline is being courted by the elegant Noel, Marquis de Maynes (Mel Ferrer), who is a favorite of the Queen (Nina Foch) and renowned as the finest swordsman in France. The Queen advises it is time Noel took to marriage and that Aline would be a suitable match. Andre runs afoul of Noel

Aline de Gavrillac (Janet Leigh) and the admiring Andre Moreau (Granger).

Philippe de Valmorin (Richard Anderson) unwisely tackles the Marquis de Mayne (Mel Ferrer). The Chevalier de Chabrillaine (Henry Wilcoxon) knows the Marquis has nothing to fear.

The Marquis has nothing to fear from Andre Moreau either—at this point.

Actress Lenore (Eleanor Parker), who loves Scaramouche in vain.

174

when he and his friend Philippe de Valmorin (Richard Anderson) meet him in a tavern. Philippe is a revolutionary, the editor of an underground newspaper and a man with a price on his head. Noel is aware of his identity and provokes him into a duel. Since Philippe has no skill with the blade he is quickly dispatched. Andre picks up the sword and furiously slashes at Noel but he too is an amateur. He makes his escape by holding Noel at pistol point and vows that he will one day have his revenge.

Andre is acquainted with an actress, Lenore (Eleanor Parker) and in need of refuge from the law he joins the theatrical troupe of which she is a member. The actor who plays the masked clown Scaramouche is a drunkard and Andre assumes his role. While with this company he also seeks out the fencing master who taught and continues to coach Noel—Doutreval (John Dehner), who sympathizes with the revolution and agrees to take Andre as a pupil. When Noel discovers Andre studying with Doutreval, the fencing master then

arranges for him to receive futher instruction from his own teacher, Perigore (Richard Hale). In the meantime Andre is approached by the revolutionary forces in the government and asked to become a minister. He agrees, but mostly in order to come face to face with Noel, who sits on the opposite side of the political barrier. The other ministers are aware of the animosity and constantly arrange for Noel to be sent away on missions. But the day of reckoning finally arrives. In attending the theatre with Aline, Noel receives a challenge from the stage. Scaramouche whips off his mask and picks up his rapier. The fight between the two brilliant swordsmen goes on and on, and Noel is eventually backed to the point where his death is certain. But something in Andre prevents him from making the final thrust and in confusion he angrily sticks his sword in the floor of the stage. The father of Philippe (Lewis Stone) then tells him why he could not kill Noel. Andre is not the son of Gavrillac but of the Duc de Maynes, the father of Noel. However, there is a compensation for Andre be-

Leeway for the most lavish of all movie duels.

Georges de Valmorin (Lewis Stone) explains to Andre why he was unable to kill the Marquis.

yond the triumph of having bested the so-called finest swordsman in France—since the loving Aline is not his sister, she can be his bride.

Scaramouche has the most important of all qualities needed for swashbucklers—a sense of flair, that sense of buoyancy which comes with filmmakers' enjoying their work. In terms of costume spectacles like this one it also comes with having the resources of a wealthy studio being readily available. The sets and costumes of *Scaramouche* are of the highest order and the Technicolor photography of Charles Rosher captures it all with great style. The beauty of color in this picture is extraordinary, as is the use of scenically gorgeous Golden Gate Park in San Francisco. Several scenes were filmed in the park and there are some marvelous sequences of brightly uniformed cavalrymen pursuing the hero through woods, across streams and lush green meadows.

Both the 1923 and the 1952 versions of *Scaramouche* are important items in any study of swordplay on the screen. The early film contained the best fencing to that time and the man responsible was Henry J. Uyttenhove, a Belgian fencing master and the coach at the Los Angeles Athletic Club. In 1920 Douglas Fairbanks hired Uyttenhove to supervise the fencing in his *The Mark of Zorro* and retained him for *The Three Musketeers*. But Fairbanks, despite his verve and his acrobatics, was not a good swordsman, being more concerned with theatrical dash than accurate fencing movements. Ramón Novarro and Lewis Stone were willing pupils and although their duel is somewhat static by later standards, it was the first to employ correct feints, thrusts, parries and lunges.

The duel in the 1952 picture is among the few classics in screen swordplay. While Mel Ferrer is seldom thought of as a swashbuckler, his handling

of the blade and his graceful moment mark him as one of the most accomplished actors with the sword. Stewart Granger, who almost had the dashing-hero field to himself by 1952, played *Scaramouche* with bravura and strength. His impressive swordmanship was due to the coaching he received from the late Jean Heremans, who staged and supervised all Granger's MGM duels. Heremans was also a Belgian fencing champion and at the time of being hired by MGM to direct the swordplay in *The Three Musketeers* (1948) he too was the fencing master at the Los Angeles Athletic Club. Heremans coached a number of actors and actresses, including Lana Turner from *Diane* (1956) and Grace Kelly in *The Swan* (1956), but his prize pupil was Stewart Granger.

As an actual contest the climactic duel in *Scaramouche* is ridiculous. It runs six and a half minutes and no two swordsmen could engage each other so furiously as do Granger and Ferrer for that length of time. However, viewed purely as fantasy the duel is a delight. It begins in the corridor behind the boxes of the Ambigu Theatre, then proceeds through the boxes and onto the ledges, with Granger swinging out over the auditorium on a thick cord sash. He then drives Ferrer back through the boxes, down the corridor to the Grand Stairway and into the foyer. From there they move through the theatre, over the seats and onto the stage. Once behind the stage Ferrer, sensing that he is losing the match, starts to employ props and hanging weights to deflect the onslaught of his determined opponent. Granger backs Ferrer against a theatrical flat but fails to follow through on his advantage. This is the longest duel so far staged for a film and by far the most elaborately staged and choreographed.

Lewis Stone as the Marquis and Ramon Novarro as Andre Moreau in the 1923 version.

179

The Adventures of Robinson Crusoe

1954

A Tepeyac–United Artist Picture. Produced by Oscar Dancigers and Henry Ehrlich. Directed by Luis Bunuel. Screenplay by Philip Roll and Luis Buñuel, based on the novel by Daniel Defoe. Photographed in Pathecolor by Alex Philips. Music by Anthony Collins. Running time: 90 minutes.

CAST

Robinson Crusoe, Dan O'Herlihy; *Friday,* James Fernandez; *Capt. Oberzo,* Filipe De Alba; *Bosun,* Chel Lopez.

The most venerable of all adventure tales is *The Life and Strange Adventures of Robinson Crusoe,* published in 1719 by Daniel Defoe (1660–1731), the novelist-journalist-political commentator whose picaresque stories and witty style set the pattern for novel writing. His own life could well be the subject of a movie; Defoe was the foremost religious dissenter of the day and was at one time put in the pillories for his satirical pamphlets on the subject of the Church. He traveled widely, speculated and lost badly, was employed by the British government as a political spy, and for a nine-year period published *The Review,* a most important example of early journalism. His *Robinson Crusoe,* written in the latter part of his long career, is basically a story of survival—as much over loneliness as isolation—and yet it seethes with a substratum of political satire, as well as making wry comments on

human nature. The novel has been the subject of plays, sketches and various films but the only really intelligent movie version is the one made by Luis Buñuel in Mexico.

The hero of Defoe's story is a young Englishman, the son of a prominent family, who rebels and runs away to sea. Buñuel's film sticks closely to the plot and adds its own dimensions of splendid isolation in beautiful scenery and the anguish of being alone year after year. Crusoe (Dan O'Herlihy), a sailor, is washed up on a desert island when his ship is caught in a storm and wrecked. He is the only survivor and he uses whatever he can salvage from the wreckage to build a home for himself. Little does he realize that this is the beginning of twenty-eight years on the island, the first eighteen of them entirely by himself. At first he takes pleasure in having survived and in having come across such a tropical paradise. He occupies himself building a home, with the ship's cat and dog as his companions, and gathers a group of goats. Crusoe keeps himself busy and feels pleased with having proven himself self-sufficient. But then comes illness, against which he has little defense. Fever brings with it

Crusoe (Dan O'Herlihy) prepares for a long stay on the island . . .

the first real twinges of fear—the fear of being totally alone, removed from civilization and forgotten. Despair slowly overcomes him and causes depression. He fingers the cloth of a woman's dress from the wreckage and it brutally reminds him of the absence of women. The dog dies and in burying it Crusoe becomes bitter at the loss of a friend. The only voice he hears is his own and even that is a form of companionship. Wildly he runs to a valley and shouts The Lord's Prayer at the top of his voice, just to hear the echo.

In the cave-home he has fashioned for himself, Crusoe gets drunk on his homemade wine and acts like a patron in a tavern, carousing and imagining himself with others. Eventually it wears off and makes him realize all the more how lonely he is. Depression replaces fear and at one point he walks into the sea at night, holding a torch in his hand. It drops and in being extinguished by the water it seems to symbolize his bitter plight. His long years alone turn him into an eccentric. He pretends he is still part of society and dresses grandly in goatskins, with an umbrella to protect him from the sun. Then a big change comes into his life . . . eighteen years

after being alone. Cannibals visit the island and as part of a ceremony prepare to kill and cook one of their own men. Crusoe intervenes, scatters the cannibals and rescues the man. Since it happens on a Friday, that is the name he bestows on the man (James Fernandez).

At first Crusoe treats the man like a lesser being, in a "lord and master" situation, imperiously requiring him to be a servant. Crusoe's mind is warped by his years of solitude and he gradually assumes that Friday may murder him in his sleep and eat him. As time goes by, sanity settles on Crusoe's mind and he starts to treat Friday as a fellow human, instructing him in the ways of civilization and teaching him skills. Another ten years go by but they are easier than the previous ones. Finally a ship appears on the horizon and makes its way to the island. The crew are English privateers and it is they who return Crusoe to civilization.

The Adventures of Robinson Crusoe is a kind of delightful "odd man out" in the films of Luis Buñuel. The brilliant Spaniard has concerned himself with bizarre views on mankind, often surrealistic and bitterly mocking in their treatment, but *Crusoe*

181

Occasionally he rails at God.

... and spends years looking at the horizon.

At last, some other humans—cannibals ...

is a true adventure yarn, tinged with compassion for the lonely man's plight, and beyond that, a comment on the anguish of being an individual in an indifferent world. The interiors for the film were shot at the Tepeyac Studios in Mexico City and the exteriors on the lushly tropical west coast of Mexico at Manzanillo. For a full sixty of the ninety minutes of running time, Dan O'Herlihy is alone on the screen—and never lets the interest sag for a moment. The Irish actor was then thirty-five and had been in the United States for several years following his success in Dublin with the Abbey Theatre. He jumped at the opportunity to play Crusoe for Buñuel and told his agent to accept any fee, even nothing, in order to get the role. The painstaking Buñuel kept him in Mexico for months and the Manzanillo location proved very uncomfortable.

Recalls Dan O'Herlihy, "That location was rugged. The temperature was over one hundred—and I can't agree with Defoe that goatskins were the things to wear in the tropics. There were scorpions —little, but with a deadly bite—and peons would beat a path for me every time I had to walk in my bare feet. Once a longboat overturned, badly injuring two of the cast. But Buñuel was the most exciting director I ever worked with; he often made things up out of his head as we went along, things not in the script. Up to then I had always thought of the stage as more creative; Buñuel convinced me otherwise . . . with a work of art that is also entertainment."

. . . one of whom he saves, and names Friday (James Fernandez).

It takes time to learn to trust . . .

. . . but then comes friendship, and the education of Friday.

183

20,000 Leagues Under the Sea

1954

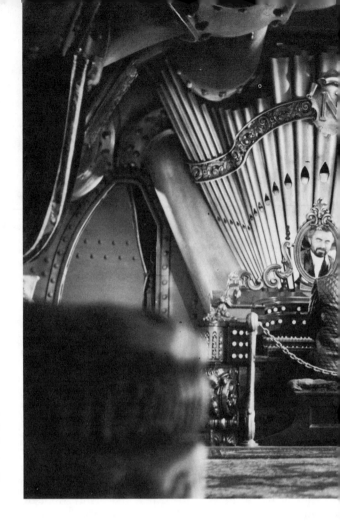

A Walt Disney Production. Directed by Richard Fleischer. Screenplay by Earl Fenton, based on the book by Jules Verne. Photographed in Technicolor by Franz Planer. Special Effects photography by Ralph Hammeras. Music by Paul Smith. Running time: 120 minutes.

CAST

Ned Land, Kirk Douglas; *Captain Nemo,* James Mason; *Professor Aronnax,* Paul Lukas; *Conseil,* Peter Lorre; *Mate on* NAUTILUS, Robert Wilke; *John Howard,* Carleton Young; *Captain Farragut,* Ted de Corsia; *Diver,* Percy Holton; *Mate on* LINCOLN, Ted Cooper; *Shipping Agent,* Edward Marr; *Casey Moore,* Fred Graham; *Billy,* J. M. Kerrigan.

Jules Verne (1828–1905) was a Frenchman with an incredible imagination and a passionate interest in science. He was also something of a seer. His stories told of scientific and technical developments long in the future and involved trips around the world, to the moon and the center of the earth. He prophesied aircraft, rockets, dirigibles, submarines, superbombs and television. Just about the only thing Verne did not foresee was the large sums of money people in the twentieth century would earn from turning his stories into films.

Perhaps the most astounding thing about Verne is that he wrote all his highly descriptive fantasy voyages without leaving his home town of Nantes. In 1869 he published his *20,000 Leagues Under the Sea,* after studying everything that had so far been learned about oceanography, and startled readers with a story about a weird and wonderful submersible ship that explored the mysteries of the deep. In 1954 Walt Disney chose this as the first live-action film to be produced at his Burbank studio and spent five million dollars matching the imagination of his artists with that of Verne. The result was a hearty success—for a producer who barely knew the meaning of failure.

Earl Fenton compressed the Verne story but preserved the spirit of the original, with much help from the Disney Special Effects and Processes Department. The story begins in 1868 as news of an awesome, monstrous and aggressive "thing" sweeps the nautical world. Tales of vessels being swiftly destroyed by this apparition reach the American government and an armed frigate is sent to destroy the mysterious craft. Instead, the monster sinks the frigate and three survivors—Ned Land (Kirk Douglas), an harpoonist, Professor Pierre Aronnax (Paul Lukas), a distinguished authority on undersea life, and Conseil (Peter Lorre), his assistant—find

The elegant Captain Nemo (James Mason).

themselves aboard the submarine. They also find that their host, Captain Nemo (James Mason) is himself a rather strange creature. He is a cultured, hospitable gentleman but possessed of an ambition to destroy the world, which he despises. His splendid ship, the *Nautilus,* is operated by atomic power and equipped with electrical and mechanical wonders. In their involuntary roles as prisoner-guests, the trio make a trip around the world, observing at first hand the marvels of the ocean's depths.

Although the professor and Conseil are content to remain aboard and take advantage of the knowledge gained, Ned Land is eager to escape and get back to his own way of life. He tries once when the *Nautilus* stops at a lonely island but savage cannibals chase him back to the comparative safety of Nemo's ship. Seizing every opportunity to get away, Ned inserts notes containing the location of Nemo's secret island, Vulcania, in bottles and tosses them hopefully into the sea. One of the notes finds it way to the Navy, and after being shelled by a warship the *Nautilus* sinks thousands of feet before Nemo and his crew can repair a broken shaft and regain control. While they are deeper than man has ever before ventured, they observe the strange and magical wonderworld of life miles down in the ocean. As they head for Vulcania the submarine is attacked by two giant squid. In fighting them off Nemo becomes entangled in a huge tentacle and Ned saves his life by freeing him. The grateful captain afterwards confides that he intends to use his prisoners as emissaries to negotiate peace with the outside world. But it is too late. As the *Nautilus* enters the harbor at Vulcania she finds herself trapped by enemy warships. Determined not to share his secrets Nemo gets ashore and sets a time bomb to destroy the island. On the way back to his ship he is mortally wounded and in his final movements he orders a straight-down course as the last voyage of the *Nautilus.* Ned, Conseil and Aronnax manage to escape the vessel and from a distance they later watch as the enormous explosion obliterates the island and the warships. They then muse about some future time when man will know how to use such ingenuity and force for more reasonable and intelligent purposes.

. . . and his guests, Ned Land (Kirk Douglas), Conseil (Peter Lorre) and Professor
Aronnax (Paul Lucas).

Something amiss!

186

Prepare for action!

The attack of the giant squid.

20,000 Leagues Under the Sea is the finest visualization so far of a Jules Verne fantasy. The many underwater sequences called for the building of a huge tank at the Disney studio, where art director John Meehan and Disney's Special Processes genius Ub Iworks brought their talents to bear. The biggest problem was the creation of the *Nautilus*. Verne made things difficult for Disney by requiring that the vessel resemble a sea monster, so that Nemo's enemies would suppose they were being attacked by something other than a man-made machine. According to Verne, the *Nautilus* had a battering-ram snout, electric eyes, a series of metallic ridges along its spine and an enormous tail. When the Disney artisans had completed their craft it was 200 feet long and twenty-two feet at the widest point. To accommodate Verne's esthetic skipper, it also had a main lounge with a pipe organ, a library, rare paintings, plush, ornate furniture and aquariums full of unusual fish. The company went on location—to Jamaica to shoot the cannibal is-

land sequence, and to the crystal-clear waters of the Bahamas, off Nassau, to get the extensive diving footage. All the various kinds of effort are apparent in this fine bit of action entertainment, including good performances from Kirk Douglas as a roguish sailor and James Mason in one of his many film forays into stylish villainy. At one point in the picture Douglas sings a lively chanty called "A Whale of a Tale," which, if nothing else, neatly sums up this whole Disney venture.

Perhaps the single most exciting sequence in the film is the attack on the *Nautilus* by a giant squid, which takes place during a ferocious storm. As first filmed it was done in a quiet sea but when Disney saw the footage he felt it lacked impact and ordered the whole elaborate segment restaged and completely reshot. The idea of the storm was his, and a good example of the "touch" that made all the difference to his films and made his loss to the studio with his death in 1966 a most severe one.

Attacking headhunters are easily disposed of by sending an electrical shock through the body of the *Nautilus*.

The Court Jester

1956

A Paramount Picture. Produced, directed and written by Norman Panama and Melvin Frank. Photographed in VistaVision and Technicolor by Ray June. Music by Victor Schoen. Songs by Sylvia Fine and Sammy Cahn. Running time: 101 minutes.

CAST

Hawkins, Danny Kaye; *Maid Jean,* Glynis Johns; *Sir Ravenhurst,* Basil Rathbone; *Princess Gwendolyn,* Angela Lansbury; *King Roderick,* Cecil Parker; *Griselda,* Mildred Natwick; *Sir Griswold,* Robert Middleton; *Sir Locksley,* Michael Pate; *Captain of the Guards,* Herbert Rudley; *Fergus,* Noel Drayton; *The Black Fox,* Edward Ashley; *Giacomo,* John Carradine; *Sir Brockhurst,* Alan Napier; *Sir Frisdale,* Lewis Martin; *Sir Pertwee,* Patrick Aherne; *Archbishop,* Richard Kean.

The Court Jester a great adventure film? Well, perhaps not but it is a great spoof of adventure and as a piece of entertainment it needs no defending. Norman Panama and Melvin Frank, who wrote, directed and produced it, made it with an obvious fondness for the genre and with a stylishness that makes it more entertaining than many of the films it lampoons. The sets and costumes are the equal of any Hollywood swashbuckling epic and the dialogue is far wittier than most. *The Court Jester* was a timely jest—1954 had produced such medieval clinkers as *Prince Valiant,* with Robert Wagner; *The Black Knight,* Alan Ladd; *The Black Shield of Falworth,* with Tony Curtis; and even lesser items. Panama and Frank stepped up to prove that all was not lost in the art of filming the Age of Chivalry.

A legend sets the tone of the picture: "This is the story of how the destiny of a nation was changed by a birthmark—a royal birthmark on a royal backside." The backside in question belongs to a baby and he is the rightful heir to the throne of England, as venal King Roderick (Cecil Parker) and his greedy band of barons well know. The baby is in the care of The Black Fox (Edward Ashley) and his forest outlaws, one of whom is lovely Maid Jean (Glynis Johns). Another is Hawkins (Danny Kaye), valet to the Black Fox but eager to become a fighter for the cause. Jean holds the rank of captain and declares the cause must come before all personal feelings, which distresses the shy Hawkins because he loves her. She proudly claims, "My father made me everything I am." Replies Hawkins dreamily, "He does lovely work."

Sir Ravenhurst (Rathbone) takes offense at Sir Brockhurst (Alan Napier).

Jean and Hawkins are assigned to sneak the baby into the royal palace. En route they meet Giacomo (John Carradine) who boasts of being "King of Jesters, and Jester to the King." They see him as their means of getting into the castle, so they knock him out, take his clothes and Hawkins presents himself at court as Giacomo. King Roderick, anxious to strengthen his position in the realm, commands his very independent daughter, Princess Gwendolyn (Angela Lansbury), to form an alliance with the powerful Sir Griswold (Robert Middleton). She refuses and he commands, "You'll marry him if it please me." Snorts Gwendolyn, "If it pleases you so much, you marry him." The real power behind the throne is Sir Ravenhurst (Basil Rathbone), who has been expecting Giacomo, actually a professional assassin, which is something the scared Hawkins does not know. He is helped by Gwendolyn's maid, Griselda (Mildred Natwick), loyal to the cause, who is a hypnotist and capable of turning Hawkins into a hero by a

flick of her fingers. She commands Hawkins to woo Gwendolyn in order to forestall the marriage with Sir Griswold. She snaps her fingers and says, "Now go, make love." The confident Hawkins sweeps into Gwendolyn's chambers and informs her, "I am Giacomo, lover of beauty and a beauty of a lover." When she warns him that the brutish Griswold is likely to "snap your neck like a twig," he scoffs, "Speak not of twigs when you look at an oak."

Sir Griswold arrives at the castle and challenges his rival to combat on the jousting field. Unfortunately there are others around the castle who are in the habit of snapping their fingers and poor Hawkins keeps slipping out of his heroic trance. An aide of Ravenhurst informs him that the man he thinks is Giacomo isn't, so Ravenhurst encourages the joust. In order to partake, Hawkins has to be knighted and when the King is advised that it takes years to become a knight, Roderick bellows, "Knight that nincompoop by noon tomorrow."

The king greets a newcomer to the palace (Glynis Johns), not knowing she is an officer of the rebel cause.

The jester confuses his king (Cecil Parker) and the princess (Angela Lansbury).

The jester amuses his king.

Hawkins is put through a crash course in knighthood and at the ceremony of investiture everything is done in double time, confusing and exhausting the poor man. At the tournament Griselda sidles up to him and tells him she intends to kill Griswold, who has to drink a toast to his opponent and vice versa, "I've put a pellet of poison in the vessel with the pestle," which Hawkins strives to remember as he lumbers onto the field in his heavy armor. She cautions him to remember that "the chalice from the palace has the brew that is true." Just as he thinks he has it, she comes up and warns him that "they have broken the vessel with the pestle" and the poison is now in the "flagon with the dragon." One of Griswold's men overhears this and both knights walk onto the fields desperately trying to commit the gibberish to memory. The irritated King allows them to dispense with the toast and Hawkins, by fluke, wins the contest but cannot bring himself to kill Griswold.

Sir Ravenhurst declares Hawkins to be The Black Fox and to be seized, but at that moment the real Fox and his men arrive disguised as monks and the battle commences. Ravenhurst takes out after Hawkins, who is scared silly until Griselda snaps her fingers and tells him, "Be not afraid, you are the greatest with the blade." Ravenhurst also snaps his fingers during the duel and Hawkins keeps switching from cool dexterity to quivering clumsiness. The victorious outlaws interupt the duel and catapult Ravenhurst and the other villains into the moat. In the final scene Hawkins, with the approval of the now loving Jean, stands on the throne and flashes the baby's bottom, with its purple pimpernel birthmark, to each of the loyal subjects as they parade by to pay their respects.

The Court Jester is a delight. A good claim can be made for it being the best of Danny Kaye's films, although some people may feel *The Secret Life of Walter Mitty* is an even better send-up of heroism. As the man who longs to be a hero but who trembles when the opportunity presents itself, Kaye is touchingly funny. And when under Griselda's spell he becomes struttingly confident, he is marvelous. He moves with Flynn-like grace and agility. A major asset to the picture, as Panama and Frank clearly knew when they cast him, is Basil Rathbone as Sir Ravenhurst—veritably Sir Guy of Gisbourne eighteen years later. Rathbone was then sixty-four and looking rather gaunt, but still in full command of his elegant voice, crisply mouthing threats and sneers. One of the most memorable moments in this beautiful burlesque on swashbuckling is the exchange between Ravenhurst and Giacomo (Hawkins in a courageous trance), when the latter has outlined his plan to kill the king. He asks, "Get it?" Ravenhurst replies "Got it." Giacomo nods, "Good!" The words are delivered like a snap of the fingers. In the hilarious duel between the two, Ralph Faulkner doubled for Rathbone in some of the shots. Rathbone still knew how to handle a sword but age had slowed his reflexes a little and the choreography of the comic duel was more complicated than a serious one, and the timings more acute. Rathbone was amazed at Kaye's ability with a sword: "He had never fenced before but after a couple of weeks of instruction Danny could completely outfight me. Even granting the difference in our ages, his reflexes were incredibly fast and nothing had to be shown or explained to him a second time. His mind worked like a camera."

Sir Ravenhurst thinks he has won the day. Little does he know.

Knighting the nincompoop.

The jester jousts.

Around the World in 80 Days

1956

A Michael Todd Company Picture. Produced by Michael Todd. Directed by Michael Anderson. Screenplay by S. J. Perelman, James Poe and John Farrow, based on the novel by Jules Verne. Photographed in 70 mm Todd-AO and Technicolor by Lionel Linden. Music by Victor Young. Running time: 178 minutes.

CAST

Phileas Fogg, David Niven; *Passepartout,* Cantinflas; *Princess Aouda,* Shirley MacLaine; *Inspector Fix,* Robert Newton; and cameos by Charles Boyer, Joe E. Brown, Martine Carol, John Carradine, Charles Coburn, Ronald Colman, Melville Cooper, Noel Coward, Finlay Currie, Reginald Denny, Andy Devine, Marlene Dietrich, Luis Miguel Dominguín, Fernandel, Sir John Gielgud, Hermione Gingold, Jose Greco, Sir Cedric Hardwicke, Trevor Howard, Glynis Johns, Buster Keaton, Evelyn Keyes, Beatrice Lillie, Peter Lorre, Edmund Lowe, A. E. Matthews, Mike Mazurki, Col. Tim McCoy, Victor McLaglen, John Mills, Robert Morley, Edward R. Murrow, Alan Mowbray, Jack Oakie, George Raft, Gilbert Roland, Cesar Romero, Frank Sinatra, Red Skelton, Ronald Squire, Basil Sydney and Harcourt Williams.

When Mike Todd died in an airplane crash in 1958, aged fifty-one, show business lost a rare man. Todd was the kind the industry needs most of all —the producer with boundless energy and enthusiasm, imagination, charm, muscle and nerve. He was a magnificent con man and for him there were no such things as impossible odds. In a previous age he would probably have been a buccaneer. Todd once said, "You can't teach showmanship— because there are no rules. If there were rules it would not be showmanship." His career was built on that viewpoint and *Around the World in 80 Days* stands as a monument to Todd's ability to pull off a great piece of entertainment despite the lack of sufficient backing at the start and in the face of incredible production requirements. The script called for locations in a dozen countries, actors by the hundreds and a huge budget for period props and costumes. Todd was always able to raise money, even though he was declared bankrupt in 1947. At that time he owed more than a million dollars but managed to pay it off by raising large sums during the time of his debt and producing shows on Broadway.

Damon Runyon said of Todd, "He is the greatest natural gambler I've ever known." This film was

his greatest gamble. He liquidated his assets in order to raise front money and then set about tapping other sources for the rest. During production he sold stock in the property, wrote I.O.U.'s by the score and sometimes handed out dud checks. Such was his charm that he was able to persuade several dozen celebrities to play bit parts. Few were able to deny him. Even Cantinflas finally had to agree to play Passepartout. Reputedly one of the wealthiest and most independent performers in the world, Cantínflas had previously refused all offers to appear in American films. After a meeting with Todd, the great Mexican comic accepted the role without discussing the terms. Todd also persuaded the legendary Spanish matador Luis Miguel Dominguín to come out of retirement to appear in the film and when Todd touched on the subject of money, millionaire Domingúin asked, "How much do you need?" Noel Coward was another of the many who were shoe-horned into the picture: "Todd bullied me over an inferior lunch and I gave in for the devil of it."

Todd had become familiar with the Jules Verne story in 1946 when he set out to produce a Broadway musical of it. Cole Porter provided the score and Orson Welles did the script, as well as the direction, in addition to playing Inspector Fix. Wells and Todd were not a compatible team and when the egocentric actor-director refused advice about improving the script Todd pulled out. Todd lost forty thousand dollars in so doing but his instincts were sound. The musical ran for only seventy-four performances. However, Todd still had the rights to the Verne material and the idea of a movie gradually jelled in his fervid mind. The more he thought about it, the bigger it became. The end result delighted moviegoers and made a large profit, as well as winning an Oscar as the best film of 1956. Oscars also went to the scenarists, the editors, photographer Lionel Linden and composer Victor Young.

Around the World in 80 Days lives up to its title. It is a marvelous travelogue and a splendid adventure. It begins in Victorian London as the wealthy, punctilious, supremely confident Phileas Fogg (David Niven) accepts a wager from his fel-

low members at the posh Reform Club that he can traverse the globe in the amazingly short time of eighty days. The wager is set at twenty thousand pounds and off he goes with this nimble manservant Passepartout. Nothing fazes the imperturbable Fogg —all crises are coolly dealt with, all hurdles and obstacles surmounted.

Fogg and Passepartout employ almost every means of conveyance known to man at the time. They make their way through France, Spain, across the Mediterranean, through the Suez Canal to India, across Southeast Asia, across the Pacific, the United States and the Atlantic back to London. In the course of their adventures they take a variety of trains and boats, but also a balloon, a stagecoach, a sailmobile and several animals, including an elephant and an ostrich. The trip is made the more difficult by the hounding of Inspector Fix of Scotland Yard (Robert Newton), who believes Fogg has robbed the Bank of England. In India they save the Princess Aouda (Shirley MacLaine) from being burned alive in a suttee ceremony and she becomes their companion for the remainder of the adventure. When they arrive in London Fogg is jailed by Fix as the suspected robber but shortly cleared of the charge when the real culprit is caught. The delay leads Fogg to think he has lost his wager, until he realizes that in going around the world he has crossed the International Date Line and gained a full day. He then appears at the Reform Club with only seconds to spare, thereby winning his claim. He also wins the Princess as his wife, she having turned the frosty Fogg into a warmer and less imperious man.

Around the World in 80 Days has lost some of the sparkle it seemed to have when it was first flashed on the screen in 1956 in the magnificence of 70 mm Todd-AO photography. Seen now in television, Fogg's adventures appear a little tedious and implausible, and the sight of many once-famous faces popping up in bit parts is less interesting with time. The business of hyping movies with cameos became familiar after this picture and the public tired of it. However, there is still much to recommend *Around the World,* including beautiful visuals of exotic locations and fine action sequences, such as the trip in the balloon over France, the rescue of Fogg from Indians by a company of U.S. Cavalry led by Col. Tim McCoy (John Wayne wanted the part but Todd opted for McCoy, a genuine colonel as well as actor), and the frantic trip across the Atlantic, in which the S.S. *Henrietta* is stripped to its metal framework as every piece of

En route through India (Sir Cedric Hardwicke and Ronald Colman).

Passepartout and the Indians.

wood is used to keep the furnaces going. In a sense the whole fantastic trip was a parallel of Mike Todd's determination to keep the production going. A logical man could not have done it.

Part of Todd's strength was in firmly believing in his own decisions and rarely being deflected by the advice of others. He was convinced that Michael Anderson was the man to direct *Around the World* despite the Englishman's never having worked on a movie of such massive proportions, and he felt

199

Phileas Fogg (Niven) and Passepartout (Cantinflas) depart from Paris.

Having arrived in the nick of time with his cavalry, Col. Tim McCoy is thanked by Fogg, Fix (Robert Newton) and the Princess (Shirley MacLaine).

The triumphant Fogg and the relieved train conductor (Buster Keaton)

The prairie schooner.

Mike Todd.

the only actor for the role of Phileas Fogg was David Niven, who was at that time far from being a box-office figure. Just prior to this he had taken second billing to George Gobel in the feeble *The Birds and the Bees*. However, Todd knew Niven would be ideal as Fogg since he was an actor with a fairly classy British background and had the kind of impish charm that would make Fogg a little more appealing than the rather cold character created by Verne in 1872.

Recalls David Niven in an interview with the writer: "I got a call from Mike Todd to come over to his house. I was sitting in my back yard with Humphrey Bogart at the time and since I didn't know anything about Todd I asked Bogie for his advice. He said, 'Watch out for him.' So I went over to Todd and he immediately began questioning me, did I know about Jules Verne and did I know about this book *Around the World in 80 Days*? I told him honestly that I admired Verne and adored the book—I didn't know he intended filming it. He looked me in the eye and asked, 'How'd you like to play Phileas Fogg?' I was ecstatic and said 'I'd play him for nothing.' With that Todd said, 'You've got a deal' and dived into his swimming pool. After a stunned moment I dived in the direction of my agent, hoping he could persuade Todd not to hold me to the terms I had just rashly declaimed. I played Fogg for a good price but it was such a marvelous picture I think I might have been tempted to play him for nothing."

202

The *Henrietta,* prior to being stripped.

War and Peace

1956

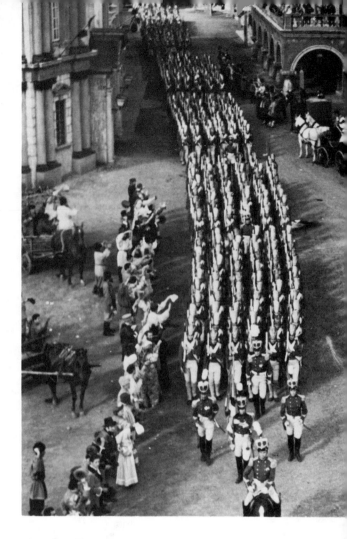

A Paramount–Ponti–De Laurentiis Picture. Produced by Dino De Laurentiis. Directed by King Vidor. Screenplay by Bridget Boland, King Vidor, Robert Westerby, Mario Camerini, Ennio De Concini and Ivo Perilli, based on the book by Leo Tolstoy. Photographed in VistaVision and Technicolor by Jack Cardiff. Music by Nino Rota. Running time: 208 minutes.

CAST

Natasha Rostov, Audrey Hepburn; *Pierre Bezukhov,* Henry Fonda; *Andrey Bolkonsky,* Mel Ferrer; *Anatole Kuragine,* Vittorio Gassman; *Helene Kuragine,* Anita Ekberg; *General Kutuzov,* Oscar Homolka; *Napoleon,* Herbert Lom; *Platon,* John Mills; *Dolokhov,* Helmut Dantine; *Lise,* Milly Vitale; *Sonya,* May Britt.

The first film to be made from Leo Tolstoy's *War and Peace* was a Russian production of 1916. By then the great author-reformer had been dead for six years, although still a powerful force in the thinking of the Russian masses. Tolstoy had been born into the landed gentry but much of his life was spent in criticizing the Czarist regime and urging greater understanding of the common people. To this end he devised social reforms and educational programs, and eventually gave away his estates to the peasants. He also sprinkled his political views throughout his prolific writings and incurred the wrath of the government, the Church and his own class, which resulted in his being excommunicated in 1901. He wrote *War and Peace* in the years 1864 to 1869 and strove to point out in this massive panorama of the Napoleonic invasion of Russian that the French were beaten not so

much by the Russian generals but by the courage and loyalty of the common soldiers. Tolstoy knew what he was writing about; in his eighty-two years he came to know every level of Russian life and he was deeply involved in its political tides. As a young aristocrat he had caroused with the masochistic abandon that seems to be part of the Russian character and he learned firsthand of war as a soldier in the Crimea. Everything that was Tolstoy is apparent in *War and Peace.*

The truly great film version is the one released in 1967 after years of production and directed by Sergei Bondarchuk (who also played the role of Pierre), with unlimited aid from the Soviet government as part of the celebration of the fiftieth anniversary of the Bolshevik revolution. In its original version the Bondarchuk film runs more than seven hours but for the American release it was cut by seventy minutes and released in two separate parts. Its battle scenes are the finest ever filmed and the dreadful but spectacular retreat from Russia seem-

The Russian army marches to meet Napoleon.

ingly employs the same number of men as did Napoleon and can be taken as a reenactment of history. However, Bondarchuk's film is rather heavy going for non-Russians or those not sympathetically understanding of the Russian tendency to wallow in quiet anguish. A much more comprehensive filming of *War and Peace* is the French-Italian-American production directed by Hollywood's King Vidor. It has flaws, and its backers obviously wanted it to be as commercial as possible, but as an introduction to Tolstoy's book it has much to recommend it.

Tolstoy and Vidor tell the epic story through a handful of major characters. As Napoleon prepares to invade Russia, Pierre Bezukhov (Henry Fonda), an aristocratic liberal, visits his friend Count Rostov (Barry Jones) and his lovely young daughter Natasha (Audrey Hepburn), with whom he falls in love but to whom he hesitates to propose because he is illegitimate. But when his father, Count Bezukhov, dies, he acknowledges Pierre and leaves him

a fortune. The somewhat naive Pierre comes under the influence of the beautiful but unscrupulous Helene Kuragine (Anita Ekberg) and marries her. His closest friend, Prince Andrey Bolkonsky (Mel Ferrer), achieves success as a soldier under General Kutuzov (Oscar Homolka) but returns wounded, a condition made the worse by the death of his wife in childbirth. With his own marriage ended by the adultery of his wife Pierre introduces the grieving Andrey to Natasha, and the pair fall in love. Before they can marry, Andrey is sent into battle against the invading French and the pacifistic Pierre goes along as an observer. He is horrified by the carnage at the battle of Borodino and it breeds in him a resolve to assassinate Napoleon. He returns to Moscow and aids his friends in evacuating the city but stays behind as General Kutuzov pulls his forces out in order to allow the French Emperor the hollow victory of taking the empty capital.

The Rostovs take refuge in a monastery to the

205

Pierre (Henry Fonda) carouses
with the Russian cavaliers.

east of Moscow and there Natasha is reunited with
the badly wounded Andrey, who soon dies. In the
meantime Pierre fails in his attempt on Napoleon's
life and is taken prisoner and forced to march with
the French. As a prisoner he observes much grief
and agony, an experience which greatly matures
him. He sees at first hand the misery of the French
defeat, as winter freezes and kills Napoleon's invasion. The Emperor orders his men back to France,
but with no supplies and little protection from the
extreme cold and the blizzards, thousands of
Frenchmen die along the hundreds of miles of retreat. At the battle of Berezina the Russian army
delivers the final, paralyzing blow. Pierre manages
to escape his weary captors and returns to Moscow,
together with hordes of soldiers and civilians intent
on rebuilding their country in the wake of their
victory. And Pierre finally finds himself in Natasha's
loving arms.

Any short synopsis of *War and Peace* is bound
to seem absurdly inadequate. Even this three-hour
version required half a dozen writers to synthesize
Tolstoy's complicated strands and multiple characters. The sets, the costumes, Nino Rota's music
and the actors all deserve credit. Andrey Hepburn
is a radiant young Natasha and Henry Fonda, who
himself felt he was wrong for the part, communi-
cates the confusion of the nice but lumbering Pierre,

caught up in an angry swirl of history and groping for answers, trying to find out "what happiness is —what value there is in suffering—why men go to war." His adventures lead him to understand at least partly the mysteries of life, humanity, love and loyalty.

Vidor was fortunate in getting the services of ace photographer Jack Cardiff, shortly before he gave up the camera and became a director himself. This *War and Peace* contains many marvelous pictorial moments—colorfully uniformed regiments marching through the streets of Moscow and deploying themselves on battlefields, snowy landscapes, a magnificent ballroom sequence, and most of all, the epic and tragic retreat of the Napoleonic armies through the Russian winter. Even allowing

for the relatively inexpensive use of Yugloslavian locations and extras in the mid-1950s, the film cost more than six million dollars. That it all works as well as it does is very much due to King Vidor. His ability to handle massive subjects was demonstrated as early as *The Big Parade* in 1926 and repeated in such spectacular pictures as *Northwest Passage* and *Duel in the Sun*.

Vidor accepted the invitation of Dino De Laurentiis and Carlo Ponti to direct the huge undertaking and then found himself being urged to get it into production as quickly as possible. He managed to get the cameras rolling in mid-1955, about a year after taking the job, and thereby halted the plans of David O. Selznick, Michael Todd and MGM to proceed with their versions. All three productions

Natasha (Audrey Hepburn) and Prince Andrei (Mel Ferrer) at the ball.

had announced intentions to film in Italy, as was much of the Vidor film, and all of them sought Audrey Hepburn. Vidor was the only one who impressed her with clear concepts of the Tolstoy story. The difficult task was made even more difficult for Vidor by having to start production before a final script was ready and before the complicated financial backing from several countries had been settled. Vidor was not able to keep daily track of his filming by the usual procedure of watching the "rushes"—the quick printing of the previous day's shots—because the VistaVision stock had to be processed in either England or America. Despite the pressures Vidor was able to complete the principal photography in four months, an astonishing fact in view of the multiple locations and the scope of the battle sequences. It is difficult to determine which is the greater adventure—Pierre Bezukhov's tough time with Napoleon's retreat or King Vidor's efforts to turn Leo Tolstoy's mighty tale into a good movie.

Andrei leads his regiment, and loses his life.

Napoleon (Herbert Lom), the master of all he surveys—to this point in time.

208

Pierre observes the battle
of Borodino.

The Russian winter, the real enemy.

The Bridge on the River Kwai

1957

A Horizon–Columbia Picture. Produced by Sam Spiegel. Directed by David Lean. Screenplay by Pierre Boulle, based on his novel. (Co-scenarists Michael Wilson and Carl Foreman uncredited) Photographed in CinemaScope and Eastmancolor by Jack Hilyard. Music by Malcolm Arnold. Running time: 161 minutes.

CAST

Shears, William Holden; *Col. Nicholson,* Alec Guinness; *Major Warden,* Jack Hawkins; *Col. Saito,* Sessue Hayakawa; *Major Slipton,* James Donald; *Lieutenant Joyce,* Geoffrey Horne; *Col. Green,* Andre Morell; *Captain Reeves,* Peter Williams; *Major Hughes,* John Boxer; *Grogan,* Percy Herbert; *Baker,* Harold Goodwin; *Nurse,* Ann Sears; *Captain Kanematsu,* Henry Okawa; *Lieutenant Miura,* K. Katsumoto; *Yai,* M. R. B. Chakrabandhu.

At the end of *The Bridge on the River Kwai,* as the bridge is blown up and many of the film's principal characters go to their deaths, a British medical officer (James Donald) looks on appalled and says, "Madness! madness!" It is as good a comment on war as can be spoken and the film itself serves to clarify that view while also being a splendid piece of entertainment. *Kwai* has been criticized in some quarters as glorifying war but its director, David Lean, defends it as "a painfully eloquent statement

on the general folly and waste of war." It achieves this by presenting an interesting story in an *exotic* setting, with a truly believable set of characters, devoid of mock heroics and questionable patriotism. More than most of its kind it is a film about the down-to-earth business of war and how men adjust themselves to its circumstances.

Pierre Boulle wrote the screenplay from his novel, although he was greatly assisted by Carl Foreman and Michael Wilson, who took no credit because of their political blacklisting. In order to accommodate William Holden as the star the lead role of Shears, the sailor who escapes from the Japanese prison camp and later leads a commando party back to it, was changed from British to American, and in involving himself in the production Holden astutely worked on a small salary with a percentage-of-profits spread over a long period. This resulted in his becoming a millionaire, as did producer Sam Spiegel. However, the major change from the book to the film was the decision to destroy the bridge. In the original it remains intact but for a lengthy film, partly structured on a strain of suspense, Lean and Spiegel opted for a climax that would satisfy audiences. It also pointed up the heart-rending waste of time and effort that is so much a part of warfare.

Boulle based his story on fact—the Japanese building of a railway connecting Bangkok and Rangoon in 1942, the infamous "Death Railway," in which Allied prisoners were used as laborers, often to exhaustion and death—and embellished it with a philosophical confrontation between East and West. The protagonists are the British Colonel Nicholson (Alec Guinness) and the Japanese Colonel Saito (Sessue Hayakawa). Nicholson and a company of British soldiers are marched into Saito's prison camp, with the object of using them to build a railway. Nicholson is a proud, traditional soldier who immediately reminds Saito of the Geneva Convention and refuses to allow his officers to work as laborers. The objection means nothing to Saito and the two colonels come to an impasse. Saito humiliates the dogged Briton in front of his men and when Nicholson still refuses to cooperate he is subjected to confinement in a punishment hut, where he suffers grievously from the extreme heat and the lack of food and water. His courage makes an impression on Saito, who compromises in the use of officers but insists that the company of prisoners must be used for the construction of a bridge across the river. It now occurs to Nicholson that his men are in dreadful condition and that in order to save

Col. Nicholson (Alec Guinness) reviews his men for Col. Saito (Sessue Hayakawa) . . .

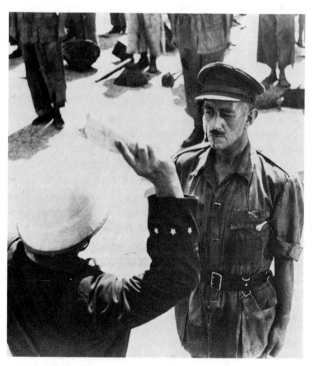

. . . and gets put in his place.

their lives they need organization, discipline and purpose. He agrees to build the bridge for Saito, insisting on his personal supervision and that it must be "a proper bridge."

Life for the prisoners assumes a sense of order and the work progresses in a manner that pleases both colonels. Nicholson comes to enjoy the project and rationalizes what he is doing as being for the good of his men. The thought that he is actually aiding the enemy does not seem to cross his mind. News of this bridge comes to British Intelligence and Major Warden (Jack Hawkins) is given command of a unit to destroy it. In doing this the British seek the aid of Shears (Holden), an American who has escaped Saito's camp and has the knowledge needed to locate it and gain entry. But Shears is a war-weary cynic who needs much persuasion in order to lead the unit. However, he later finds some purpose and value in the mission, although he does not live to enjoy any reflection on his contribution. His unit arrives at the bridge, after a tortuous trek through the jungle, on the day the bridge is completed. Nicholson proudly installs a plaque on a nearby tree to mark the accomplishment of his men and in the evening the British soldiers celebrate with a talent show. As they do this the commandos wire the bridge for detonation. In the morning Nicholson discovers the wires and in a misguided loyalty to his bridge he advises Saito. They frantically search for the source of the wires and when Nicholson finds the men poised to charge the explosives he tries to stop them. In the scurry and the confusion it is Nicholson himself, cut down by British bullets, who falls on the plunger and blows up the bridge, carrying with it a trainful of Japanese troops.

Kwai's ending has sparked conjecture. Did Nicholson fall on the plunger by accident or on purpose? If it is an accident it is poetic justice albeit very glib. But it is a fair assumption that the deluded colonel had come to his senses in his final moments and realized what he had done by building his bridge. In either case it is an interesting reflection on the anguish of men in combat making decisions under extreme circumstances, particularly those subjected to long confinement in brutal prison camps. The film also touches upon military ethics and how they have been changed by time: Nicholson, the professional, trying to live by a code of honorable conduct and finding in war a sense of

Building the bridge.

Shears (William Holden) guides the commandoes to the bridge.

purpose he probably would never find elsewhere, and Major Warden, a wartime officer, purely pragmatic and unconcerned with gentlemanly considerations in winning a war. Nicholson, the proud Briton, and Saito, the proud Japanese—seemingly hero and villain but actually not—seemingly symbols of opposing cultures but actually men with much in common.

Kwai is a handsome example of the adventure film. Lean's careful direction gives it both flair and quality, and with the luxury of a large budget and a totally sympathetic producer he was able to take his time in getting precisely what he wanted on the screen. He and Spiegel had scouted locations in Malaya, Siam and Burma but could not find the right combination of settings and accessibility. The decision was finally made to film in Burma, where the terrain was similar to settings described by Boulle and where the government was cooperative. The bridge, was as Colonel Nicholson demanded,

"a proper bridge." A quarter of a million dollars were spent in building it over the course of eight months. It was 425 feet long, ninety feet high and more than a thousand large trees were felled to supply the lumber. The destruction was handled by explosives experts brought from England and the whole thing was demolished in thirty seconds. No models were used. The train which crashes into the river after the explosion was a sixty-five-year-old group of engine and six coaches that had belonged to an Indian maharajah.

The Bridge on the River Kwai registered David Lean as one of the few directors capable of making a massive action movie and doing it with great intelligence and style. Lean loves everything about picture making but perhaps his greatest talent lies in presenting credible people in his stories. No one seeing this film could ever forget Colonel Nicholson and Colonel Saito.

Shears and Major Warden (Jack Hawkins) pause on the trek through the jungle.

The Magnificent Seven

1960

A Mirisch Picture. Produced and directed by John Sturges. Screenplay by William Roberts, based on the Japanese film *Seven Samurai*. Photographed in Panavision and DeLuxe Color by Charles Lang, Jr. Music by Elmer Bernstein. Running time: 126 minutes.

CAST

Chris, Yul Brynner; *Calvera,* Eli Wallach; *Vin,* Steve McQueen; *Chico,* Horst Buchholz; *O'Reilly,* Charles Bronson; *Lee,* Robert Vaughn; *Harry Luck,* Brad Dexter; *Britt,* James Coburn; *Old Man,* Vladimir Sokoloff; *Petra,* Rosenda Monteros; *Hilario,* Jorge Martinez De Hoyos; *Chamlee,* Whit Bissell; *Henry,* Val Avery; *Robert,* Bing Russell; *Sotero,* Rico Alaniz; *Wallace,* Robert Wilke.

Akira Kurosawa's *The Seven Samurai* (1954) holds a firm place in any listing of classic films, although its three hours in a very alien culture are probably a bit much for most Occidental viewers. But for film students it is an exciting lesson in cinematic art, with brilliantly filmed battle sequences involving charging horses, swarms of arrows and spears, flashing knives and swords and graphic bloodshed. The idea of turning it into a Hollywood western resulted in many snorts of disgust from the more august critics, who conveniently overlooked Kurosawa's admission that he had been strongly influenced in making *The Seven Samurai* by studying the westerns of John Ford, Howard Hawks and others. Kurosawa might also have mentioned John Sturges, whose *Bad Day at Black Rock, Gunfight at the O. K. Corral* and *Last Train from Gun Hill* are all stylish items. Sturges' work is marked by a cool, detached and unsentimental attitude and it was precisely right for *The Magnificent Seven*.

The basic plot of *Samurai* translated to a western setting quite easily. Instead of being about a group of medieval Japanese warriors hired by villagers to protect them from plundering bandits, *The Magnificent Seven* is about some American gunslingers coming to the aid of Mexicans for the same reasons. The time is somewhere around the end of the nineteenth century and William Roberts' screenplay indulges in a little too much philosophizing about the end of the age of freewheeling adventures. However, it is the fact that these men feel at odds with a changing society and with the diminishing opportunities for hell-raising that they accept the meager offer of the Mexicans, a mere twenty dollars apiece and food. It begins when three villagers

220

from Ixcatlan journey north for American help and meet a noted gunfighter, Chris Adams (Yul Brynner). Having nothing better to do, he agrees to "chase some flies from a little Mexican village." He seeks out some former comrades—Vin (Steve McQueen), Britt (James Coburn), Harry (Brad Dexter), Bernardo (Charles Bronson) and Lee (Robert Vaughn)—all either drifters or renegades. En route to the village they meet a young Mexican, Chico (Horst Buchholz), who persuades them to take him along. The villagers are at first suspicious of the mercenaries, who fear they are no better than the bandites of Calvera (Eli Wallach), who have been pillaging the village for years.

After the first bandit attack, in which three of Calvera's men are killed, the villagers change their mind and submit to being taught the tactics of defense, the use of firearms and the building of barricades. The furious Calvera decides to make a major attack on the village and rid himself of the hired gunmen but in this endeavor he is thoroughly trounced. The bandits are surprised to find themselves outmaneuvered and outfought, and Calvera is captured, although he manages to escape. The

confident villagers assume that the regime is over but they reckon without graft and corruption in their own ranks. A few villagers in Calvera's employ enable him to assume command of the village and the seven hirelings find themselves prisoners. Calvera, feeling generous in his victory, allows them to leave and has his men escort them to the outskirts of the village. The idea of defeat sits badly with the seven and they decide to return for a showdown, in the furious course of which Calvera is killed, along with most of his bandits, and Harry, Britt, Lee and Bernardo also lose their lives. With peace settling on Ixcatlan, young Chico decides to stay with the girl with whom he has fallen in love, and Chris and Vin ride off into the horizon.

The public loved *The Magnificent Seven* but critical reaction varied greatly, with a few critics seemingly unable to forgive Sturges his temerity in making a western of *The Seven Samurai*. Howard Thompson in *The New York Times* thought it "a pallid, pretentious and overlong reflection of the Japanese original," but "Tube" in *Variety* considered it "a rip roaring, rootin' tootin' western with lots of bite and tang and old-fashioned aban-

221

Yul Brynner and Steve McQueen.

Conferring with the bandit chief (Eli Wallach).

don," although disapproving somewhat of "a great deal of verbal thunder about fear, courage and the hopes and hazards of the gunslinging profession." Arthur Knight made an interesting comment in reviewing the picture for *Saturday Review:* "Despite the Orozco peasants, native potteries and semitropical vegetation of the hill country near Cuernavaca . . . the film remains closer to the spirit of *Shane* and other big-budgeted cow-country epics than to the exotica of its Japanese source. Kurosawa gave over a good deal of his footage to the backgrounds and motivations of his seven samurai; in the adaptation, true to Western tradition, the men appear out of nowhere and work for "the cause" on impulse. As a result, their selfless nobility in sacrificing themselves for an increasingly unappreciative community becomes a little hard to believe. Nevertheless, when the action takes over, Sturges guides it with a firm hand and a sharp eye for pictorial excitement."

The Magnificent Seven should not be made the subject of academic discussions. It's an adventure yarn with some fine action sequences, good color photography by Charles Lang, Jr. of rugged Mexican settings and most conspicuously a music score by Elmer Bernstein that is not so much background as up-front. The music is an integral part of the spirit of the picture and its rhythmic, lilting main theme—later used on television commercials as the Marlboro Country music—remains one of the most popular tunes ever written for the movies, and deservedly so.

Horst Buchholz and McQueen.

The instructors (Brynner, Charles Bronson and Brad Dexter).

223

Swiss Family Robinson

1960

A Walt Disney Picture. Produced by Bill Anderson. Directed by Ken Annakin. Screenplay by Lowell S. Hawley, based on the novel by Johann Wyss. Photographed in Panavision and Technicolor by Harry Waxman. Music by William Alwyn. Running time: 128 minutes.

CAST

Father, John Mills; *Mother,* Dorothy McGuire; *Fritz,* James MacArthur; *Roberta,* Janet Munro, *Pirate Chief,* Sessue Hayakawa; *Ernst,* Tommy Kirk; *Francis,* Kevin Corcoran; *Captain Moreland,* Cecil Parker; *Pirate,* Andy Ho; *Pirate,* Milton Reid; *Pirate,* Larry Taylor.

The problem with Walt Disney's version of *Swiss Family Robinson* is that it is likely to mislead those who have not read the book. Turning from the picture to the original material is bound to be a disappointment. The Disney film is a merry romp in a tropical paradise, and while the novel by Johann Rudolf Wyss (1781–1830) is a solid framework of adventure, it is, by modern standards, rather tedious. The prose is long-winded and heavy with moralizing about the values of family life and puritanical beliefs. The book is all that keeps Wyss's name alive. He was a Swiss professor and a collector of folklore, and the plot of his famous book was actually invented by his father. Wyss wrote it down and embellished it, and no film scenarist need feel badly about doing the same thing. However, for this account Lowell S. Hawley did a little more than embellish—he dropped one of

the four Robinson brothers and invented a band of pirates as the family's major problem. Also, as clearly dictated by Disney policy, he added many incidents about animals, with the end result being only a few steps away from one of Disney's *Wild Life Adventures.* The previous Hollywood filming of the story was in 1940, with Thomas Mitchell, Edna Best and Freddie Bartholomew but it had first been tackled by Universal in 1925 as a fifteen-chapter serial.

The Disney picture opens with excitement but with very little explanation for the predicament in which the Swiss family find themselves. The scene is a fierce storm at sea and a badly battered sailing ship is being tossed toward the rocky coast of an island. Mr. and Mrs. Robinson (John Mills and Dorothy McGuire) and their sons Fritz (James MacArthur), Ernst (Tommy Kirk) and Francis (Kevin Corcoran) are trapped in their cabin by fallen debris in the corridor, and they are the only people on board. All the others have departed, presumably after having been driven off course by pirates and lost in the storm. The ship runs

aground and settles half submerged on the rocks. The Robinsons manage to break their way out of their cabin and with the storm abated and the sun shinning, they survey their situation and find it far from disastrous. They are on the coast of a lush tropical island in the South Seas, probably not too far from their destination, New Guinea. The ship is full of supplies, including animals, and once having made their raft, father and sons proceed to transport all manner of things from the wreck to the shore.

The Robinsons have left their hometown of Berne, to escape the conformities of Swiss life and the dangers of Napoleonic Europe. Father expresses some doubt about uprooting his family to start a new life is a distant colony but Mother assures him it was the right thing—and the boys, enjoying every hour of life on the island, never had any doubts. The Robinsons build an elaborate tree house (three rooms) and construct a fortress at the top of a hill in order to ward off any return of the pirates. Once they have taken everything they need from the wreck, including a pipe organ and an arsenal of

weapons, they blow it up to destroy the evidence of their presence. After constructing a small boat Fritz and Ernst try to circumnavigate the island but they run into heavy surf and are washed up at some distant point. There they see a British naval officer, Captain Moreland (Cecil Parker) tied up on a beach, with a young boy beside him as a band of pirates argue about what to do with them. The two boys creep up behind the prisoners and Moreland tells them to take the boy and leave him for ransom. The trek across the island is difficult and the boys soon discover that the boy they have rescued is a girl, Roberta (Janet Munroe), a niece of Moreland. The three arrive at the Robinson homestead on Christmas Eve, with Roberta welcomed as one of the family, particularly by Mother. But a problem arises—jealousy between Fritz and Ernst over Roberta—until a bigger one arrives— the pirates, who want her.

The Robinsons, a most ingenious family, are prepared for the pirates. They have positioned guns at every point in their fortress, made dozens of hand grenades out of cocoanut shells, placed dynamite

225

Papa (John Mills), Mama (Dorothy McGuire) and the boys—Ernst (Tommy Kirk), Fritz (James MacArthur) and Francis (Kevin Corcoran).

No problems too big for the Robinsons.

226

charges on the hillside, dug concealed pits and prepared slides of rocks and logs. The attacking pirates are thoroughly confused and eventually withdraw, at which point Captain Moreland, having been ransomed, appeared with his ship and finishes off the pirates with broadsides. Then, faced with the choice of staying or leaving, the Robinsons decide to remain in their paradise, all except Ernest, who, having conceded romantic defeat in losing Roberta to Fritz, leaves for Europe to go to a university.

This handsome and happy adventure yarn was filmed on the island of Tobago, West Indies, whose beauty is fully apparent in Harry Waxman's Technicolor photography. The Wyss novel goes into great detail in describing the means of survival on the island but the Disney picture makes it all look like a well-organized tourist jaunt to a land of milk and honey. It was obviously designed to entertain children of all ages, which it did and continues to do. The only serious objection might be raised by zoologists, who could point out that an island, supposedly in the South Pacific, would hardly be the home of an elephant, a tiger, a zebra, South African ostriches and a South American anaconda, in addition to hyenas, monkeys and a Galapagos

The pirate leader (Sessue Hayakawa)

227

tortoise. But raising such an objection would be like complaining about the lack of a staff psychiatrist at Disneyland. This is a fantasy, and one of its many charms is the tree house the Disney engineers built in a huge samaan tree, with the living room in the center and two bedrooms on the right and left on higher levels. Decked out with fine furniture from the shipwreck and replete with all manner of gadgets, it is no wonder that the Robinsons decided to stay on the island. Disney reportedly spent five million dollars making the picture, which was in production for half a year, with interiors filmed in England. Like almost everything else he did, this investment paid off splendidly, leaving the rest of us not only envious of his Midas touch but wondering how to get shipwrecked in the South Pacific on Disney terms.

The Robinson defenses . . .

. . . and defenders.

Captain Moreland (Cecil Parker) the rescuer. His niece Roberta (Janet Munroe) prefers to stay on the island with Fritz.

The Sundowners

1960

A Warner Bros. Picture. Produced by Gerry Blatt-ner. Directed by Fred Zinnemann. Screenplay by Isobel Lennart, based on the novel by Jon Cleary. Photographed in Technicolor by Jack Hilyard. Music by Dimitri Tiomkin. Running time: 124 minutes.

CAST

Ida Carmody, Deborah Kerr; *Paddy Carmody,* Robert Mitchum; *Rupert Venneker,* Peter Ustinov; *Mrs. Firth,* Glynis Johns; *Jean Halstead,* Dina Merrill; *Quinlan,* Chips Rafferty; *Sean,* Michael Anderson, Jr.; *Liz,* Lola Brooks; *Herb Johnson,* Wylie Watson; *Bluey,* John Meillon; *Ocker,* Ronald Fraser; *Jack Patchogue,* Mervyn Johns; *Mrs. Bateman,* Molly Urquart; *Halstead,* Ewen Solon.

Australia, a visually stunning continent, remains a challenge for filmmakers. The Australians, like the Canadians, have struggled to maintain a film industry but always in the face of insufficient financing, with the result that few of their pictures do justice to the country. The fantastic landscapes and a history of rugged individuals hacking out a living against epic odds gives Australia much in common with the American west, and the best example of this on film is *The Overlanders.* Starring the late Chips Rafferty, who seemingly appeared in every movie made Down Under, it was made in 1946 and told of the movement of cattle from the northernmost area of Australia to the south in the face of possible Japanese invasion in the first years of the Second World War. Had the actors been

dubbed with American voices it would have been difficult to spot this massive trekking of cattle over mountains, deserts and rivers as not being one of the better Hollywood accounts of western Americana. This is no discredit to *The Overlanders,* an admirable film in many ways. It stands as an example of what can be done with Australian subjects.

Hollywood has not been entirely unmindful of Australia. One of the best movie adventure yarns is *Captain Fury* (1939), with Brian Aherne as a kind of Aussie Robin Hood of colonial days, but not a foot of it was shot in Australia. *Botany Bay* (1953) deals with the shipment of convicts from England to Australia, with James Mason as a Bligh-like captain and Alan Ladd as a mysterious felon, but the film bogs down in cheap dramatics, as does *Kangaroo* (1952), filmed entirely in Australia,

with Maureen O'Hara and Peter Lawford braving the hellishly hot Outback as ranchers. But by far the best film so far made in and about Australia is *The Sundowners.*

The Sundowners is a beautiful piece of filmmaking, giving a compassionate account of an Australian family of some fifty years ago and revealing much about their life-style and the land in which they live. In one of the less exotic examples of Aussie jargon, a "sundowner" is a wanderer whose home is wherever he happens to be when the sun goes down. Paddy Carmody (Robert Mitchum) is a hale and hearty specimen of this breed, who takes his wife Ida (Deborah Kerr) and their son Sean (Michael Anderson, Jr.) with him as he wanders the Outback as a drover and sheep shearer. It's a cheerful, loving family whose whole life is one of adventure. Most of the adventures are conven-

tional, dealing with the constant shifting as they trek sheep, traveling in their wagon and pitching their tents in a different place every night, but sometimes danger faces them, as in the case of fires in the dry forests. Paddy and Ida are a warm and well-adjusted couple, except for one thing—the conflict between his love of being a wanderer and her basic desire for the stability of a home. The film itself makes a great appeal for the open, itinerate way of life; it also adds up to a rather wistful comment on a life-style available to fewer and fewer people in an increasingly populous and shrinking world.

The film owes much to the intelligence and good taste of director Fred Zinnemann. Zinnemann spent three months in Australia on reconnaissance tours, then brought his company over in December of 1959 and filmed until the following March. He

231

Paddy (Robert Mitchum) needs to be helped out of the Australia House.

Paddy the shearer.

Paddy, his son Sean (Michael Anderson, Jr.), his wife Ida (Deborah Kerr) and his aristocratic employee Venneker (Peter Ustinov) move the sheep.

purchased five thousand sheep for his droving scenes and learned that the sheep is possibly the least tractable, albeit the mildest, of animals. In order to draw performances from them he resorted to the special schooling of one sheep, who then became the directorial bellwether of the herd. Zinnemann also used man-conceived ruses to lure them one way or another, including a stereo recording of sheep "baas."

The company quartered first in the community of Cooma, in the Snowy River Mountains of New South Wales, where it rained and sleeted and left the crew numb. They next moved twelve hundred miles to South Australia, to Port Augusta, on the Gulf of Spencer, where they were broiled in the sun and whipped by hot winds. This was the scene of the shearing shed sequences. All the actors required to shear underwent an intensive indoctrination course in shearing in the sheep station at Carriewerloo, including Robert Mitchum, who arrived an innocent and departed with enough skill to qualify as a "gun" shearer. A gun shearer can strip 260 sheep in an eight-hour day. However, Mitchum declined all offers to stay on in this profession.

Mitchum looks upon *The Sundowners* as one of the very best of his films, possibly because he had such a good time with the Australians. His talent for accents, rarely used in his film career, enabled him to assume the peculiar voice of the Aussie working man—that strange mixture of southern drawl and Cockney vowel distortions. Deborah Kerr, in a delightful performance, also colored her gentle voice with a local lilt, and gave the role

both a touch of gentility and a touch of sensuality. Zinnemann added a number of excellent Australian actors—Chips Rafferty included, of course—to his stars, and surrounded them with genuine Outback types. By the end of the filming Mitchum, Kerr and Peter Ustinov were drawling their speech and sprinkling it with worlds like tucker (food), cobber (friend), fair dinkum (genuine) and shickered (drunk).

The film, splendidly photographed by Jack Hildyard, reveals much of the spacious Aussie landscape and the life on sheep stations. For his music Zinnemann chose Hollywood's Russian-born Dimitri Tiomkin, long famous for scoring westerns and sometimes for overdoing it with symphonic bombast. In this instance Tiomkin opted for a subdued approach and spiked his score here and there with folk tunes. In the pub sequence in which Mitchum gets "shickered," filmed in the village of Nimmatabel in New South Wales, Mitchum needed no persuasion to join the beery habitués in singing songs like "Botany Bay" and "Lime Juice Tub."

It is interesting to note that the script for this sympathetic and knowledgeable look at Australia, a country almost notorious for its male camaraderie, was written by a woman, Isobel Lennart. The script shows an understanding of the Aussie's love of beer, buddies and sports but it also sheds light on the distaff side, particularly in showing the Australian woman's compassion for the problems of women in a largely male society. Memorable is Glynis Johns as the hearty pub-hotel owner, who likes men and knows how to deal with them. Outstanding is a scene in which Deborah Kerr, as an

Venneker, Mrs. Firth (Glynis Johns) and the Carmodies relax at Mrs. Firth's public house.

233

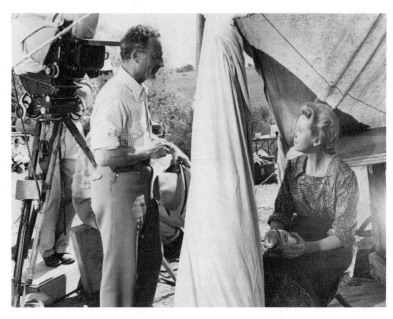

Director Fred Zinnemann chats with Deborah Kerr.

Venneker, Sean and Ida exhausted by fighting the forest fire.

Outback wife sans makeup, sits on a railway platform and spots in the window of a stationary train a woman who obviously has all the things she doesn't. They look at each other for a moment as the affluent woman applies powder to her face. Deborah automatically lifts her fingers to her cheeks. They size each other up and we instantly realize their thoughts.

The most interesting character in *The Sundowners* is that played by Peter Ustinov—as Rupert Venneker, an educated but slightly mysterious Englishman, the kind of elegant drifter who was once a prominent figure in the halcyon days of the British Empire. Venneker signs on as a drover with Mitchum, seemingly not so much for employment but for something to do. Throughout the film he wears a nautical cap, a deft device that serves to limn his character. On the first morning of the job, there is this telling exchange between the aristocratic hired man and his rough-hewn employer:

CARMODY: Do me a favor, will you? If you're gonna be a drover, get rid of that silly, flaming hat.
VENNEKER: Let me tell you about this silly hat, my good man.
CARMODY: Quit calling me that—I'm not your good man.
VENNEKER: Would you prefer "boss"?
CARMODY: Wouldn't be a bad idea.
VENNEKER: I was about to say, Carmody, that this cap of mine has seen places you don't even know exist. It started life on the head of a ship's master in the China Trade.
CARMODY: Yeah? What happened to him?
VENNEKER: Nothing happened to him. He is just not going to call you boss, that's all.

Ride the High Country

1961

An MGM Picture. Produced by Richard E. Lyon. Directed by Sam Peckinpah. Screenplay by N. B. Stone, Jr. Photographed in Metrocolor by Lucien Ballard. Music by George Bassman. Running time: 93 minutes.

CAST

Gil Westrum, Randolph Scott; *Steve Judd,* Joel McCrea; *Heck Longtree,* Ronald Starr; *Elsa Knudsen,* Mariette Hartley; *Billy Hammond,* James Drury; *Joshua Knudsen,* R. G. Armstrong; *Judge Tolliver,* Edgar Buchanan; *Kate,* Jennie Jackson; *Elder Hammond,* John Anderson; *Sylvus Hammond,* L. Q. Jones; *Henry Hammond,* Warren Oates; *Jimmy Hammond,* John Davis Chandler; *Saloon Girl,* Carmen Philips.

When MGM released *Ride the High Country* they did it with no promotion or ballyhoo, thinking it too offbeat a western to gain much approval on the circuits. To their astonishment the most esteemed movie critics throughout the country took it upon themselves to give the film the kind of praise film producers pray for. It was a gem of picture-making, with truly empathetic characters and a storyline that ebbs and flows spellbindingly from the opening shot to the last. Its quality is basically due to its director, Sam Peckinpah, but he had the advantage of a superb original screenplay by N. B. Stone, Jr., gorgeous color photography by Lucien Ballard, and as his stars, a pair of western past masters—Joel McCrea and Randolph Scott. Ballard has distinguished himself particularly with filming

awesome western landscapes, and Peckinpah used him for both *The Wild Bunch* and *The Ballad of Cable Hogue. High Country* was Peckinpah's second feature film, following *The Deadly Companions* the year before, but he had already shown his affinity for western stories writing and directing episodes of the television series *Gunsmoke, The Westerner, The Rifleman* and *Klondike.* A Peckinpah film that would rate inclusion in any consideration of major adventure films had it not been severely shortened and thereby damaged is the one he made after *High Country—Major Dundee,* a realistically gritty saga of the cavalry in pursuit of Apaches. It shares some of the same qualities as this one—a genuine feeling for the Old West, its landscapes and its individuals, and a mellow kind of regretfulness about a lost and gone era in American history.

Ride the High Country is about a couple of old-timers, past middle age and washed aside by the waves of encroaching civilization in the turn-of-the

The bride, Elsa (Mariette Hartley) arrives in Coarse Gold for her wedding, followed by her groom (James Drury) and his family.

century West. Both are heroic figures, having been noted lawmen, and yet they are now reduced to taking whatever comes their way in order to live. Steve Judd (McCrea) rides into the town of Hornitos on the invitation of a banker, who needs a guard to escort gold from the mining community of Coarse Gold. Judd does his best to hide the frayed cuffs of his shirt from the banker and he goes to the bathroom to read his contract, so that the banker cannot see his need for glasses. Judd takes the job and asks that he recruit a needed second man. Walking around the town he stops at a carnival and notices Gil Westrum (Scott), an old friend now earning money by being a sharpshooter in a sideshow and spouting Buffalo Bill-type nonsense about the Wild West, Westrum accepts the job and brings along his young, scrap-happy friend, Heck Longtree (Ronald Starr). Despite their friendship, Judd and Westrum are different kinds of men. Judd is a moral rock of Gibraltar with an ironclad code of honor. Westrum is not. His cheerful smirk hides a bitter-

ness about the latter stages of his life and he takes the job with the intention of stealing the gold.

On their way through the mountains they stop for a night at the home of Joshua Knudsen (R. G. Armstrong), a farmer and a religious fanatic. Heck takes a shine to his daughter Elsa (Mariette Hartley), who is repressed by her stern father. To escape home she has accepted the proposal of Billy Hammond (James Drury), one of a family of four sons and a father who live in Coarse Gold. The three men agree to take Elsa to her bridegroom but when they get there they are disgusted to find the Hammonds to be a wild and filthy bunch living in squalor. Billy is the most presentable of them and Elsa timidly agrees to go through with the wedding, which takes place in the only building in town, the saloon-bordello. The rest of the community is made up of dirty tents and shacks. On her wedding night, with Billy drunk, Elsa has to fight off the advances of his brothers, who seem to regard her as community property. She escapes and turns to Judd,

237

Gil Westrum (Randolph Scott) and Steve Judd (Joel McCrea)—relics of the old West.

Westrum and Heck for protection. They agree to take her with them on the trail back to Hornitos. Now comes a double-barrelled problem—the Hammonds want Elsa back and they also want the gold. And for Judd there is one more hazard—Westrum and Heck intend to take the gold for themselves.

Elsa and the three men are tracked by the Hammonds as they make their way through the mountains. They attack and are routed, with one of the Hammonds losing his life. Heck, who has fallen in love with Elsa, changes his mind about stealing the gold but Westrum takes it and leaves. At the Knudsen home Judd, Heck and Elsa find her father murdered and the remaining three Hammond brothers firing at them from the house. Heck is wounded and it remains for Judd to hold off the Hammonds— but not for long. Westrum, having had a change of heart, appears on the scene and takes his place beside Judd. The two then agree to fight it out in the old way—in the open, with guns firing in a showdown. Their challenge to the Hammonds is accepted and it costs all three brothers their lives. Westrum escapes unharmed but Judd is mortally wounded. Knowing that he is dying he asks Westrum to take care of the two youngsters and to see that the gold arrives at the bank. Westrum promises that the gold will be delivered and Judd says, "I know that, I always did . . . So long partner." Then, with Westrum, Heck and Elsa gone, he quietly lies back and dies.

Even for those who generally do not appreciate westerns, *Ride the High Country* is an absorbing and moving piece of entertainment. For western buffs it is an item of study, with its accurate period detail and the vistas of the California Sierras, near Mammoth Lakes. It firmly established Peckinpah as a director of unusual style, a man with the ability to create a seething sense of danger in seemingly peaceful settings—although his talent in staging scenes of violence is shockingly impressive. Many of the actors who appeared in *High Country* appeared in following Peckinpah pictures. Three of the actors playing the Hammonds—Warren Oates, L. Q. Jones and John David Chandler—appear as grotesque characters, horribly grubby, semi-demented, comic but frightening. And they are typical of Peckinpah's technique of creating strange images, often ugly ones in beautiful settings. His mining community in this film is memorable for its spirited and dangerous atmosphere, with its one true gold mine being the whorehouse, an almost Hogarthian experience. The madam is a cheerful nightmare and tucked away in a corner is the whisky-sodden relic

Elsa decides to quit her marriage and leave with Heck Longtree (Ronald Starr), Westrum and Judd.

of a judge (Edgar Buchanan), who comes alive every now and then to mouth words of wisdom jarringly at variance with the wild and tawdry surroundings.

But the real gold of *Ride the High Country* lies in the presence of Joel McCrea and Randolph Scott, for both of whom this was a final film. Each had come to specialize in westerns and each had been in the business for more than thirty years. McCrea was fifty-six at the time of filming and Scott fifty-eight, although the parts required them to be somewhat older and more lifeworn. It was the perfect film for each to end his career and yet there is a wry quality about the characterizations. No two actors in Hollywood had less in common with the roles of the two penniless has-beens of the story. McCrea and Scott were, and still are, two of the wealthiest products of the picture business, millionaires many times over with their land investments. As in the case of Bob Hope and Bing Crosby, it is a toss-up as to which one is the richest. Not that it matters. What matters is that McCrea and Scott, in many fine westerns, set an admirable style in quiet heroism, always courageous, ever dignified, never vulgar. Ideal figures in celluloid mythology.

The showdown with the Hammonds.

The end of the trail for old Steve Judd.

239

El Cid

1961

A Bronston-Dear-Allied Artists Picture. Produced by Samuel Bronston. Directed by Anthony Mann. Screenplay by Fredric M. Frank and Philip Yordan. Photographed in Super Technirama and Technicolor by Robert Krasker. Music by Miklos Rozsa. Running time: 184 minutes.

CAST

El Cid, Charlton Heston; *Doña Chimene,* Sophia Loren; *Count Ordoñez,* Raf Vallone; *Princess Urraca,* Genevieve Page; *Prince Alfonso,* John Fraser; *Prince Sancho,* Gary Raymond; *Arias,* Hurd Hatfield; *Fanez,* Massimo Serato; *Ben Yussuf,* Herbert Lom; *Al Kadir,* Frank Thring; *Moutamin,* Douglas Wilmer; *Don Diego,* Michael Hordern; *Count Gormaz,* Andrew Cruickshank; *Don Pedro,* Tullio Carminati; *King Ferdinand,* Ralph Truman; *Don Martin,* Christopher Rhodes; *King Ramiro,* Gerard Tichy; *Bermudez,* Carlo Giustini.

The easiest way to describe *El Cid* is by calling it a Spanish *Ivanhoe.* It shares the rich historical grandeur, the spectacles of massive medieval battles, and the central figure of a knight who comes to the aid of his country. But whereas Sir Walter Scott's knight was pure invention, *El Cid* was at least based on history, although controversy swirls around him as to the exact facts. He was a Castilian aristocrat named Rodrigo Diaz de Bizar (1040–1099). An anonymous poem written a few years after his death is the source of most of the literature written about him, but the historians claim it to be a dubious source. In writing their screenplay Fredric M. Frank and Philip Jourdan conferred

with the eminent Spanish historian Don Ramón Menendez Pidal, as did composer Miklos Rozsa and art directors Veniero Colasanti and John Moore. Pidal's contributions are not listed in the credit titles but his influence was profound. He introduced Rozsa to everything available about eleventh century Spanish music and the composer, who had already performed yeoman service in the cause of ancient Roman music in *Quo Vadis, Ben-Hur* and *King of Kings,* produced a score rich with Spanish flavors, as well as meeting all the requirements of the spectacles, romance and drama. Rozsa's score is best appreciated by educated ears but the work of Colasanti and Moore is readily apparent to the eye. Their sets and costumes are stunningly beautiful, and fully captured by the Technicolor photography of Robert Krasker, who had long ago proved his talents in this line of picture-making with Olivier's *Henry V.*

Spain barely existed as a country in the eleventh century. It was an array of kingdoms warring between themselves and threatened from the south by the Moors, who intended to spread the doctrines of Islam throughout Europe. *El Cid* focuses on this

240

The tournament at Calahorra, staged before the castle of Belmonte.

troubled situation and pinpoints the strife in the kingdoms of Castile, Leon and Aragon. A hero arises from the political chaos—Rodrigo Diaz de Bivar (Charlton Heston), whose bravery in battle and wisdom in council earns him the Arabic name of Al Seid (the Lord), or in Spanish, El Cid. After one decisive battle he allows several Moorish emirs to return in safety to their country but with the vow they will never again attack Castile. This generosity is misunderstood by many Castilians and used against him by his enemies at court. The powerful Count Ordoñez (Raf Vallone) brands El Cid a traitor and Count Gormaz (Andrew Cruickshank) challenges him to a duel. El Cid kills Gormaz in defending himself and incurs the wrath of his bride-to-be, Doña Chimene (Sophia Loren), the daughter of Gormaz. King Ferdinand (Ralph Truman) urges her to continue with the marriage for political reasons but she enters it with hatred for her husband. The King dies shortly thereafter and his kingdom is divided between his two sons, Alfonso (John Fraser) and Sancho (Gary Raymond), and his daughter Urraca (Genevieve Page), all of them shallow, selfish people.

The ambitious Alfonso arranges the assassination of his brother and when El Cid refuses to swear allegiance to Alfonso unless he declares himself innocent of Sancho's death, he is ordered to leave Castile. In the years that follow, Chimene bears El Cid two sons and gradually comes to understand his integrity and the nobility of his purpose in uniting Spain. This eventually leads to her love of her husband. In all this time he has continued to fight the Moors and increase the ranks of his followers. When the leader of the Moors, Ben Yussuf (Herbert Lom) makes known his intention to invade and conquer Valencia, Alfonso recalls El Cid from exile and places him in command of his army. The battle for Valencia rages for days, with the decision dangerously in the balance. On the eve of the final Moorish assault on the city, El Cid is mortally wounded. Realizing he will soon die and that his army will not survive without his leadership, he makes Chimene promise that his body will be strapped in his saddle and his horse positioned at the head of his charging brigades. She does as he asks, and when the Moors see the invincible El Cid leading the massive attack they panic. The victory

241

is Spanish and the Moors withdraw from the country.

El Cid is a film of enormous cinematic scope, full of marvelous images and splendid action sequences but marred here and there with ponderous dialogue and some wooden characterizations. The critical consensus was that as a spectacle it had few equals but that at three hours it was too long. Charlton Heston, who by this time had already donned the mantles of Moses and Ben-Hur, was the logical choice for the lead, partly for lack of any other male star of suitably heroic stance and larger-than-life machismo. It is easy to be snide about Heston's playing of historical figures but they are greatly difficult roles and beyond the credibility range of most actors. His physique and manner enable him to wear costumes and wage ancient warfare, and there are moments in *El Cid* that would be almost impossible to believe without Heston's commanding presence. He looks every bit the man to lead a legion of warriors against the Moors and to engage in tournaments. One outstanding early sequence is his contest with Don Martin (Christo-

El Cid (Heston) spares the lives of the captured Moors.

242

King Ferdinand (Ralph Truman) grants El Cid the right to champion his cause, to the disgust of daughter Urraca (Genevieve Page), sons Sancho (Gary Raymond), and Alfonso (John Fraser), and court plotter Arias (Hurd Hatfield).

pher Rhodes), a fight to determine whether the King of Aragon or the King of Castile shall rule the city of Calahorra. The tournament lasts for ten minutes of screen time, first with lances on horseback and then with swords on foot, and it is staged in front of the handsome castle at Belmonte, with a full panoply of medieval heraldry arrayed to watch the knightly combat.

Anthony Mann's direction gave *El Cid* its much-needed spine, with a steady flow to the action and an elegance of style in handling huge scenes of brightly costumed extras in grand settings. However, the magnificent battle sequences were the work of the second unit director, Yakima Canutt, ex-cowboy, rodeo champion and Hollywood's foremost stunt man. When his bones became too brittle for stunting Canutt used his knowledge in devising stunts for others, and soon established himself with a military sense of tactics and an imaginative mind. His triumph in *El Cid* is his staging of the battle of Valencia, with the dead hero leading an avalanche of cavalry and putting the Moors to rout. For this long sequence the company selected the ancient

El Cid prepares to defend the honor of Castile against the champion of Aragon, Don Martin (Christopher Rhodes).

The Cathedral at Burgos (replica).

243

El Cid, the saviour of Valencia.

The army of El Cid approaches Valencia—actually Peñíscola.

El Cid and his beloved Chimene (Sophia Loren).

244

walled city of Peñíscola, since Valencia itself was scenically unsuitable. The art directors dressed up the city with buntings and backdrops and the company was on location for a month. For the battle, Canutt used 1,700 soldiers of the Spanish Army, 500 horsemen from Madrid's Municipal Honor Guard and more than three thousand people from the locality.

El Cid is quite literally a movie about castles in Spain. In addition to those of Belmonte and Peñíscola the film used several in the province of Valladolid. Scenes were also shot in the mountains of Guadarrama and when producer Samuel Bronston was discouraged from using the actual cathedral at Burgos, he ordered a replica built on the backlot of the Sevilla studios in Madrid. The film required the manufacture of thousands of costumes, weapons, tapestries, banners, pennants, mock jewelry and, for the battle of Valencia, the construction of a dozen wooden war machines and the conversion of thirty-five fishing boats to look like a Moorish fleet. If nothing else, *El Cid* is a course for prospective art directors. It is, of course, much more—a truly spectacular account of the adventures of Spain's legendary knight in shining armor, Rodrigo Diaz de Bivar. Any intimation that he probably was nothing like Charlton Heston will not be tolerated.

The view from Valencia.

Lawrence of Arabia

1962

A Horizon-Columbia Picture. Produced by Sam Spiegel. Directed by David Lean. Screenplay by Robert Bolt. Photographed in 70 mm, Panavision and EastmanColor by F. A. Young. Music by Maurice Jarre. Running time: 222 minutes.

CAST

Lawrence, Peter O'Toole; *Prince Feisal,* Alec Guinness; *Auda Abu Tayi,* Anthony Quinn; *General Allenby,* Jack Hawkins; *Turkish Bey,* Jose Ferrer; *Colonel Brighton,* Anthony Quayle; *Mr. Dryden,* Claude Rains; *Jackson Bentley,* Arthur Kennedy; *General Murray,* Donald Wolfit; *Sherif Ali Ibn el Kharish,* Omar Sharif; *Gasim,* I. S. Johar; *Majid,* Gamil Ratib; *Farraj,* Michael Ray; *Tafas,* Zia Mohyeddin; *Daud,* John Dimech; *Medical Officer,* Howard Marion Crawford; *Club Secretary,* Jack Gwillim; *RAMC Colonel,* Hugh Miller.

Robert Bolt received sole credit for scripting *Lawrence of Arabia* but he had obviously studied the various books written about T. E. Lawrence, including Lawrence's autobiography *The Seven Pillars of Wisdom.* The screenplay is a masterful mixture of fact and artistry, hewing to the truth but going beyond it in conjuring up images and emotions probably more glorious and stimulating than those experienced by Lawrence himself. This is a film about truly great adventure and it is unique in being a film that succeeds on what are more often than not two disparate levels—vast visual splendor and action, and a witty, intelligent study of historical figures. Bolt's fine script was the blueprint for

all this but the meticulous builder was David Lean, immeasurably aided by Freddie Young, one of the most creative photographers in the history of the cinema. His photography in *Lawrence of Arabia* is incredible. In reviewing it *Time* said, "Time and again the grand rectangular frame of the Panavision screen stands open like the door of a tremendous furnace, and the spectator stares with all his eyes into the molten shimmer of white golden sands, into blank incandescent infinity as if into the eye of God."

David Lean, a man totally devoted to the art of making movies, averaged no more than one film a year prior to *The Bridge on the River Kwai* but with the success of that giant picture he discovered his true metier—the film of epic proportions and depth—and since then he has spent four and five years on each of his projects. No amount of time and effort is considered too much by Lean and only

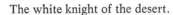

a man with that attitude could have made this picture. Lean spent more than a year studying and filming in the deserts of Egypt and Arabia and those who worked with him observed that the strange kind of fascination with the awesome landscapes that captured Lawrence seemed to have a similar affect on Lean.

Lawrence of Arabia, running almost four hours in its original presentation, ran into criticism in some quarters for not giving a more comprehensive understanding of Lawrence as a man. This is a rather luxurious view because even those who knew Lawrence claimed they never fully understood him and doubted that he really understood himself. He was an enigmatic character, a man born of an undistinguished background and possessed of a strange, driving force. He had a strong urge for adventure and he discovered remarkable things about himself, among them that he had unusual courage

and the gift of leadership, in addition to vanity and a perverse streak of sadism. In casting the role Lean wisely opted for an actor unknown to most filmgoers. Physically Peter O'Toole was wrong, being tall and handsome against Lawrence being short and plain, but emotionally he was very right. O'Toole as an actor has a cool remoteness about him. That, plus his considerable ability, made him perfect for Lawrence.

The film is somewhat remiss in revealing little of Lawrence's early years and nothing about the obscurity he chose after his Arabian adventures were over. It begins with his death, while riding a motorcycle along an English country lane in 1935, and then jumps to the memorial service at St. Paul's Cathedral, attended by various prominent people who knew him. One of them is Jackson Bentley (Arthur Kennedy, in a role modeled on Lowell Thomas) and his discussions with the others lead to

249

Lawrence (Peter O'Toole) is chosen to approach the Arabs. Prince Feisal (Alec Guinness) approves of the choice made by Mr. Dryden (Claude Rains) and General Allenby (Jack Hawkins). Col. Brighton (Anthony Quayle) looks dubious.

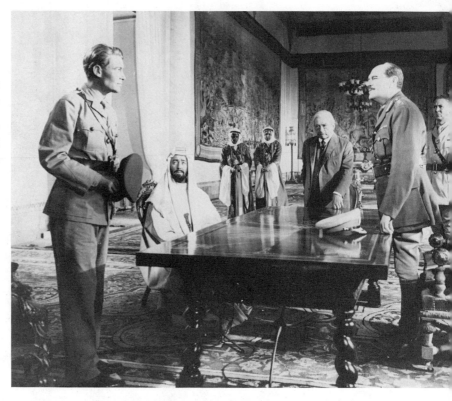

Lawrence and his friend Sherif Ali Ibn el Kharish (Omar Sharif).

Auda Abu Tayi (Anthony Quinn) warns Lawrence of trouble.

a flashback. It is 1916 and Lieutenant Lawrence, an untidy and far from dedicated soldier, is serving at the British headquarters in Cairo. His passion for the desert and knowledge of Arabian affairs comes to the attention of the head of the Arab Bureau (Claude Rains), who arranges to have him sent as an emissary to Prince Feisal (Alec Guinness) in an attempt to promote means of subduing the conflicts among the Arab tribes. On the way he meets Sherif Ali (Omar Sharif), who becomes his strongest ally in the cause to unify the Arabs. Feisal agrees to his forces being absorbed into the British campaign but he believes, as do others, that only a miracle will bring about unity. Lawrence provides the miracle. He inspires the Arabs by accomplishing an arduous trek across the Nefud Desert with a small force of guerillas and capturing the Turkish garrison at the port of Aqaba. His victory makes him a hero. And he is well publicized by Bentley.

Lawrence is eventually captured by the Turks and brutalized by a Bey (Jose Ferrer). The film at this point clearly alludes to sodomy and Lawrence's homosexual tendencies. It also touches upon his discovery of pleasure in killing, after finding it necessary to shoot one of his own men. The sensation becomes acute when he leads his men in an attack on a Turkish regiment in the desert and savagely takes part in killing every last Turk. Lawrence is sickened by this aspect of his psyche but with the urging of the British commander of the area, General Allenby (Jack Hawkins) he agrees to lead his devoted Arabs into Damascus to set up a tribal council to rule the city. But the ancient tribal animosities are too strong to be reconciled and Lawrence sees his hope of a permanent understanding among Arabs die away. He accepts the rank of colonel from Allenby, who shares the official view that Lawrence has outlived his usefulness, and he returns to England. He turns the situation over to Allenby and Feisal, who arrive at an expedient Anglo-Arab entente but one that is doomed to failure, as Lawrence well knows. Hero-worshipped by the Arabs, he leaves with a bitter feeling of shame.

Sam Spiegel acquired the rights to Lawrence's *The Seven Pillars of Wisdom* while he and Lean were in India mapping out a concept of a film about Mahatma Gandhi. The project loomed more and more difficult and it was abandoned in favor of doing the Lawrence picture. What this required at the very outset was a definite point of view and Lean was well aware his film would provoke criticism. He told Canadian interviewer Gerald Pratley: "To say that Lawrence was a complex character is to state the case mildly. There is enough action, enough psychological and thematic material in *Seven Pillars* for a dozen films with a dozen different points of view. On top of that Lawrence and his book have enjoyed, or endured, the comments and interpretations of some scores of historians, soldiers and journalists, often with an axe

Lawrence and his Arabs, in a rare moment of unity.

The attack on Aqaba.

Waylaying a Turkish train.

253

of their own to grind. We met and engaged play-wright Robert Bolt to write the screenplay, and together we worked out our point of view upon the man and the theme to be drawn from his story."

Lean and his crew spent almost two years on various locations. They shot first in the desolate areas along the Saudi Arabian frontier, with its red sand dunes stretching to the horizon, and then moved two hundred miles west to Aqaba, working in temperatures too hot to be recorded on a thermometer. The actual city was far too modern to fit the requirements of the script and a replica, as it appeared in 1916, was built in Spain, near Seville, as were sets calling for scenes in Cairo, Damascus and Jerusalem. The spectacular scenes showing Lawrence's attacks on railways were also done in Spain but the fearful and bloody sequence in which the Turkish regiment is liquidated was shot in Morocco. This sequence lingers in the memory, along with many others, such as the ferocious sandstorm, the painful winter trek across the desert, the long shot of Omar Sharif as a speck in the distance emerging and coming closer through shimmering heat waves, Lawrence proudly strutting for the first time in his Arab robes and the ethereal vistas of brilliantly colored but merciless deserts. *Lawrence of Arabia* can lay good claims to being the greatest of all adventure films.

Director David Lean (in the foreground in a white jacket) and photographer Freddie Young (in front of Lean with his hands on his hips) filming the British advance. The officer in front of the camera and riding a camel is Anthony Quayle.

The Great Escape

1963

A Mirisch-Alpha Picture. Produced and directed by John Sturges. Screenplay by James Clavell and W. R. Burnett, based on the book by Paul Brickhill. Photographed in Panavision and DeLuxe Color by Daniel L. Fapp. Music by Elmer Bernstein. Running time: 170 minutes.

CAST

Hilts, Steve McQueen; *Hendley,* James Garner; *Bartlett,* Richard Attenborough; *Ramsey,* James Donald; *Danny Velinski,* Charles Bronson; *Blythe,* Donald Pleasance; *Sedgwick,* James Coburn; *Ashley-Pitt,* David McCallum; *MacDonald,* Gordon Jackson; *Willie,* John Leyton; *Ives,* Angus Lennie; *Cavendish,* Nigel Stock; *Goff,* Jud Taylor; *Sorren,* William Russell; *Griffith,* Robert Desmond; *Nimmo,* Tom Adams; *Haynes,* Lawrence Montaigne; *Von Luger,* Hannes Messemer; *Werner,* Robert Graf; *Strachwitz,* Harry Riebauer; *Kuhn,* Hans Reiser.

The Great Escape is one of those films which prove that style is something more important than subject matter. The prospect of making a killing at the box office with a movie about prisoners of war trying to escape from a German stalag was not a very likely one for 1963. There had been so many of them. But *The Great Escape* had the advantage of a fine source, Paul Bricknell's book, plus excellent scenarists in James Clavell and W. R. Burnett, and producer-director John Sturges in command of a big budget and a splendid bunch of actors. The

Mirisch Company also astutely decided to film the story in Germany on the actual site of Bricknell's experiences, reproducing the stalag precisely and enlisting the aid of men who were there during the war. To this was added a marvelous sense of adventure, excitement, suspense and humor, backed up with a jaunty score by Elmer Bernstein and some fine color photography of Bavarian landscapes by Daniel Fapp. The reviewer for *Time* neatly summed it up: "*The Great Escape* is simply great escapism."

The picture opens with several truckloads of Allied officers, mostly aviators, being delivered to a maximum security stalag. Commandant Von Luger (Hannes Messemer), a Luftwaffe colonel and a gentleman, tells the senior British officer, Group Captain Ramsey (James Donald), "We have put all our rotten eggs in one basket and we intend to watch that basket very carefully. With your cooperation, we may all sit out the war very comfortably." But since all the British and American officers in his charge are men who have made numerous attempts to escape from other prison camps, Von Luger knows his words are meaningless. The German idea

to group all these "rotten eggs" in one basket immediately begins to backfire on them. Since they are all enterprising and determined, they pool their ideas on the planning of a massive escape. Their leader is Squadron Leader Roger Bartlett (Richard Attenborough), who directs them in the building of three tunnels, any one of which will enable hundreds of men to escape. The other officers in the planning each bring various talents to bear; Hilts (Steve McQueen) in a breezy sportsman, who wins the title The Cooler King by getting himself put in solitary confinement time after time for his cheeky attitude toward the Germans, thereby creating a lot of surface show; Hendley (James Garner) is the scrounger of the team, a man with an ability to devise and fabricate almost anything; Blythe (Donald Pleasance) has the talents of a forger, and makes visas and passports; and Polish-American Danny Velinski (Charles Bronson) is the experienced foreman who supervises the digging. Others are in charge of making maps, civilian clothes, compasses and stockpiling rations.

The plans proceed in an orderly fashion, with a great deal of attention placed on caution and ruses to deflect German attentions. Von Luger and his officers suspect that something is going on but they do not realize it is directly under their feet. The captives involve themselves in much surface activity, which masks the underground work. When picking at concrete inside a hut is done, it coincides with hammering outside and with men clinking horseshoes in a pitching contest—and so on. The tunnels are marvels of ingenuity, with wooden tracks and dollies, electric lights and bellows-operated ventilation. The first day of the escape arrives—and never goes beyond the first day because the Germans discover the operation. But by then seventy-six men have escaped and dispersed into the surrounding countryside. Hendley and Blythe appropriate a small German plane but crash-land short of the German border. Hilts steals a motorcycle and leads the Germans a harrowing chase right up to the Swiss frontier but fails to negotiate the jumping of the bike over the barbed wire. Bartlett and other British officers are captured in various towns and rounded up into a group. The Gestapo have now moved into control of the stalag and the mild-mannered Von Luger is relieved of his

Velinski (Charles Bronson) shows Bartlett the way to break through the floor.

Squadron Leader Bartlett (Richard Attenborough) outlines his plan. In front of Attenborough is Charles Bronson, and to the right—James Coburn, John Leyton and James Donald.

Blythe (Donald Pleasance) and Hendley (James Garner) prepare to snatch a Luftwaffe plane.

post. Fifty men, including Bartlett, are driven into the country and ordered from their trucks, and are then mowed down by machine-gun fire. Twenty-three others are returned to the stalag. Only Velinski and two others actually escape Germany.

The Great Escape is a wry title. More precisely it might have been called *The Great Attempt to Escape*. On the other hand it graphically shows

what enterprising men can accomplish under the most unusual circumstances, as well as pointing out that it is the duty of prisoners of war to harass the enemy, to make themselves a nuisance and to cause problems for their captors, putting as much strain on their war effort as possible. The film states this case very boldly but it does it in the form of rattling good entertainment. It makes no bones about war being hell but it also presents war as man's greatest crack at adventuring. And with the highest of stakes—life and death, victory or defeat, submission or surmount.

It must be admitted that the film overdoes the "rover boy" aspects of the prisoners high-heartedly banding together for their nose-thumbing of their captors. The circumstances described in Bricknell's book are tougher, more grim and tedious than the movie suggests. John Sturges steers it all with a firm hand but the long picture is crammed with detail and characters, and creaks a little with the weight of them. However, as a movie about bravado and ingenuity in wartime, *The Great Escape* is in a class by itself. It benefitted by being filmed in Germany and by employing several men who were prisoners in the stalag of the actual story. All of them said that the reconstruction of the camp was so exact that they felt continually queasy, feeling that they had slipped back twenty years in time.

258

MacDonald (Gordon Jackson) and
Bartlett make like Germans . . .

. . . until spotted by the Gestapo.

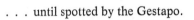

Hilts (Steve McQueen) makes a grand attempt at
escape—and fails.

Director John Sturges (in glasses) lining up a sequence
with Garner and Attenborough.

Zulu

1964

A Diamond-Embassy Picture. Produced by Stanley Baker and Cy Endfield. Directed by Cy Endfield. Screenplay by John Prebble and Cy Endfield. Photographed in Technirama and Technicolor by Stephen Dade. Music by John Barry. Running time: 135 minutes.

CAST

Lt. John Chard, Stanley Baker; *Otto Whit,* Jack Hawkins; *Margareta Whit,* Ulla Jacobsson; *Pvt. Henry Hook,* James Booth; *Lt. Gonville Bromhead,* Michael Caine; *Colour-Sergeant Bourne,* Nigel Green; *Pvt. Owen,* Ivor Emmanuel; *Sgt. Maxfield,* Paul Daneman; *Cpl. Allen,* Glynn Edwards; *Pvt. Thomas,* Neil McCarthy; *Pvt. Hitch,* David Kernan; *Pvt. Cole,* Gary Bond; *Pvt. Williams,* Peter Gill; *Lance Corporal,* Tom Gerrard; *Surgeon Reynolds,* Patrick Magee.

A generation after *The Four Feathers* and long after Hollywood had ceased glorifying the British Empire, Welsh actor Stanley Baker and American director (resident in England) Cy Endfield managed to raise the large amount of money needed to make *Zulu.* It took a lot of effort to get it. A movie about the nineteenth-century British army fighting natives in Africa was not considered a likely item in the cinema of the sixties. Baker made it tough for himself by not compromising—it *had* to be done on location and it *had* to be done grandly. His breakthrough came in Rome after a meeting with Joseph E. Levine, who was intrigued with the idea of a lusty military adventure picture to be shot in the land of the Zulus. Baker straightaway proceeded to South Africa to scout locations and enlist the assistance of the various government bureaus,

all of which he got. Prior to shooting, he and Endfield girded their loins to tackle what they thought would be their most difficult task—getting hundreds of Zulus to play their warrior ancestors in a battle which they lost, and at great expense of blood. The philosophical aspects proved of little concern. The main problem was in explaining to the tribesmen what a film was all about. None of them had seen one and the only movie Baker could lay his hands on was an old Gene Autry western. He claims it won the day for him and that the Zulus almost split their sides with laughter. After that, the tribesmen eagerly joined in the games of make-believe.

Zulu is a vivid reenactment of one of the most hazardous and glorious days in British military history—January 22, 1879, when one hundred and five men of B Company, 2nd Battalion, 24th Regiment of Foot, South Wales Borderers, withstood the siege of four thousand Zulu warriors. John Prebble's story, which he adapted into a screenplay with the help of Cy Endfield, is a meticulous account of that day's facts and figures, although the by-play

The Zulu's mating dance, on a grand scale.

between the various characters is supposition for the sake of entertainment. The story begins with the Reverend Otti Witt (Jack Hawkins), an alcoholic missionary, and his daughter Margareta (Ulla Jacobsson) attending a Zulu ceremonial dance of marriage between hundreds of couples. The impressive dancing and chanting takes on a different connotation when Witt learns that a large band of warriors have wiped out an army detachment of twelve hundred men, taken their rifles, and that the tribesmen are heading for his premises at Rorke's Drift.

Rorke's Drift is an army outpost, in addition to being Witt's mission, and the soldiers, mostly Welshmen, are relaxed in going about their duties in the balmy climate. Witt arrives and explains the situation to the officers, advising an immediate evacuation. To his horror, they decide to make a stand. Witt becomes increasingly neurotic with the prospect of the advancing warriors and his rantings wear on the nerves of the men, so he is locked up. His daughter takes it upon herself to be a nurse to the men already in the infirmary and for those who

will soon fill it. The regimental officer in charge is Lt. Gonville Bromhead (Michael Caine), a slightly foppish gentleman who reminds all who need to be reminded that his family has served in the army for generations. He is miffed to discover that Lt. John Chard, (Baker), on assignment with the Royal Engineers, is his senior by dint of longer service and that regulations therefore place him in command. The situation is made the more tenuous by the fact that Chard has had no combat experience and, on a subtler level, he is obviously not from an aristocratic background. But necessity compels the two officers to work together to set up the defense of the station, constructing makeshift barriers and deploying their men tactically to cover every point.

The Zulus soon arrive, the unseen advance heralded by an ominous chanting—a dull, chugging sound somewhat like a slow train shunting, as the tribesmen beat their shields with their spears. Then they come into sight and put the fear of God into the hearts of the soldiers—long lines of black figures coming down the grassy slopes of the hills like ripples in water. The Zulus prove to be capable

261

soldiers, attacking in ranks with skill and with complete disregard of death and injury. The British rifle fire mows them down and the warriors retreat. Then they come again—and again and again—each time getting nearer to the buildings and cutting down more and more Britons. Every retreat is followed by a deathly silence, during which the officers and men take stock of their situation. It seems highly unlikely that any of them will survive, as the attacks take their toll and the ammunition diminishes. Wearily they prepare for yet another onslaught. Again the hideous noise suddenly alerts the soldiers—by now just a handful—to another attack. Most of the men in the infirmary are too ill to fight but a few are malingerers. One of them, Private Hook (James Booth), decides to fight, and performs heroically in hand-to-hand combat with the tribesmen. The battle goes on and on—and then it stops. The Zulus in this wave all lie dead. The exhausted Britons slump in their positions and prepare for what must be the final attack, one which they cannot possibly ward off. Instead they hear a massed yell from the Zulus—their signal of acknowledgment to the victor, as they withdraw from the scene.

The battle at Rorke's Drift was a decisive one in the British campaign to pacify South Africa for settlers, coincidentally at the same time the American army was performing similar service west of the Mississippi. As a page in British history it has the distinction of being the battle which produced the most Victoria Crosses in one day—eleven were awarded, including those to Chard, Bromhead and Hook. The film is a superb account of that battle, with a realistic point of view from the producers which wisely salutes the heroism of the Zulus, so well organized and fearless in their attacks, and the cool discipline of the Britons, quite obviously masking their justified fear of bloody annihilation. *Zulu* is *Gunga Din* for real, with not a shred of cavalier larks and quips. Cy Endfield's direction stresses the physical exhaustion of nonstop killing and the effect it has on men, making some furious with rage, others tremble with dread and still others applying themselves calmly to the horrifying situation.

Zulu was filmed in the Royal Natal National Park and Stephen Dade captured the lushly flowing, colorful landscapes and the sense of strange isolation. The acting is near-perfect for such a tale. Stanley Baker, the man who most wanted to make the picture, is solid as Chard, the engineer forced into becoming a combat officer, and Michael Caine, in

Lt. Chard (Stanley Baker) tries to control the frightened Margareta (Ulla Jacobsson) and her father, Otto Witt (Jack Hawkins).

The tribesmen approach Rorke's Drift.

Lt. Bromhead (Michael Caine) near exhaustion.

The black tide against the thin red line. The figure in the lower left corner is solid old pro, Sergeant Bourne (Nigel Green).

his first major screen appearance, almost steals the film as the disdainful aristocrat. Most memorable is the late Nigel Green as a sergeant of the old order, sternly watchful and understanding of his men but compassionate, as in the last roll call when he lines the weary survivors up for a head count. He looks them over like a father and quietly advises, "Steady, men." For the Welsh, *Zulu* has added charms, with little bits of humor about some of the soldiers' concern over what the loss of men will do to their choral group. And in answer to the chanting of the Zulus, a group of redcoats break into "Men of Harlech." At the end of the film the mellifluous voice of Baker's friend, Richard Burton, intones the list of heroes. But the most arresting moment in *Zulu* is just before this, as the camera pans over a field containing the dead warriors. It becomes apparent to the soldiers, and to us, just what price the tribesmen have paid. The carnage is appalling. The field is carpeted with black corpses, side by side and many piled on top of each other, a few quivering in last contortions. It is an incredible, heart-stopping view.

The
Naked Prey

1966

A Theodora–Sven Persson Film. Produced and Directed by Cornel Wilde. Screenplay by Clint Johnston and Don Peters. Photographed in Panavision and Technicolor by H. A. R. Thomson. Musical Advisor: Andrew Tracey. Running time: 96 minutes.

CAST

The Man, Cornel Wilde; *Second Man,* Gert Van Der Berg; *Warrior Leader,* Ken Gampu; *Safari Overseer,* Patrick Mynhardt; *Little Girl,* Bella Randels.

Cornel Wilde enjoyed a decade of popularity as a movie star following his success as Chopin in Columbia's juicy account of the composer's life, *A Song to Remember* (1945), but seldom received critical acclaim. Critics who reviewed his work in swashbuckling items as *The Bandit of Sherwood Forest, Forever Amber* and *At Sword's Point* sometimes remarked that he was better than his material but few would probably have guessed he would later emerge as a distinguished film maker. No one was unhappier with his material than Wilde himself and by the mid-1950s he had determined to change the course of his career, setting up his own production company and making *Storm Fear,* which he both starred in and directed. In 1957 he made *The Devil's Hairpin and Maracaibo,* in both of which he was the star-director-producer, although neither added much luster to his name. However, with *Lancelot and Guinevere* in 1963 the critics began to take notice. This was exactly the kind of ma-

266

The hunter (Cornel Wilde) captured.

terial in which Wilde had won his spurs—romance and derring-do—and yet it was done with style and conviction. His playing of the gallant Lancelot was believable and his staging of the battle scenes, shot in Yugoslavia, was remarkable. Then, with *The Naked Prey* three years later, Wilde fully established himself as a man with a distinct sense of cinema.

The Naked Prey is among the few really great films made about Africa. It lacks the grandeur of *King Solomon's Mines* or the humor of *The African Queen* but it surpasses both in realism. Its sense of reality is quite shocking and it is a graphic adventure, entirely free of romanticism. The story is simple—about a man running for his life, and the script by Clint Johnston and Don Peters is a rarity because it contains no dialogue, other than a few words by the hero to himself and the shouts of native tribesmen. And the music score is made up of tribal chants and drumming. The hero (Wilde) is the leader of a safari but we never get to know his name. At the start of the expedition he feels concerned because his employers refuse to consider the natives as worth bothering with or showing any token of friendliness. Their cavalier attitude soon causes their death. The tribesmen ambush the safari and quickly wipe it out, saving half a dozen members for torturing ceremoniously. One of the carriers is basted with clay and roasted on a spit, another is decked out with feathers for a ritualistic butchering and the white boss of the safari is staked out in a ring of fire, with his head positioned at the only point a trapped cobra can escape. The only man spared is the safari leader. Out of respect for his bravery they give him a bare chance for escape, although it is actually more of a game on their part. He is stripped naked and allowed to run a few hundred yards. Then a half-dozen young warriors with spears pursue him and the hunter becomes the hunted.

The man surprises the tribesmen by being as fleetfooted as they are. One of them dashes ahead of the others to claim his prey but the man outwits him, dodges a spear and uses it to kill the tribesman. He takes the spear, the shield, a pair of sandles and a loincloth, and runs. The tribesmen are angered by the killing and the pursuit becomes even more deadly. The man uses his wits, his knowledge of the landscape and every ounce of strength he can squeeze from himself to elude his pursuers. Having no food, he scrounges for roots, weeds and any form of animal life. He scores a tactical victory by setting a brush fire and cutting

The chief warrior (Ken Gampu) gives the hunter a sporting chance.

off the tribesman, which enables him to rest. He next observes a village being pillaged by slave traders and discovers a little girl in hiding. She is bright and friendly, and the two becomes fellow travelers for a few days. When she decides she has reached a place where she feels safe, the two part company, having enjoyed a feeling of mutual trust despite the lack of a common language. He then makes his arduous way across the severe country-side, only to find the tribesmen have caught up with him. Two of them die in fighting him and the remaining three doggedly keep up the chase, until they come within sight of a fortress. The man makes the last desperate part of his run and the leader of the tribesmen makes a last desperate attempt to stop him. A rifle shot from the fortress fells the tribesman and makes the man safe.

The Naked Prey is a skillful piece of fluid action and a touching account of a terrible struggle for survival. The credit for the film belongs very much to Cornel Wilde, whose idea it was to make the picture and whose performance as the hunted hunter gives it credence. It is largely a physical performance and only an actor with an athletic background would have been capable of giving it. Wilde won the National Intercollegiate Fencing Championship in foils in 1934 and two years later was a member of the U.S. Olympic Training Squad in saber. As a fledgling actor he earned money with displays of swordsmanship, which led to his being chosen to play Tybalt in Laurence Oliver's production of *Romeo and Juliet* on Broadway in 1940. Once established in Hollywood, it was apparent that Wilde was the only leading man who did not need coaching in swordplay when cast in swashbucklers. Wilde kept himself in good shape over the years but *The Naked Prey* caused him considerable sickness. He became ill while scouting locations but after recovering in California he returned to Africa to make his film. Not long after filming commenced he came down with tick fever, a condition similar to malaria and caused by minuscule ticks entering and poisoning the body. Those who worked with him claimed that much of his on-camera work was done while suffering with high temperatures and that he took advantage of his ailing condition to give his characterization greater reality.

The film was shot in the North Transvaal, close to Mozambique, with parts done in Bechuanaland and what used to be known as Southern Rhodesia. Much of its violence is raw and grisly but it is not contrived. It is a film about primitive people in a harsh landscape and Wilde captured it masterfully. This is a study in elemental existence and the tribesmen are not made out to be villains, but simple people with their own codes of conduct, including a sense of fair play and deep attachment to their comrades. Wilde took great care in casting the tribespeople: "I wanted unsophisticated people who would act in front of the cameras as they acted in everyday life. There was an uninhibited vitality about them that you just can't get in urbanized areas. They know nothing about movies and only a few chiefs understood English but once they knew what we wanted, they enjoyed this game of make-believe. Their tribal dances included reenactments of bravery in battles and in hunting, so they were used to a kind of dance mock-fighting. The man who played the leading tribesman in the chase is Ken Gampu, a legitimate actor in South Africa, and with his help we were able to show the others want we wanted."

As with all film crews going into Africa, those on *The Naked Prey* suffered severe discomforts and a few were gravely ill. Recalls Wilde, "We had just about everything happen to us. The whole crew was put to rout by a swarm of bees on one location and we had five men treated for shock—one had over a hundred stings on his head alone. The results of all this lasted for days and some of the people had delayed reactions to the stings, swelling up with the poison two weeks later. The land itself was beautiful but terrifying. One of the things I most wanted to show was the danger of the terrain. I got a special lens from Panavision, which could take extreme closeups of the almost unseen hazards facing anyone moving through this landscape—the thorns, four and five inches long, that can go right through a shoe sole, and the barbed hooks in the acacia trees that tear the flesh off a man or animal who runs into them by error. And there were all kinds of flower pods containing great needles, in addition to millipedes a foot long, large scorpions and lizards with spikes all over them. So as the man runs through all this, it's not just a pretty landscape but a very dangerous one."

Cornel Wilde received wide acclaim for *The Naked Prey*, although there were a few critics who felt it was a picture that needed a strong stomach. A year later he followed it with *Beach Red*, again as star-director-producer, a vividly realistic account of a World War II battle in the South Pacific. In 1971 he directed and produced *No Blade of Grass* in England, a disturbing look into the future with civilization falling apart in the wake of pollution. Both films were hard-hitting—and vastly different from the romantic milieu in which Wilde had first made his name in Hollywood.

Director Wilde lining up the slave village sequence.

Jean Wallace (Mrs. Cornel Wilde) with some of the tribespeople who appeared in the film, all of whom were amazed at her platinum blonde hair and her tiny little Chihuahua, neither of which they had ever seen before.

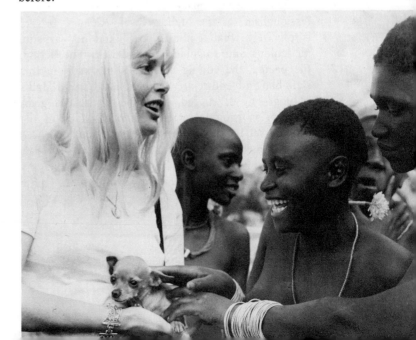

The Professionals

1966

A Pax-Columbia Picture. Produced, directed and written by Richard Brooks. Based on the novel *A Mule for the Marquessa* by Frank O'Rourke. Photographed in Panavision and Technicolor by Conrad Hall. Music by Maurice Jarre. Running time: 117 minutes.

CAST

Bill Dolworth, Burt Lancaster; *Henry Rice Fardan,* Lee Marvin; *Hans Ehrengard,* Robert Ryan; *Jesus Raza,* Jack Palance; *Maria Grant,* Claudia Cardinale; *J. W. Grant,* Ralph Bellamy; *Jacob Sharp,* Woody Strode; *Ortega,* Joe De Santis; *Fierro,* Rafael Bertrand; *Padilla,* Jorge Martinez De Hoyes; *Chiquita,* Marie Gomez; *Revolutionary,* Jose Chavez; *Revolutionary,* Carlos Romero; *Banker,* Vaughn Taylor.

The Professionals is an aptly titled picture. It refers to four soldiers-of-fortune but it also applies to the people who made it. This is Hollywood professionalism on the highest level. Richard Brooks is precisely what a filmmaker should be—artistic, meticulous and singularly firmminded. The acting, the pacing, the editing and the stunt work in this slam-bang adventure are flawless, and Conrad Hall's photography of rugged, awesome landscapes gives the film an exciting sense of fantasy. Much of the story is set in Mexico but Brooks decided to shoot on the American side of the line, mostly in Nevada's Valley of Fire State Park, and thereby avoid any possible objections from Mexicans, who, quite rightly, had long resented Hollywood depictions of

their history. In this case they might not have minded, since Brooks treated the Mexican aspects with respect, perhaps even going a little too far in philosophizing about the politics of revolution. The only real villain of this yarn is an American capitalist and the sentiments favor the revolutionaries. At one point, as a lull in the fight between a Mexican rebel captain and one of the American adventurers, they talk about causes. The Mexican sadly refers to a revolution as being something like a love affair, that time is the enemy of both, and the American cynically replies, "When the dead are buried and the politicians take over, it all amounts to the same thing—a lost cause."

This is a movie about one of the last frontiers of adventure, the Mexico of the early years of this century when Pancho Villa and other colorful rebel chieftains led their people in the fight against fascism. Many Americans either took advantage of the situation or for more noble reasons joined the

270

Raza (Jack Palance) wipes out the Federales.

revolutionaries to help them. Either way it was pure adventure. *The Professionals* deal with four such men: Bill Dolworth (Burt Lancaster), a cheerful rogue and an expert with dynamite; Henry Fardan (Lee Marvin), a gunnery expert making a living demonstrating new automatic weapons; Hans Ehrengard (Robert Ryan), a wrangler and breeder of horses, and Jacob Sharp (Woody Strode), an expert guide, bounty hunter and champion archer. They are hired by a wealthy businessman, J. W. Grant (Ralph Bellamy), to go into Mexico and recover his beautiful, young, abducted wife, Maria (Claudia Cardinale). The mission is absurdly dangerous but Grant believes the courage and the combined skills of these four men, plus the inducement of ten thousand dollars apiece, will get him what he wants. He also knows that Dolworth and Fardan fought for Pancho Villa and that they are acquainted with the man who has taken the wife—Jesús Raza (Jack Palance), contemptibly described by Grant as "the bloodiest cutthroat in Mexico."

The men make their precarious way one hundred miles to the camp of Raza. Their knowledge of the country and the people, and their skill with arms and strategy enable them to retrieve the girl. They attack the camp at night and explode all the crucial points by firing sticks of dynamite on arrows and raking the Mexicans with crossfire. They then discover their biggest problem. Raza and the girl are lovers, and that there was no abduction. Grant had practically purchased Maria in marriage, even though she had grown up with Raza. She is still devoted to him and objects to being taken back to Grant. The ransom money demanded by Raza for her release is their way of raising money for the revolution, with her returning to Raza afterwards. Says Dolworth to Fardan, "We've been had!" Be that as it may, Fardan, a man of moral fiber, insists on going through with the deal and taking Maria back to Grant.

The exit is far more hazardous than the entrance, with the furious Raza attempting to retrieve his love and she doing her best to escape. Raza and his men are defeated when Dolworth explodes a narrow canyon he dynamited on the way to the camp and when he holds the Mexicans at bay while the others head for the border. Dolworth, a crack shot, picks off the Mexicans until only the wounded Raza is left.

At the border the girl and the three rescuers are met by the happy Grant but it soon becomes obvious that the only way he can detain Maria is by force. She denounces him as a vicious scoundrel and promises to run away again. Then Dolworth turns up, bringing with him the almost exhausted Raza. Maria runs to his side and Grant orders one of his men to kill him. Before the order can be obeyed Fardan fires a shot at the Grant employee and saves Raza. The adventurers now turn their guns on Grant and allow Maria to make her escape with Raza, thereby forfeiting their pay but apparently gaining satisfaction in doing the right thing.

Whether the kind of men depicted as soldiers-of-fortune in this film would have shown a generous change of heart is debatable but such is the sleekness of Brooks' direction and the skill of the four actors that the point is not one to ponder. *The*

J. W. Grant (Ralph Bellamy) hires the professionals to retrieve his abducted wife in Mexico.

Professionals is a prime example of an adventure picture but it also adheres to accuracy in setting its story. This looks like the Mexican border country of 1917, with its trains, cars and tough, grubby people. The four professionals are all men of sharp instinct, men who live by their wits, close to the earth and always within a hair's breadth of death. Ehrenberg, the horseman, can accept the killing of humans but the slaughter of horses is abhorrent to him. Sharp, the black giant and champion archer, conceals all feelings, knowing that to show emotion would be fatal for him. Fardan, the ex-soldier who still wears an army stetson, is laconic in his opinions on life but his code is simple and incorruptible. Dolworth, first seen making a hasty retreat from the bed of another man's wife, is admittedly corruptible but he does his job in loyalty to his friend Fardan. They may all be rough and unsociable but they take pride in being professional in what they do and each man knows he can entirely rely on the other.

No film dealing with Mexico in the revolutionary years can avoid violence and brutality. The most horrifying sequence in *The Professionals* occurs when the four are on their way to Raza's camp and observe him and his men attacking a train carrying government troops. The battle is loud and vicious and it ends with Raza hanging the officers and shooting the surviving soldiers. From the distance Ehrenberg expresses his disgust with these barbarians but then Dolworth tells him the reasons for the hatred, that the troops had liquidated a village, pillaging, raping and torturing. The explanation partly satisfies Ehrenberg but he still expresses disgust with revolution, causing Dolworth to muse that perhaps the whole theme of revolution has only just begun, a polemic probably a little too grand for such a man to mouth.

The Professionals is about men and its mood and its dialogue are markedly masculine, although without the kind of scatology that the permissiveness of later years would have allowed. These are men with a certain fatalism about them and the film is shaded with subtle regrets about the dubious rewards of idealism and free-wheeling. When Fardan explains the mission to Dolworth, the latter shakes his head and says, "I'll be damned." Intones Fardan, "We all are." But the best line is the last one. After letting Raza and the girl escape, the furious J. W. Grant snarls at Farden, "You bastard!" Without even looking at him Fardan replies, "Yes, sir. With me, an accident of birth. But you, you're a self-made man."

Fardan and Dolworth size up their objective.

Cameraman Conrad Hall, to the right of the camera, lines up a shot.

Having captured Maria Grant (Claudia Cardinale), the pros have to fight off the man she really loves.

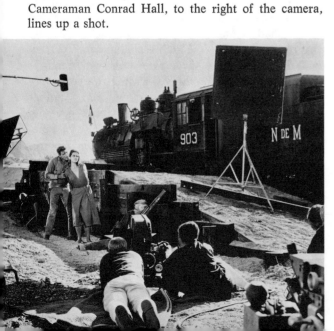

The Man Who Would Be King

1975

An Allied Artists/Columbia Pictures Production. Produced by John Foreman. Directed by John Huston. Screenplay by John Huston and Gladys Hill, based on a story by Rudyard Kipling. Photographed in Technicolor and Panavision by Oswald Morris. Music by Maurice Jarre. Running time: 129 minutes.

CAST

Daniel Dravot, Sean Connery; *Peachy Carnehan,* Michael Caine; *Rudyard Kipling,* Christopher Plummer; *Billy Fish,* Saeed Jaffrey; *Kafu-Selim,* Karroum Ben Bouih; *District Commissioner,* Jay May; *Ootah,* Doghmi Larbi; *Roxanne,* Shakira Caine; *Babu,* Mohammed Shamsi; *Mulvaney,* Paul Antrim; *Ghulam,* Albert Moses.

1975 was not a conspicuous year for commercial movies, either in quality or quantity, and such was the moralistic and/or realistic nature of the year's output that seemingly half of the films were issued with restricted ratings. The likelihood of any old-fashioned, slam-bang adventure films emerging in such a year was far from great and yet two of the best in a very long time appeared in 1975—*The Wind and the Lion* and *The Man Who Would Be King.* Both starred Sean Connery and both were largely filmed in Morocco. The former concerned an incident during the presidency of Theodore Roosevelt, when an American woman was kidnapped by Moroccan rebels and held for ransom. *The Wind and the Lion* is an action-packed yarn but in the High Adventure sweepstakes it is dwarfed by *The Man Who Would Be King,* which takes us back to Queen Victoria's India and the ambitions of a pair of ex-army roustabouts to set up their own empire.

John Huston, who co-scripted the film as well as directed it, claims the Kipling story had taken his cinematic fancy in the early days of his career and that he had wanted to film it as far back as twenty years ago, obtaining the rights at that time. "Originally I wanted to do the movie with two friends—Clark Gable and Humphrey Bogart. However, every time I started to think about the film, another project came up and finally I just about gave up hope. Then suddenly in 1974, producer John Foreman interested Allied Artists and Columbia Pictures in jointly financing the movie. I think it's one of the greatest adventure stories ever written." Filming it was also a bit of an adventure. Huston and Fore-

Sean Connery—and the magic arrow.

man chose Morocco because of that country's variety of racial strains and for an astonishing range of scenery. Kipling's tale is set in India, Afghanistan and Kafiristan (a region of eastern Arghanistan, now known as Nurestan), and Huston was able to match the physical requirements within a portion of Morocco. Marrakech was used to depict Lahore of the 1880s and the Kafiri village of Er-Heb was brought to life in the foothills of the Atlas Mountains. Later the cast crew flew into the actual mountains for scenes of snow and glaciers, and to stage the action sequences supposedly to take place in the Khyber Pass. A crucial setting in Kipling's story, the Holy City of Sikandergul, was built on a hilltop only an hour's drive from Marrakech.

Kipling's short story (some 12,000 words) dates from a time when he was working as a young journalist in India. Many of his earliest stories

apperaed in the Allahabad Pioneer, which he edited between 1887 and 1889, when he was in his early twenties, and one of them was *The Man Who Would Be King*. Later it appeared in a book of short stories of his put out by A. H. Wheeler and Company, who supplied inexpensive books to Indian railway bookstores. It was from these small volumes that Kipling's reputation grew, as travelers took the books back to Europe and America.

Of particular interest in this handsome film is the fact that Kipling himself is a leading character —as a first-person storyteller—and shrewdly portrayed by Christopher Plummer, eschewing his usual leading-man image and submitting himself to a remarkably good makeup facsimile of Kipling, with bushy moustache, steel-rimmed glasses and thinning hair. To get closer to the characterization, Plummer studied accounts of the author and

Christopher Plummer and Michael Caine

Michael Caine, Christopher Plummer and Sean Connery

managed to get, from the BBC, a recording of a broadcast in which he appeared. From this he was able to approximate Kipling's manner of speaking.

The story begins as a crippled, mangy old beggar shuffles into Kipling's office at the Northern Star in Lahore late one night and unfolds an incredible tale. The beggar is actually Peachy Carnehan (Michael Caine), or rather, what is left of Peachy, now horribly aged and a little mad. Kipling, after the shock of recognition, recalls their first meeting, when the brash and larcenous Peachy pickpocketed his watch at the Lahore railway station and later returned it when he realized Kipling was a brother Freemason. Peachy then introduces his friend Daniel Dravot (Sean Connery) to Kipling—both are ex-sergeants of the British Army in India—and explains their plans to proceed into the primitive areas of northern India and set themselves up as rulers.

Kipling becomes intrigued by the audacious pair and decides to help them—largely in the interests of a probable good yarn coming out of it. He gets them an appointment with the District Commissioner, who takes a dim view of their scheme and refers to their kind as "detriments to the dignity of the Empire." To which Danny replies, "Detriments you call us. Detriments! Well, I remind you that it was detriments like us that made this bloody Empire." With that they turn heel in military precision and march out of the office. Later, the two likable rogues tell Kipling something of themselves: "The less said about our professions, the better, for we have been most things in our time. We have been all over India. We know her cities and her jungles, her palaces and her jails." To which Peachy adds: "Therefore we're going away to another place where a man isn't crowded and can come into his own. We're not little men and there's nothing we're afraid of."

Danny and Peachy, after a long and arduous trek, find their Shangri-La. They acquire a rag-tag army of tribesmen and take over the Holy City of Sikandergul, once ruled by Alexander the Great. Danny assumes godlike proportions after surviving an arrow in the chest in battle; he plucks the arrow seemingly from his heart and casts it aside, to the astonishment of the natives. In fact, his Freemason medal has stopped it entering his chest. But the medal works other wonders for him; the face on its surface resembles a likeness of Alexander the Great and the population regard Danny as a reincarnation. He is crowned king and given absolute power, which includes the vast wealth of treasure accumulated over the centuries. But, as Kipling stresses in telling the tale, power corrupts —and Danny starts to assume regal bearing and the belief that perhaps he really is a descendant of Alexander and fated to be a king. The realistic Peachy, who merely wants to gather up the loot and transport it back to civilization, fails to knock sense into Danny and finally decides to leave. Danny asks him to stay for his wedding to a local princess —a fatal blunder. The terrified girl, almost catatonic at the wedding, bites Danny's face as he attempts to kiss her. She draws blood and the priests and attendants gasp—a God does not bleed! With this they realize he is a fraud and decide to put him to death. Danny is driven onto a rope bridge over a high gorge and they cut it out from under him. They crucify Peachy and leave him for dead. Miraculously he survives and months later turns up in Kipling's office to relate the incredible adventures.

That a picture of the *Gunga Din* ilk, adventuring into imperialistic and unfashionable waters, should turn up in the mid-seventies was highly improbable. Its success was a blow to the general belief that "they don't make pictures like that any more." What it takes, as it always has in the film industry, is the abiding passion of someone with the stamina to persevere with a project and see it through, in this case John Huston—and the inspired casting of Michael Caine and Sean Connery as the men bent on cutting themselves a large slice of life's pie. The cheeky quality of Caine and the stolidity of Connery perfectly match the requirements of the bold yarn. However, the 1975 stamp marks *The Man Who Would Be King*. The picture does not glorify the British Empire, as it would have done thirty years previously, and the language and characterizations are more earthy.

In reviewing the film for the *Los Angeles Times*, Charles Champlin touched up on the political message in Kipling's story, pointing out that Huston, in

Caine and Connery

Connery—about to be put to death but saved when the tribesmen see his Freemason medal

depicting all the fun and adventurous games, does not avoid the underlying theme: "His pals who would be king are also the advance scouts of an exploitative society invading an older and more primitive culture with no wish to stay, understand or share but only to grab and split. It won't work, Kipling was saying nearly a century ago, and here, shuffling along ruined and mad, is the symbolic consequence—the barely living reminder, as the Caine character says, not to come again. The tale carries itself, and neither Kipling nor Huston drumbeat the message, but it is there and there is no other."

Other critics seemed less willing to embrace *The Man Who Would Be King,* feeling that it should have been more exciting and splendid. Perhaps, but if nothing else, it proves that the art of making films of great adventure has not been completely lost. We need more accounts of bold humans who, like Peachy Carnehan and Daniel Dravot, are not afraid to stand up and say, "We are not little men."

Connery and Caine, beating retreat.

Michael Caine and Sean Connery, as the man who would be king.

Connery, as the would-be king, going to his death. ▶

Index

280